Tiny Dancer

Anthony Flacco

Tiny Dancer

The Incredible
True Story of a Young
Burn Survivor's Journey
from Afghanistan

THOMAS DUNNE BOOKS
St. Martin's Press
New York

THOMAS DUNNE BOOKS.
An imprint of St. Martin's Press.

TINY DANCER. Copyright © 2005 by Anthony Flacco with Dr. Peter and Rebecca Grossman. All rights reserved. Printed in the United States of America. No part of this book may be used or reproduced in any manner whatsoever without written permission except in the case of brief quotations embodied in critical articles or reviews. For information, address St. Martin's Press, 175 Fifth Avenue, New York, N.Y. 10010.

www.stmartins.com

Design by Kathryn Parise

Photos courtesy of Dr. Peter and Rebecca Grossman

LIBRARY OF CONGRESS CATALOGING-IN-PUBLICATION DATA

Flacco, Anthony.
    Tiny dancer : the incredible true story of a young burn victim's journey from Afghanistan / Anthony Flacco.
        p. cm.
    ISBN 0-312-34333-7
    EAN 978-0-312-34333-0
    1. Hasan, Zubaida. 2. Burns and scalds in children—Patients—Afghanistan—Biography. I. Title.

RD96.4.F53 2005
362.197'11'0092—dc22   2005045525
[B]

First Edition: September 2005

10   9   8   7   6   5   4   3   2   1

To Sharly

for the magic of believing

Introduction ✣

In March 2002, when we first were notified of a badly burned little girl from Afghanistan whose name we didn't even know, we could not have imagined the course of events that were soon to transpire, and how it would indelibly affect our lives. Zubaida's journey is truly a story of the human spirit; how good can come from bad, how charity can run through each of our hearts, and how love can be a gift without parallel.

This is a story of inner strength. How a little girl fought against all odds to live.

One might ask why: Why fight so hard? What is it that you really have to live for? When Zubaida was burned, her family was impoverished, and she lived under the oppressive reign of the Taliban. A disfigured, poor female living in pre-9/11 Afghanistan could only expect to live a miserable life, if she were allowed to live at all. And so perhaps she was blessed to have a child's naïveté, and to have a father whose love for his child was stronger than the zealous cultural extremes of his place and time.

Zubaida's story is also one of irony and humanity. When we are asked about the tragedy that struck Zubaida, it is often assumed that she was a casualty of the American military invasion of Afghanistan. In fact, it was the American military that turned out to be her savior. If something good has transpired from the devastating events of September 11, 2001, it is that the resultant American policy placed American soldiers in Afghanistan after Zubaida got burned. Had there not been an American military presence, Zubaida would surely have perished.

Getting Zubaida to America was a multifaceted and complex process and could only have been accomplished through coordinated efforts, strong individuals, and Non-Government Organizations, as well as the State Department and the military. Once in the United States, Zubaida's presence inspired the best of intentions by all those who were lucky enough to have Zubaida touch their lives.

However, there were times when even those with the best of intentions clashed. While all who came into contact with Zubaida wanted the best for her, not all of us had the same game plan. That, at times, led to conflict between individuals and organizations involved with Zubaida's journey. Over time, there were arguments between different parties as well as miscommunications. Zubaida's plight stimulated so many people on so many levels that emotions ran high, and we certainly bear our share of responsibility for that.

In addition, there was the reality of Zubaida herself. Even with allowances for the emotional trauma that Zubaida had already undergone and was continuing to go through, there was no getting around the fact that Zubaida's behavior at times could be irrational, and sometimes hurtful and mean. Nevertheless, if you stripped away all the complications, she was still a little girl, and like all little girls, she needed love, boundaries, and discipline mixed with careful guidance. She also desperately needed a level of assurance that she would not be abandoned. It is here, at this basic level, that the true beauty of Zubaida's story can be told.

While her physical transformation was exceptionally rewarding for all of us involved, it was her transformation as a person that was most noteworthy, and her transformation transformed us. In the end, Zubaida gave to us a love that transcended miles, cultures, religions, and language. While many of the dealings we have had with Zubaida before, during, and after her journey to America have been complex, frustrating, aggravating, and sometimes maddening, they have always been enriching. Zubaida rightfully is another man's child, another mother's daughter. But a part of her will always be our little girl.

There have been many children who have crossed our path, some of whom have been patients in the burn center. Each one is very special in their own right. Zubaida, however, took us completely off guard. Here she was, a ten-year-old girl in a foreign country, with no family, surrounded by a strange culture and unfamiliar people, having to deal with countless surgeries, physical scars, and language barriers. But through her iron will, strong personality, and keen ability to adapt, Zubaida was able to learn, give back to others, and even lead her peers. All Zubaida needed was support and opportunity, ironically, something she may not have had had she not been injured. We feel Zubaida will go on to do great things. She is a born leader.

There are so many people who did not get the credit that they deserve for helping this child. We just want to let them know that we recognize what they did and are forever grateful. We also know that Zubaida will never forget their kindness. Among these wonderful people are the U.S. soldiers who served in Afghanistan CJCMOTF; members of the State Department; Michael Gray; the Non-Government Organization that helped bring her to America; the Children's Burn Foundation; the Sherman Oaks Hospital; the original host family; Dr. Mike Smith; Col. Robert Frame; the American Red Cross; Russell Roten; Alan Goldstein; the doctors, nurses, technicians, and staff of the Grossman Burn Center; Sandy and Mitch Francis; Jeff Grossman; Dr. A. Richard and Elizabeth Grossman; Dorothy English; Henri, Patty, Mona, and Nina Moayer; the administration, faculty, and students of Round Meadow Elementary School, including her best friend, Emily Hegel, whose beautiful spirit, love, and total acceptance of Zubaida also helped to rebuild Zubaida's self-esteem and support her already strong sense of individuality and confidence; friends and family members who all embraced her and extended their love; the Afghan and Iranian communities of Los Angeles; Zohra and Captain Daoud; Anne Bodine; Sergeant Shannon Para; the members of the Provincial Reconstruction Team and UN personnel in Herat, Afghanistan; John Oerum; Julia Dunphy; ABC News; Dr. Mo and Nadjia Qayoumie; the Hegel family; Tina Bahador; Mahnaz, Gabby, and Miriam, the caretakers and translators who lived in our home; Federal Express; Swiss Air; Sharlene Martin; Anthony Flacco; the numerous individuals who opened their hearts and offered help; and the hundreds of people who have donated to Zubaida's Fund to secure a better future for her.

We, along with all of them, have come to realize that the gift belongs to the giver.

—DR. PETER AND REBECCA GROSSMAN

Tiny Dancer

1 🌿

In July of 2001, Zubaida (*Zu-BAY-dah*) was only nine and a half years old, but she was already well aware that her remote desert village in southwestern Afghanistan was an ancient place. She couldn't avoid knowing that hundreds of years earlier, the village of Farah had been a major site of the region's trade activity—her daily life was carried out amid tall mud-brick ruins that hadn't seen their true form since back in the thirteenth century when Genghis Khan swept through the region with the Mongol hordes.

She didn't care; Zubaida's existence was punctuated by the cultural music and dance that had surrounded her every day of her life. And as music will do with some people, the melodies and rhythms managed to pass into her blood and soak into her bones, so that a major portion of her waking existence took place while she hummed without thinking about it or danced without self-consciousness. It was within her love of music and dancing that Zubaida found something to lift her out of boredom and steer her away from depression whenever she found herself alone amid the ancient and isolated ruins.

Lately, she felt her music carrying a special power over her. Her time in this life for carefree dancing was soon to end; under prevailing laws of the ruling Taliban forces, she would never again be allowed to run and play in public with other girls, or to have a boy for a friend under any circumstances, with the coming of her tenth birthday. She knew that, and she felt time shrinking itself tighter around her.

So despite the crushing mantle of heat on this July afternoon, Zubaida felt rhythms and melodies playing inside of her wisp-thin body that helped her to pass the closing days of her childhood with a measure of personal happiness. Zubaida sang out, "I am the girl from Herat, I can hear the music from over the mountain," a line from a very old song that is still commonly sung by Afghan women.

It was still early in the day, and she was alone at home while all of her siblings were scattered around the village at their tasks. Her mother and older sister were visiting neighbors. It was a perfect opportunity to let loose her urges to openly sing and dance. It was wonderful to be so free and to give herself over to the music. After all, there were no brothers and sisters around to trip over, no grouchy parents to tell her to keep down the noise, and best of all, no Taliban cleric glowering down his disapproval that a female child should dare to give vent to a moment of youthful joy.

Zubaida felt herself surrounded by a bubble of time and opportunity that presented an ideal setting for some intense young girl exuberance. All she had to do was tap into the music and glide on its waves; it animated her from head to toe. It moved her through the house in wiggling gyrations and twisting leaps. Once she started, there was no stopping her. She was well aware of the endless cruelty of the Taliban enforcers and knew that they would violently disapprove if they saw her like this—but she also knew that the Taliban tended to ignore this desert region most of the time, in favor of seeking higher numbers of converts amid Afghanistan's larger towns and cities. And so as long as she remained hidden behind the thick mud-brick walls of the family home, she was safe from all of them.

The temporary solitude also offered her a good opportunity to take a bath with some privacy, so she burned off excess energy by humming and skipping and twisting her way through preparing the bath and filling the small tub. When she bent to light the heater's pilot flame, she noticed that the little fuel tank was nearly empty. So she stood up again and danced away, singing one of her favorite passages over and over while she retrieved the household's kerosene can and carried it back to the heater.

Lost in her music, alone in the house, it was easy for a girl who was not yet ten years of age to lose track of little details—like making sure the pilot light was out before she tried to fill the heater with fuel. Instead, even though she knew better than to risk sloshing the fuel by jumping around with the can in her hands, she was still able to improvise a few fancy footsteps and hold the can steady while she moved toward the heater.

Zubaida could control her movements so well that if she hadn't been a forgetful, barefooted kid who had neglected to kick her shoes out of the way before approaching the heater, there would have been no problem for her that day.

In that first instant, when the toes of her first foot hit the edge of the first shoe, she instinctively shifted her weight to the other foot to retain her balance. It should have worked, but the other shoe was waiting to foil her. It tangled itself between both of her feet and caused her balance to shift just enough that she couldn't find any stability to the floor. Instinct opened her arms and she let the kerosene fall away, so that all she had to do was balance her own weight. That move, at least, was successful—instead of sprawling headlong onto the water heater, she only fell to her hands and knees.

If the small tidal wave of kerosene had not splashed directly over the heater's pilot light, she probably would have jumped right back to her feet without so much as a bruise. Instead, a sheet of fire roared up from the pilot and leaped into the air, igniting the fuel that had spilled on her.

It turned the nine-and-a-half-year-old tiny dancer into a blazing human torch.

꙳ ꙳

Her first sensations were mostly emotional—she screamed in fear to the empty house while she tried to beat out the flames that were already enveloping the top half of her body. But when she inhaled, the superheated air immediately scorched her throat and lungs, cutting her cries into terrified yelps.

It was only then that the first full wave of physical pain hit her, and it came with the force of a vicious animal attack. Flaming orange teeth bit through her hair, tore through her skin and into her flesh, digging toward her bones. She lost all control of herself and gave in to mortal panic, flailing at her clothing and staggering around the room, colliding with the thick mud walls.

Next door, her mother, Bador, and her second-eldest sister, Nacima, both heard Zubaida's initial screams. Even though they didn't recognize her contorted voice, the tone was so gut-wrenching that it brought them running; they arrived in time to see her collapse. The two women were products of their age, essentially uneducated and seldom allowed to travel beyond their neighborhood, deliberately kept ignorant of as much of the world as could be withheld from them. But within the confines of the home walls, they were fiercely independent and there was no situation where they would react in any way but to immediately attack it themselves. "The water, quickly!" her mother exclaimed. Fortunately, they had the presence of mind to grab the tub of bathwater, hoist it between them, and pour it over the burning child—who had now been on fire long enough that the hungry flames were not only feeding on the spilled fuel, but on the oils of her flesh itself. The impact of the water snuffed the flames, but for the women, the sight of what remained in that smoking pile dropped them to their knees.

The girl inside of the burned heap was consumed by terror and pain. She never lost consciousness, but the combination of terror and agony concentrated her attention so completely that she was barely aware of the larger question of what had actually happened to her. In those first moments, all she knew was that the initial wave of fear had been replaced by such a relentless, evil pain that there was no possible reaction other than to inhale with scorched lungs, scream all the air out of her body, then inhale and scream again. It didn't matter that the fiery air burned her inside; her body was running on instincts that needed to scream the pain away, needed to force the pain through her lungs and back out into the air.

It didn't work, but her instincts wouldn't let her stop.

An hour after the flames were extinguished, Zubaida lay writhing on the floor while her sixteen-year-old brother Daud frantically searched the town for their father. There was no phone anywhere in the village of Farah; the only way to search for anyone was to run, call out, spread the word. Back at home, Zubaida's agonized sounds were fully joined by those from her mother and sister and even a few of the neighbor women. They lent their throats to her suffering and helped her to scream the pain away, just as the women of their families have done for centuries.

In such a remote place, no one had any better medical treatment for catastrophic burns than to continually drizzle water over the burned area in the attempt to cool the skin. There were no strong drugs and not even any alcohol to ease Zubaida's pain in this region of devout Shiite Muslims. But although the girl was deep in shock by this point, for some reason she never passed out and remained fully conscious.

For her mother, Bador, that fact was a source of both reassurance and torture. It was reassuring to see life in Zubaida's eyes, but any attempt to touch her daughter sent fresh waves of pain flashing through the girl, causing more of Zubaida's screams to fill the air.

Finally, after that first hour, the lethargy of shock began to settle in. With no IV to keep up Zubaida's fluid levels, she lapsed into bouts of uncontrollable shaking. Her family grew alarmed by the low, weak moans that began to rise up from a body that was too exhausted to protest any louder.

What no one could hear was Zubaida's voice inside of herself, where she was still screaming at full force. She screamed like a desert animal being eaten alive. She screamed her horror and her shock and her pain, and most of all she screamed her molten rage that this thing was happening to her. It was only because her body's strength was nearly gone that the screams emerged as little more than those long halting groans that hung in the air like questions no one could answer.

Now Zubaida's father arrived, gasping. Mohammed Hasan stared down in horror at his little girl while he fought to make his brain believe his eyes. He was gazing at a burned cinder of a child, barely recognizable. He shrieked in horror. Then he cried, unashamed, right along with the women. He begged for help from Allah, from the Prophet Mohammed, and from Ali—Mohammed's anointed one, champion of the Shiite Muslim people.

If the prayers worked, the intervention they brought was only a small consolation. The way that events played out made it seem as if Allah had agreed to keep Zubaida alive, but only alive enough so that she didn't die on the spot. Everything else, it seemed, was being left up to their own humble earthly actions.

For Hasan, as an Afghan husband and father, this could only mean that everything else was up to him. His wife Bador couldn't take Zubaida to seek the help she needed—under Taliban law, a married woman was only allowed to offer help inside of the home and behind private walls, but without a father or brother to chaperone her, she couldn't even take her own injured child to a hospital.

In the Taliban-ruled provinces, a woman caught trying such a thing by herself might be judged an "adventuress." And since an adventuress is a temptress and a temptress is a whore, a woman so judged could easily receive a sentence of death by public stoning—or perhaps a simple beheading as a quicker alternative, if her crime was less severe.

One of Hasan's strong young visiting cousins had already carried Zubaida down the street to the local clinic, but it had produced no effective treatment and no pain-killing medicine. It was clear that everyone expected her to die within hours. The impoverished clinic had no meaningful help to offer, anyway.

Mohammed Hasan began to pack a few meager belongings for a trip to Herat, the closest city. "I must take Zubaida and find good doctors," Hasan told his wife and family. By now the entire community knew that something had gone terribly wrong in the Hasan house, and had gathered outside in concern. Even though no one had the skill to offer any sort of medical help, the tribal culture rose up around them.

Within the town and the province of Farah, the people either call themselves *Afghan*, like the Hasan family, or *Pushtun*, the area's majority. Both groups have survived by clinging to their tribal structures over the centuries, and have done so along a continuous timeline while the civilizations of numerous conquering races rose and fell around them. That same tribal unity rose up to help the family now.

Word went out that Zubaida had to be transported to the closest medical clinic in Herat, roughly a hundred and twenty miles away, an impossible trip either by foot or by camel for one so badly injured. But one of the families related to the Hasans was fortunate enough to own an old car that sometimes ran. They agreed to attempt to drive Zubaida and Mohammed to Herat, if he could fill the nearly empty tank and pay for all of the trip and perhaps pay something for the wear on the vehicle.

Their neighbor drove while Hasan held Zubaida's shrieking form flat on the backseat and her mother rode in front. The trip took nearly seven hours. It sent the burned girl into fresh shrieks every time the truck bed bounced over the rutted dirt road. Zubaida had still not gained the release of passing out, so her mother continually cried and begged Allah to intervene, or to at least let Zubaida fall unconscious and give her some relief.

But Zubaida's ability to maintain a stranglehold on life, surprising as it was after those around her began to give her up for dead, didn't appear to include the option of relief from consciousness. Some part of her that was more ancient than the mud-walled village ruins was sending her the continuous, unspoken message that in order to remain alive, she had to stay alert. She was in that desperate and primal state where her instincts filled her nervous system with the fear that once she let go of the world and allowed herself to sleep, there would be no stopping the downward slide. So with every ounce of alertness left to her, she felt every bump while they pushed along through the relentless desert until the hot day descended into a mercifully cool night.

When they finally arrived at the clinic in Herat, Hasan pulled out the small wad of currency that represented much of his family's cash and pressed it into the hands of a doctor. "Please save my little girl," he begged. His passion for her well-being may have been a surprise to the staff at the clinic, since the region's growing fundamentalism—followed by its takeover by the Taliban forces—was accompanied by commensurate losses in the social standing of females in general, and of female children in particular.

The kind of deep concern that Hasan showed for his little girl was more typically reserved for sons. Under Taliban fundamentalism, many parents would be expected to simply abandon their dying daughter in the wilderness, or, if the family patriarch was of a more kindly nature, dispose of her in some quick and painless method like a stealthy bullet to the head and then bury the body with a little respect.

A female child, after all, does little to protect her parents from poverty in their old age when she is taken away at marriage and sealed behind thick walls.

Still, the doctors agreed. "We will do what we can." But the look on their faces showed little hope. Despite their lack of essential supplies, they realized that the charred skin had to be scraped and washed if Zubaida was to have any chance of surviving the infections that would inevitably follow. And so even though they had no anesthesia to offer her, there was nothing else to do but peel away her blistered and oozing skin.

That procedure began less than eight hours after the accident, but Zubaida found that she still had plenty of energy left for shrieking with every cell of her body while the skin was flayed off her. The staff had to hold her down just as they would a torture victim. From Zubaida's standpoint there was no difference. "No, no, please stop, please don't," she cried out in desperation.

She found that the initial pain had not diminished at all, and now—impossibly—it became worse when they pulled the burned skin away. In the deeper areas of her burns, where the flesh of her chest was essentially destroyed, the nerve endings were also gone. Therefore her pain in those spots wasn't as bad as it was across her neck, throat, and arms. There, the burns had left live nerve endings beneath the scorched flesh. And those singed nerves were now sending awful messages to her brain. Agony blasted up out of her—every new shriek was like steam through a tight valve.

Once the torture session was finally over, there was nothing left in the little clinic's arsenal to offer her as treatment, other than to rub her with salve to keep the raw flesh somewhat protected. They released her back into her father's care. The kindly doctor, moved by the father's unusual concern for his female child, took Hasan aside and said, "The injuries are certainly not survivable. Death could come tonight or tomorrow, or maybe in a week or two." The only remaining question was how long a nightmare Hasan's little girl would have to endure before death inevitably claimed her.

The doctor urged, "Take your daughter home and pray for her end to come quickly."

Hasan did take Zubaida back home after sharing the dreadful prognosis with his wife, but no matter how deep Zubaida's agony, he could not find it in himself to pray for her to be taken, lost to the family. He and Bador directed the rest of the family not to pray for her death at all. Instead, they asked them to pray for a miracle.

And if a miracle was too much to ask, Hasan prayed aloud, "Please Allah, take me instead of this innocent child." He cycled the plea to his God in the back of his mind and repeated it over and over while he made the helpless motions of caring for her.

Twenty-four hours after the fire, Hasan called upon their neighbors for a small loan to pay for gas so that another borrowed rolling wreck could be employed to take Zubaida and seek help in other places. He traded off some of the family possessions to raise the meager cash and set out with her toward the Afghanistan-Iran border, with a loose plan of making their way to one of the larger hospitals there. Surely, he thought, the doctors in such places would know what to do. Mohammed Hasan had served his country's army in the long war against the Soviet invaders. He knew about the kinds of elaborate medical care that could be found, for the right people. No doubt one such place would have the right kind of medicine to save his daughter.

By now, Zubaida was lost to a thick fog of fatigue after a full day and night of screaming her way through pain so intense that she would never have words to express any of it. Her parents kept drizzling cool water over her tortured flesh. The relief mostly came from the attention that they showered upon her and its effect of easing her terror. No matter what they did for her, the pain was unrelenting. The only thing that stopped her cries for brief periods was when sheer exhaustion overwhelmed her.

This time they drove late at night, avoiding the worst of the desert heat while they rolled along over parched stretches of land under a pitch-black sky. Once they reached Herat, they continued north until they crossed the border into Iran and headed for the small Iranian city of Moshad.

At least the occasional Taliban roadblocks were manned by devotees who seemed to understand the girl's plight and who felt no threat from her. They let the moaning child and the half-hysterical father pass on. The black-turbaned fanatics may not have understood a father's unwillingness to leave his daughter's fate up to Allah, but they were moved enough by her condition to shrug and allow her delusional father to continue his hopeless quest.

Doctors in Moshad took a look at Zubaida, freshened her salve coating, and referred them on to the capital city of Tehran, another five hundred miles away. That meant driving for another twelve hours, while for Zubaida, nothing about traveling got any better.

The hospital in Tehran accepted her for treatment, although there wasn't much that they could do beyond rubbing her with other ointments in an attempt to ward off the worst of the infections and to keep the wounds from drying out.

She was soon past any sense of time; the days and nights began to melt into one another. The single most constant force in her awareness was agony coming from her roasted nerve endings. Whether it forced its way back out as energetic screams or exhausted moans, it continued to burn inside of her.

❧ ❧

Zubaida, all of her family, and everyone in the village of Farah knew that their poverty was worsened by an entire generation of war with the invading Soviet forces. It was a conflict that didn't end until 1989. Many of their local men died in the long struggle to repel the Soviet Army and defeat Communism.

But after the Russian foreigners were finally driven away, there was nothing to fill the vacuum; the unifying power of a common enemy was lost to the splintered interests of many different Afghan militia factions. Soon the infighting between local warlords began. No matter who won the warlords' bitter flare-ups, the result always ended up with the general population being stripped of basic goods and services and left to absorb the impact.

Under those conditions, the rise of the Taliban followed the departure of the Soviets. Black-turbaned squads of long-bearded fanatics swept over the country of thirty million. They used the name of Allah to imprison the female population and exercise twenty-four-hour control over all of the men, via a host of strict religious edicts. Zubaida's family and everyone in Farah understood how the Taliban's destructive influence on their region had drained away any international relief that might have been intended for them, long before any of it could reach the village. That relief included any medically valuable painkillers or antibiotics. More important for the Hasan family, the Soviet war and the Taliban rise to power had mutually succeeded in ending the education

of females throughout Afghanistan for so long that now not only were doctors
rare in the region, there were no trained nurses there at all.

゜゜゜

*Halfway around the planet, the grim reality of the Taliban was already the topic of a
draft U.S. Presidential Directive. It was quietly being prepared in Washington, D.C.,
to authorize one last black-ops attempt to remove a certain obscure but worrisome
Afghanistan-based Islamic terrorist named Osama bin Laden.*

*If that attempt failed, the Presidential Directive proposed that the next logical step
would have to be nothing short of the complete removal of the Taliban regime from all
positions of power in Afghanistan, because of their sympathy for Osama bin Laden's
anti-U.S. campaign.*

*At about the same time that Zubaida was burned, the last of nineteen Islamic sui-
cide hijackers arrived inside the United States and began final flight training in preparation for the attack they planned for the coming September 11.*

゜゜゜

One week after the burns, Zubaida's pain was down to a more bearable level
most of the time, but the enflamed nerve endings always raged again whenever
her dressings needed to be changed. Before long, screams and silence became
her only language. She clung to her life without painkillers inside a ruined
body that would surely never dance again. Now, the music that had always carried her through every difficult experience remained silent. Since the fire, she
hadn't heard a note.

Sometimes she could sink into mere sobs and go back to crying like any
other little girl, but most of the time she shrieked in pain with every change of
dressing and every scraping of the infected wounds.

The Iranian doctors spent twenty days giving her the best medicines that
they could make available, while Zubaida teetered in and out of her nightmare
world. But the medicines they could offer and facilities they possessed simply
weren't enough to fight back the raging infections that had begun to attack her
raw and open wounds.

Eventually, the doctors agreed that they were making no headway with her.
The hospital was crowded and the need for space was severe. So they in-

formed Mohammed Hasan that they had done everything they could for his suffering child, but it was impossible for this little girl to live much longer through the waves of infection that were now sweeping through her. Despite the doctors' greater resources and higher levels of training than those back in Herat, their ultimate response was the same as the others—*take your daughter back home and pray for death to ease her suffering.*

⚜ ⚜

Huge, unseen forces, whose power had been steadily building for over twenty years, now swirled invisibly throughout their homeland and spilled across the borders and spread all over the planet. No one on either end of the unseen storm could know how powerfully those waves were about to impact on one suffering Afghan girl huddled in an isolated desert village with her stunned and aching family.

Toward the end of July, suicide pilot Mohammed Atta contacted Osama bin Laden by courier and asked for another several weeks to complete his squad's flight training. It is apparent that his request was granted—on July 27, the CIA noted that the mounting intelligence "chatter" concerning rumors of imminent attacks on America had abruptly fallen silent.

Nobody knew why.

⚜ ⚜

Hasan took Zubaida back to their home village of Farah, but he still couldn't make himself follow the doctors' suggestions about praying for her to die. Even though Hasan was a Muslim, he didn't share the fanatic ways of the fundamentalists. Not only was he opposed to their vicious control over the population, but in an hour such as this one, he couldn't share in the belief that the same God who allowed this to happen to Hasan's defenseless daughter would take any better care of Zubaida in the afterlife than He had in this world.

Instead, Hasan continued his litany for the only end that he could desire— some sort of miracle to save his suffering child. It was a faltering prayer, propped between his refusal to embrace extreme religion and his rejection of the superstitions that pervade much of the desert nomad culture. Just as he had never believed in the militant fringes of Islamic faith, he had also never found any comfort in any of the age-old beliefs that remain prevalent in that part of the world: *To look upon the moon during the third night of a new moon is to bring bad luck. A woman carrying an unborn child must not touch her body during an eclipse, or the child will bear a mark on the part of the body that was touched. If she carries a knife during an eclipse, the child will be scarred in any part of the body where the knife touches the mother.*

Hasan knew that his more superstitious wife had avoided all such behaviors, and even so, their little girl was slowly being covered in infected scar tissue that grew more pronounced with every passing day—what good had the age-old superstitious "precautions" done? He struggled to remain faithful to his God even as he acknowledged that the realm of superstition hadn't done anything to help the family, either.

Hasan realized that he remained his daughter's only hope. He had to be willing to fight as hard as she herself was fighting. So as soon as he and Zubaida arrived back home in Farah after the twenty-day stay in the Tehran hospital, he arranged for the local folk doctor to make daily visits and rub Zubaida with homemade ointments in a continuing effort to fight off infection in her wounds.

The ointments seemed to work well enough to keep the worst at bay, but they lacked the power to bring her into a healing state. Zubaida couldn't eat well enough to sustain herself, so her flesh began to wither. The infections held her in a grip of low-grade fevers. Meanwhile the scar tissue covering most of her face and torso continued to grow thicker with every passing day, wrapping her in tight bands of stiff flesh that were beginning to bind her like fibrous ropes.

But whether it was Divine Intervention, blind luck, or simply the result of one girl's steely will to live, in the three weeks that had passed since the fire consumed so much of Zubaida, she continued to cling to life with an unyielding grip that nobody could explain.

Gradually, with the passing days, Zubaida plunged into a place where dreams, nightmares, and waking life all melted together under the late summer sun. Desert heat was a lifelong reality that usually went unnoticed—now it was a constant torment. Her scarring wounds itched almost as badly as they hurt, at least until she made any attempt to move. Then the simple act of turning over on her sleeping pad sent fresh shocks of pain shooting through her.

Family members tended to her, floating in and out of her awareness like ghosts until every part of the day and night was impossibly foreign to her. All the more so, since she found that she had lost her music. There was no desire to sing left in her, and she certainly couldn't do any dancing. The very urges, the feelings, had disappeared. There was a thick silence in her head where her constant companion of rhythms and melodies always used to be. She was no longer a little girl; she was an organism made of pain.

※ ※

Six weeks after the fire, Zubaida was still receiving daily visits from the local folk doctor, who emerged from the house every day surprised to have found a living patient to treat inside. Friends and neighbors debated whether she continued to live because Allah willed it so, or if some superstitious practice that they didn't know about was secretly protecting her. Nevertheless, visitors came away convinced that Allah wouldn't wish such a thing upon any child—and that if her condition was the product of some occult practice, then it only proved that superstition wasn't worth the trouble.

Zubaida's wounds were beginning to fill in with the granulation tissue that a burned body will make to generate a new blood supply to damaged areas. Those parts were becoming laden with bacteria in spite of the daily ointments and the dressing changes. Her left arm had been burned much worse than the right one, and the growing scar tissue caused it to feel stiffer by the day, along with her head and neck. Between the pain of movement and the stiffness of the flesh that was trying in vain to heal, her range of motion became severely limited.

While new nerves attempted to grow into the twisted and distorted flesh, there were times when the wounds actually hurt her worse than right after the fire. She spent most of her time trying to lie as still as possible; the pain was at its lowest level when she didn't move at all. The daily change of her oozing dressings remained a torture session that everyone around her dreaded as much as she did.

Most of the people of Farah survive by farming fields that are carefully irrigated by the nearby Farah River. They eke out their livelihoods with little or no margin of profit due to the region's many years of wartime destruction. Zubaida's family was no better off than the others, so there was nowhere to go but to those same neighbors to seek funds for further treatment.

Some good fortune finally found them; from various places around the village, small quantities of money that supposedly did not exist began to leak forth on behalf of the Hasan family. The sums had to be presented as loans, though. In a community that lives with the specter of hunger, everyone gave with the faith that they would see the money returned to them.

Before long, however, and to his public shame, Mohammed Hasan found that he couldn't work at his usual odd jobs enough to care for his own family, let alone save anything to pay back to his neighbors. Tending to his daughter took most of his time and all of his energy. Bador tried to keep up with the work of cleaning Zubaida's bedding and washing the many strips of dressing, along with the endless chores of tending to seven other children. She did this in the context of a culture that enforced strict limitations on her right to step outside the walls of her own home, let alone venture outside of her neighborhood, which meant that she kept up her workload inside of a tiny box of a house whose walls she could seldom escape.

Bador began to develop migraine headaches that left her nearly as debilitated as her daughter.

Hasan and his wife did their best to fight off despair, but despite their Muslim background, negative emotions sometimes took hold of them. Then, late at night after the children were asleep, they sat away from the others and slipped into talk of suicide.

In addition to the devastation of their daughter, the accident had dragged an entire family down into a deep, dark well where it was plain that there would be no future and no escape. The crushing debt load that the family was rapidly accumulating was hitting them at a time when paying work was nearly impossible to find anywhere inside of Afghanistan's Farah province.

Everyone who visited them exclaimed that they had never seen injuries such as those that Zubaida sustained. To all of them, and to Hasan himself, it seemed somehow supernatural that their daughter had not died that first day—and utterly impossible that she continued to hang on to life after weeks of such suffering.

The more superstitious visitors went away from the Hasan home with the clammy feeling that they had just witnessed something impossible inside that house—something unnatural. It was as if this destroyed remnant of a little girl were simply too stubborn to allow herself a release from attacks of pain so severe that others could not comprehend them any more than they could understand what was keeping her alive.

Nevertheless, the days kept on inching their way forward, one into the next, and still young Zubaida refused to let go.

❧ ❧

In the United States on September 4, 2001, the President's Principals Committee had their first meeting regarding international reports of the grim threat of attacks by a Muslim extremist organization calling itself Al Qaeda, "the Base," under the direction of an obscenely rich son of Arab privilege named Osama Bin Laden. The National Security Council's counterterrorism coordinator, Richard Clark, pleaded for intense White House resolve in hunting down Al Qaeda fighters. He expressed his gut fear that there were major attacks upon the American homeland coming in the very near future.

In Afghanistan on September 9, the Northern Alliance leader Ahmed Shah Massoud consented to a personal interview with two Arab "journalists" who had been waiting in his camp for days in order to see him. The pair entered his tent carrying a fake camera rigged with high explosives. They were undercover Al Qaeda operatives, and their suicide bomb killed Massoud and his staff.

On September 10, the National Security Agency's Deputy Director Stephen Hadley told the CIA to prepare for a series of covert actions against Al Qaeda. By this time, America's international security warning system was, as The 9/11 Commission Report would later put it, "blinking red."

❧ ❧

The news of the September 11 attacks on America didn't reach into the remote areas of Afghanistan right away. Even if it had, there was no way that Zubaida or her family could have any idea of the size of the impact that the aftermath would make upon them.

Summer passed into fall, and although the men in the village of Farah had heard reports of American soldiers building up their numbers inside of Afghanistan, local people were only aware of the Americans in the form of occasional U.S. Army convoys passing by on the way to Herat. They didn't feel any particular threat; it was all part of some far-away politician's problem.

Three months after Zubaida's accident, the sole sliver of good news for her was that the pain was tapering off to tolerable levels. She was never free of it, but the wrenching agony had finally left her. Whatever discomfort remained with her seemed pale next to that.

Her music, however, was long gone. She didn't expect herself to dance or sing, but it surprised her that she couldn't even hear any notes. Nowhere in her mind was the invisible radio that had always supplied her with accompaniment to her daily life, song after song after song.

She was even beginning to forget what it felt like to have the music inside of her.

Now that the pain had subsided, however, Zubaida had plenty of time to consider what this accident had cost her position in the family structure. Even at her young age, she had long since become the family's "alpha" child, assuming a role of responsibility at home that was greater than her years. Now her embarrassment over her appearance was not as great as her feeling of guilt that she could no longer be of use—her roster of daily chores had once been a substantial contribution to everyone's well-being. But not only was she of no use anymore, her constant need of help was a heavy drain on energy and resources that no one in the family or their struggling village could afford to waste.

The only defense left to her mental state was to slow her thoughts down to the point that time seemed to race by in front of her. That altered state became her full-time place of refuge.

Most of her open wounds were closed or closing, but the normal skin that had once been there was steadily being replaced by stiff scar tissue. Sometimes, if she moved too quickly, one of the healing areas would break open with a fresh surge of fiery pain, and the recovery had to begin all over again. Her left arm was now so stiff that she had to keep it tucked up against her chest, since any other position pulled at her chest wounds. Eventually the sticky healing flesh glued her arm into place.

The arm stayed there, crooked up against her left side, until the stiff scar tissue thickened so much that the arm became permanently welded to her torso.

The healing skin of her neck and lower face was now covered over with scar tissue that continued to grow, but the tissue's inability to stretch also caused it to gradually pull her head farther and farther down onto her chest. Finally, her chin rested there and became sealed in that position. Since her head couldn't move any farther downward, the out-of-control scar tissue then began to pull down on her face, her eyes, her jaw, her lower lip.

By the time three months passed, Zubaida's condition had degraded to a state so severe that most people living in the world's developed nations will never see anything like it—the masses of scar tissue surrounding her and binding up her body had progressed to a stage that is simply never allowed to develop in places that have adequate medical care. Just as the famed "Elephant Man" had been betrayed by his own bones and cartilage when they grew out of control and distorted him beyond recognition, Zubaida's flesh was now playing a similar trick on her by wrapping her in that growing blanket of unbending scar tissue.

Eventually, her mouth was pulled so far downward that she could no longer close it enough to chew her food—her mother had to mash it up for her. The difficulty in eating had already caused her to lose a fourth of her body weight, and there was no sign that she would be able to gain it back.

Zubaida herself had no clear idea why she wouldn't let herself give in to death. She could feel it tugging at her, but the strongest urge inside of her was to somehow get back on her feet and pitch in with the family. It didn't matter to her that she had older siblings—Zubaida's boundless energy had always made her invaluable to the family's day-to-day living. She couldn't imagine them being left without her.

She also felt her family's grief for her. When she overheard her parents give in to thoughts of complete despair, she felt shamed to be the cause of it. It was nearly as humiliating as the reactions of visitors when they gasped at her appearance.

But even all of that wasn't enough to soften Zubaida's grip on life. Her innate drive to hurry up and get better didn't actually work—and didn't even prevent her condition from growing worse—but it was enough to keep her alive.

She felt herself filled with the determination that if Death wanted her, it would have to come and drag her away. She didn't question where the strength came from; it felt as much a part of her as the urge to breathe. It was as if the music that she no longer possessed had left just enough of its essence inside of her to continue fueling her with the power of its life force, even if she could no longer hear a single note.

❦ ❦

When America's 9/11 Commission later issued its report on the events of that day, one of its primary conclusions was that in the post-9/11 era, individual citizens need to accept responsibility for their own well-being. It must ultimately rest with each one of them, and it's unwise to rely upon government resources to save them in times of disaster.

It was a lesson that Afghanistan's desert people learned centuries ago. Nowhere was the warning more apparent than in the Afghan village of Farah, in the house of Zubaida Hasan.

With the coming of winter, scorching desert heat was replaced by the bitter cold air that rolls down from the towering mountains to the north. They spill out of a vast range of snowy peaks bisecting all of Afghanistan: the daunting Hindu Kush. The word "Kush" comes from Persian, meaning "killers," and it perfectly describes that high and jagged range of barren peaks. The extraordinary stamina needed to cross that range is an apt symbol for that toughness of spirit which Afghanistan's tribal people have embodied through centuries of struggle.

On the high desert plain in Farah, Mohammed Hasan and his wife, Bador, agreed that there had to be some reason that their daughter was still alive, even if they couldn't fathom it. They resolved that as long as Zubaida was willing to fight so hard for her life, then they would continue to fight along with her. They kept her out of sight whenever the Taliban were around, knowing that the fanatics would have no sympathy for a father's quest to save a single female child after she had been injured to the point of being socially useless. Then whenever the coast was clear, they went to work scraping up every cent they could borrow from friends and neighbors so that Mohammed could take her on one more pilgrimage to one more city, always in the hope of finding a doctor who might know what to do for her.

The family was being torn apart from the stress of caring for her. It was killing all of them to live with her while she slowly wasted away, unable to eat enough to sustain herself. The scar tissue on her face had contracted to the point that she could no longer close her eyes—she slept with them open. She could no longer close her mouth. The scar tissue was also strangling her from the inside by contorting her windpipe. Clearly the determined struggle that Zubaida had mounted to this point was nevertheless doomed to fail.

By now everyone in the region had heard about the tragic "miracle" of Zubaida's refusal to die, and even though nobody had the wherewithal to help on their own, a number of them responded to the Hasan family's pleas for help to pool together tiny amounts. Eventually they raised the fabulous sum of ten million *afghanis*—worth a little more than three thousand U.S. dollars at that time.

Hasan gladly accepted it, even though he had no idea how he could ever repay such a fortune. All he knew was that with this sum, he could transport his dying daughter to the southern city of Kandahar, where there was a small U.S. military presence in the wake of the terrorist attacks on America. That meant that there would have to be fabulous American doctors, did it not? There would be surgeons with the great skills that ex-soldier Hasan knew would accompany any such powerful military force. Perhaps there would be someone among them who knew if there was anything at all that could be done for her.

Hasan's neighbors warned him that any military force has strict policies about not getting involved with the problems of the local population. But Hasan also remembered that Americans were rumored to sometimes show unpredictable bouts of generosity if they felt convinced that you meant no harm. It was worth the risk of another try. So he set about planning the trip to Kandahar, determined to use every last penny of the collective loan in a last desperate search for help.

Even in his remote village, he had heard stories about that pack of Muslim extremists who recently flew huge airliners into some very important buildings in America. Local gossip had it that the very word "Muslim" had become a curse to American ears. Some of his more cynical neighbors cautioned him that it would not matter to the Americans that he was no fanatic and that he hated the Taliban even more than they did. He was a Muslim, therefore he would be a suspect to American eyes.

Hasan had never dealt with an American before, and wasn't even sure what one looked like. But even in his remote village, passing travelers brought stories of American army units that were pouring into Afghanistan's mountain regions to seek out the phantom Bin Laden and flush out more of the Taliban resistance.

Some in his village warned him that it was madness to approach the Americans. They had come to fight, using all sorts of secret weapons—what reason was there for them to offer help to a man such as him? Plus, the leader of the suicide attackers in America also went by the name of Mohammed. So did that mean that Hasan's very name would draw American wrath down upon him, in revenge? Worst of all, if the Americans were anything like the Taliban "Soldiers of God," Hasan knew they might well decide that the best thing would be to shoot him and his daughter, right there on the spot.

Even so, Mohammed Hasan had to ask himself if that would be any worse than watching his girl slowly die, knowing that she would surely take her father and her grieving mother along with her anyway.

❧ ❧

The city of Kandahar lies on the southeastern edge of Afghanistan, close to the Pakistani border. It remained one of the major Taliban holdouts in mid-2002, and represented the most urban collection of fundamentalist Muslims in the country. He could not expect to find local sympathy for his lost cause of a daughter. But he could make his best attempt to approach the U.S. military. He knew that the Americans were more like the familiar Russians when it came to the way they treat their women. At least they wouldn't question his simple motive for trying so long and hard to save this one little girl, with so many other children to support at home.

❧ ❧

The anonymous American Green Beret who first assisted Zubaida wants to remain that way, not only because he broke a standing rule about not getting involved in the medical problems of the local population when there was barely enough military clinic space for the U.S. sick and wounded, but also, and more important, because he doesn't want to replace his quiet act of kindness with a media spotlight. His Special Forces work depends on anonymity.

All that those in his military unit will say is that he was in the marketplace in Kandahar one day when he spotted one of the local men walking along with a little girl who appeared to be his daughter. The soldier might not have noticed them at all, except that the scarf that was wrapped over the top of the girl's head slipped for just a moment—and revealed a hideously scarred face. He looked again and noticed that the girl was painfully thin, even by local standards, but despite her condition, she was so alert that she seemed to sense him looking at her. She raised her eyes to meet his and stared directly back at him. Such a response from a female child is almost unheard of in that land of silenced children and suppressed women. Nevertheless, her eyes met his with a mixture of curiosity and defiance.

It was all too much for him to pass by and ignore.

He spoke enough of the language to mix with gestures and ask the man what happened to the girl. Then he listened while the man explained that the girl was indeed his daughter, and that she had been terribly burned several months ago, and that he had brought her to Kandahar as part of a long journey spent in seeking help for her.

The soldier asked what was being done for her.

"Nothing," her father replied. Every doctor whom he had taken her to see judged her condition to be hopeless. He introduced himself as Mohammed Hasan, and his daughter as Zubaida. The soldier noticed Hasan's constant references to the prophet "Ali," which revealed him to be a member of the relatively peaceful Shiite Muslims, not one of the more violent Sunni Muslims from the fundamentalist Sunni regions.

Mohammed Hasan explained that he brought Zubaida all the way to Kandahar in a last bid to seek help for her, and that he had attempted to apply for some kind of help from the Americans at the military base there. They were turned away at the gates; the trip had been a waste. In the seven months since the girl's accident, her father told of selling most of the family's meager possessions and borrowing money from his neighbors to pay for their journeys throughout the region to seek help.

The soldier knew that any borrowed sum was a huge amount for a rural desert Muslim, one that he was not likely to ever be able to repay. The Green Beret marveled—in a land that places notoriously low value on females, this struggling father had ransomed his life in the attempt to help his little girl.

He looked down at little Zubaida once again—beyond the frail body and the wounded expression in her eyes, there was also a defiant streak that showed a strong spark of life. The sergeant found that the idea of walking off and leaving the child to her fate was more than he could stand. "Come with me," he said, and took the local man's arm and, in defiance of standing orders, motioned for the father to follow him. Whether it would wind up costing him a promotion or even a spell in the brig, the sergeant couldn't walk away from that spark in this dying girl's eyes.

That's when the first domino fell. It sent a wave of reaction down a long and improvised domino chain. There would be many more of them yet to fall before Zubaida would finally be under way in her impossibly strange journey, and the chain would eventually reach halfway around the world, about as far away from her home as she could go without leaving the planet.

2 ❧

In the months since the fire, Zubaida's masses of scar tissue had continued to tighten until most of her facial and bodily features took on the smoothed-out edges of a melted wax sculpture. Farah was a place of few mirrors, so she seldom had to look at her reflection. But in Kandahar, her own shocking appearance confronted her on every corner. Even when there was no glass around, her appearance didn't need mirrors to mock her—she caught her reflection in the reactions of strangers wherever they went on the ancient city's endless twisting streets. She and her father became stranded in a crowd of gawking spectators whenever they walked through the bazaar.

In a cross-fade of assaults, the physical pain was beginning to leave her at the same time that it was replaced by a throbbing sense of isolation. So far, she had survived to within a few weeks of her tenth birthday, but with that coming of age she would traditionally have to retreat into a domestic life intended to prepare her for marriage—something that Zubaida knew she was too grotesque to expect. She would lose the outer world at the same time that the potential world of a valued mother's home and hearth became closed to her.

The fire continued to rob her, over and over again. Then her whole body filled with rage that spewed out of her in a high-pressure mix of fear and long-ing and grief over everything that had been stolen from her. She could see that people were shocked when she emotionally exploded, especially when her out-bursts followed a brief moment when she had been able to react to others with wit or humor.

In those tiny moments, the good moments, she could tell that people rec-ognized her again, even if they only got a glimpse. She practically recognized herself. But some new physical pain or emotional pain always intruded.

Then the people around her, who had just recognized their old Zubaida during one of her moments of clarity, would be all the more astonished when she began to scream or cry or even strike out at them in the extremes of her frustration. Since Zubaida had no control over any aspect of her life, the only form of strength left to her was in the power to shock herself and others. Back at home in Farah, she had already overheard her parents fearfully speculating as to whether or not Zubaida was losing her mind. Now, alone in Kandahar with her father, she felt that question from him, too, while he watched her re-act to the city.

She didn't feel sure that she wasn't losing her mind. All of her shattered ideas of what anything and everything were supposed to be lay in slivers all around her. "Trust us," the adults kept telling her. "We're trying to help you," they lied. Every time the adults said they were going to help her, they tortured her by peeling at her skin. Sometimes they talked to her father as if she wasn't even there, as they had done when they told him that she had no chance to live.

Her father had repeatedly assured her, "Zubaida, my soul, we have come to this place to find help for you." But she could see that most people were only interested in staring at her with giggling fascination. Even the American sol-dier who stopped her father to ask about her seemed to stare at her. She could feel a strong need to defy them in some way, but didn't know how. Something deep inside of her utterly rejected this awful predicament. She had no choice but to accept what had been done to her body, but she needed to shriek in protest over her social isolation.

Zubaida was not going to go quietly. In private, her screams of rage were sometimes louder than her cries of pain had ever been. As soon as they were out of this chaotic city and safely back home, she would let everybody keep right on wondering whether or not she was losing her mind.

What did such words even mean, with things as they were? It was good to shock and frighten people.

It was good to make them see her.

☙ ☙

Mohammed Hasan followed along with his daughter behind the American soldier, who seemed willing to help them in some way. They walked the streets of old Kandahar, long reputed to be named for its founder Alexander of Macedon and dating back over 2,300 years. Even though Hasan was a stranger to the city, he could tell that they were heading roughly toward the American base. There was nothing else that he could do for Zubaida, now, but follow this soldier in trust and hope. When the call to prayer echoed from the minarets of the Kherqa Sharif, one of the most sacred shrines in Afghanistan, he was surprised that the American paused to allow Hasan to kneel. He wondered if the American was aware that the shrine contains a cloak believed to have belonged to the Prophet himself—was that why a Westerner would show respect for the prayer call?

He wasn't sure how to deal with these Americans. They had the power to make you rich or to turn your home to rubble. They jumped back and forth between being respectful and murderous, according to sets of rules that were baffling to him.

His previous experience with outsiders came from fourteen years of Russian occupation. The Russians were easier to contend with; the sight of them was never anything but bad news. However, when a stranger shows you courtesy and kindness, when they go out of their way to help you in need, they activate a code of Afghan behavior that obligates a person to respond in kind and treat that stranger as a friend.

But the code was meant for ancient nomad tribes—these Americans were there as an army. Even if they could be friends to him, Hasan knew that all armies serve nations that are run by politicians—which meant that armies are sometimes ordered to kill their friends.

Centuries of constant invasions across Afghanistan by marauding hordes had left the locals convinced that only a fool trusts anybody wearing a uniform. He fought the urge to cut and run. It wasn't all the papers they kept making him sign that bothered him; his experience with pieces of paper was that they didn't mean a thing. The signing of papers seemed like more of a cultural practice that the Americans nearly worshipped, so he tried to go along out of respect for these foreign ways without worrying too much about whatever was on them.

Hasan's dilemma was eased by the knowledge that he was out of options. And so far, at least, the American was treating him as a friend. The code of honor that guided the lives of Hasan's people obligated him to rise to the moment and accept the hospitality without questioning the soldier's motives.

After all, even though he was here in this partially Westernized city, he was still an Afghan, one of the four great tribes whose lands cover much of what a bunch of Western politicians once decided to call Afghanistan. The local code of law, called *Pashtunwali*, has dictated behavior for centuries. It originated with the majority Pushtun (or "Pashtun") ethnic group, but today dominates the land, regardless of an individual's tribal identity. All personal conduct and social interaction are guided by these unwritten laws, and they are impressed upon every child as soon as they are able to understand them. The code has successfully bound the tribes of Afghanistan to their common culture, in spite of the distances and separations created by their nomadic wanderings, and it has done so for longer than anyone knows.

And so in Mohammed Hasan's life, there really *were* only two kinds of people: those who ascribe to the Pashtunwali—and the Others. Most of his concept of the Others was based upon nearly fifteen years that his home region spent in bitter guerilla warfare against the invading Soviet Army—that, and a few random encounters with Europeans of one race or another over the years.

Experience had clearly revealed to him that sometimes the Others were honorable, almost as if they had a Pashtunwali of their own, but just as often the Others could suddenly change their minds and follow some other "law." This new and different law might very well make it all right for them to harm you, or even take your life and the lives of everyone around you. The Others were to be distinguished by their need to assault you with disrespect and to deal in tricks and lies.

The representatives of the Soviets were like that, all through the years of their occupation of Afghanistan. That made it easy for the locals to kill them without regret, until the Soviet generals finally realized that the tribal people have been successfully fighting off invaders for centuries. Call them the "Soviets," but Hasan's years of hardscrabble living in a permanent combat zone had made it plain to him that the real enemy of his homeland was "The Great Russian Bear." This same Bear had already devoured many of the other sovereign nations in that part of the world.

The men of Hasan's province all fought like wild animals who cared nothing for a healthy fear of death, but who were also smart enough to remember that a fighter who dies tomorrow can do more damage than a fighter who dies today. The Pashtunwali clearly dictates that the strongest and most fierce opposition possible is the only acceptable reaction when a lethal affront is committed upon one's family, or worse, one's homeland, or worse still, one's sacred religious sites.

The Great Russian Bear had launched staggering and repeated assaults upon all three. They had every reason to believe that victory was theirs for the taking. They continually captured and tortured a leading officer into declaring a "surrender" of his men, only to find that if the men didn't like what their commander told them, they might ignore him, or maybe shoot him, or perhaps—as in this case—abandon him to his captors. No one knew who was actually directing the resistance. The Soviet tanks would roll and the Soviet infantry repeatedly crushed entire "armies" of insurgents, only to find that that "army" was actually just an urban militia made up of local men. The estimates of their numbers were overblown because of the extreme violence employed by these men who were fighting for their mud-brick homes and their little shops in the bazaar and their wives and the children who depended upon them. The Soviets did not doubt that they could eventually win; they stayed longer in Afghanistan than the U.S. had in Vietnam.

But eventually the soldiers of the great Soviet Army went away, beaten and licking their wounds. The Americans, though, were new to Hasan. He realized that their military had the power to cause any sort of trouble that they wanted to make, so he would have to wait and see whether or not these pink- and

yellow- and brown-skinned strangers were nothing more than different versions of the Others.

❦ ❦

The anonymous Green Beret soldier dropped off the girl and her father for a
checkup with a Special Forces medic at the Ninety-sixth Civil Affairs Battal-
ion. It would later be explained that the U.S. Army medic, operating under a
back-unit combat situation and with constant terrorist concerns, only agreed
to see a civilian father/daughter in the first place because the Green Beret expressed concern that she might be a victim of U.S. operations. The Green
Beret, experienced in The Army Way, may have done this knowing that as
soon as a file was created on the girl, it would be much easier to pass her up the
army hospital chain to whatever sort of specialists she needed to see. It was a
point of subtlety that did nothing less than make every single event possible
that followed down the long and invisible domino chain. Otherwise, the direct
approach and The Army Way would likely have done nothing more than get
him a face full of rules and regulations.

By the time the day was over, the father and daughter had already been
guaranteed enough medical help to at least address her immediate infections.
That treatment alone might require days or even weeks, before her underlying
injuries could even be addressed.

The cautiously grateful father took his daughter off to secure guest lodgings
for a long stay, after the medics made sure that he understood them well
enough to return with the girl at the right time and place.

A few dollars quietly pressed into his hands were enough to help Hasan and
his daughter stretch their small sum of traveling money, for the moment. And
even though ancient Kandahar was not their home, they would not be without
resources in that place—every great mosque in Afghanistan has a guest house
dedicated to maintaining the custom of hospitality to wanderers, in this land
that has always been a crossroads for nomads.

Back on the U.S. base, neither the first soldier to meet them, the first
medic to treat the girl, nor the first officer to put out a few quiet inquiries on
her behalf had any way of knowing what they were starting. At the time, no-

body had enough of her story to form any sort of grand plan out of it. There was only the sight of one girl's catastrophic injuries, witnessed by common soldiers and military doctors who all know physical trauma far too well.

Once Hasan and his daughter were taken into the medical system, her father didn't need to plead for her. The sharp awareness in her eyes contrasted with the ruined state of her body to form a statement that the soldiers were unwilling to ignore. By the time the girl's story traveled far enough up the chain of command to garner some inevitable bureaucratic backlash, an invisible but compelling momentum had already formed around her.

She would need every bit of it; the potential for trouble over her was enormous—not only was it less than five months after the attacks of September 11, 2001, but bombers and cruise missiles were still pounding Afghanistan's mountain hideouts in search of Osama bin Laden, chasing shadows through the countryside. Rumors of impending terrorist assaults on Americans and their Middle East bases were suspended in the dust and inhaled with the heat.

For the U.S. forces, reliable knowledge of the enemy's ways was still in its early stages. Would the extremists be willing to use a child such as this to gain on-base access to U.S. forces?

And since the Afghan civil record-keeping system out in the war-torn provinces was nearly nonexistent, the question had to be asked—was this man who called himself "Mohammed Hasan" really even the dying girl's father?

The U.S. military policy against allowing their fighting forces to become bogged down in local humanitarian activities has plenty of justification, because even once the inherent security issues are resolved—assuming that security issues can ever be resolved by occupying forces—there is not only the lack of local infrastructure to house and feed those that the military would help, but every hour expended upon a local civilian would be one less hour available to the very American soldiers for whom those medical facilities exist.

Therefore, even if the giant logistical questions of how to physically care for local civilians could be addressed—assuming that they could ever be addressed in a country the size of the state of Texas, with twenty-five to thirty million natives and a poverty-stricken economy broken by decades of violent homeland fighting—there would still be the thorny issue of preference.

How are those to be helped initially chosen? Who does the choosing? How would the U.S. Army doctors handle the political fallout when charges of favoritism are inevitably raised by disappointed applicants? How, in short, do you keep from causing more trouble than you are trying to fix in the first place?

Every soldier and military doctor who met Zubaida over the next few weeks knew all of these Perfectly Good Reasons not to get involved. None of them needed to be reminded that if somebody up at Central Command got wind of what they were doing and decided to make an issue of it, CentCom could make permanent trouble for them. They could wind up having accomplished nothing more than jeopardizing their careers while still failing to get the girl's health into a survivable condition.

But the unseen momentum rising up underneath all of those Perfectly Good Reasons not to get involved had already grown too strong to hold back.

❦ ❦

Mike Smith was a U.S. Army physician stationed in the capital city of Kabul when he got notice of Zubaida's case. Almost immediately after she entered the system in Kandahar, her files were transmitted to him along with a set of digital photos. What he saw there stopped him in his tracks.

Smith's official position toward any local medical case was the same as the one constraining the Special Forces soldiers; his primary mission was military in nature—helping to oversee medical services provided for American soldiers. He had an obligation to resist any abuse of medical services.

However, this anti-Taliban war was taking place amid the new technology of digital photography and the Internet, and it was the photos that convinced him.

He contacted Robert Frame, a U.S. Army colonel who worked in the region to coordinate the activities of the Civil Affairs units that worked to secure the interests of the local civilian population. Frame's job function straddled the needs of the peaceful local civilians on one hand and the obligation to protect the soldiers under him. For him, the Hasan story raised potential security issues of nightmarish proportion. What if, in an attempt to respond humanely to this little girl's plight, he unintentionally aided a terrorist who could be using an injured girl as a calling card to pass American checkpoints? Was it unreasonable to fear such a thing, he wondered, following the success of the 9/11 hijackers in capitalizing on American openness? The luxury of a purely humanitarian response was something that Frame simply couldn't indulge.

The Perfectly Good Reasons not to get involved with Hasan and his daughter hung over him like knives on threads.

Even so, the photos were more than he could ignore. He booked a trip to Kandahar and brought an able translator to help him interview the pair in person.

It only took one visit. After that, Frame helped balance Mike Smith's need to maintain consistent medical treatment for Zubaida's wound infections with the humanitarian side of taking care of the political and logistical realities behind taking two locals into the military system. A large part of his job was to see to it that he did nothing to invoke a backlash of outrage among so many other needy people in that impoverished country.

Quietly, using informal means of communication, word of the Zubaida case reached the State Department in Washington when officials at Central Command in Florida contacted the State Department about this sticky medical/political case.

At the State Department, Michael Gray was coordinating humanitarian relief into Afghanistan, working under General Tommy Franks' regime, when he learned that efforts were being made to find American medical expertise for a local Afghan case. The word was that doctors on the ground in Afghanistan wanted someone in the United States to attempt some sort of heroic intervention on behalf of a girl who had been so horribly burned that her own scars were slowly killing her.

At forty years of age, Gray's boyish good looks belied the casual ease with which he grasped complex political interests. He was already aware of all of the Perfectly Good Reasons that U.S. forces must not tie up military assets with medical help to local populations, so he realized that the case had to be extraordinary for it to have landed on his desk. It quickly became clear that certain Americans in Afghanistan were willing to take on this girl's case despite the fact that if anything went wrong, there would be an explosion of negative propaganda for the military, and ultimately for the U.S. government.

And that was before he got copies of her medical photos. Once he did, it was clear to him that there were dozens of things that could go wrong with a child as fragile as this one, stranded as she was inside a country that was hovering dangerously close to tribal anarchy. If she was to survive, she had to be pulled out of the area and placed under extraordinary medical care right away. It appeared to Gray that things had gone too far to be halted at this point, but he knew that if any major politician decided that this case could land on his or her doorstep in a hail of "scandal," they wouldn't hesitate to shut down the entire operation.

It didn't matter. If anyone was going to decide to break the domino chain, Gray already knew that it wasn't going to be him. At least he had the luxury of knowing that this was precisely the kind of case that his bosses wanted him to pursue. The explosive political and security risk elements were a dangerous and unpredictable part of the picture, but since Gray's main job was to coordinate the movement of humanitarian goods and services into Afghanistan, he could see the case clearly against the backdrop of lifelong misery that was guaranteed for Zubaida if some form of radical intervention wasn't created.

He fired up the complex processes of security checks, visas, and the endless signing of sheets of paper that even Afghan desert nomad Mohammed Hasan recognized as a central part of the American way of doing things.

Soon the efforts spread outside of the military and governmental realms. A powerful but nearly secret Non-Government Organization agreed to take on the chore of coordinating events in Afghanistan with potential supporters in America. The NGO caseworkers insisted on anonymity in return for their efforts, keenly aware of the need to avoid the rush on their services that publicity could generate—which would then require them to expend their resources in handling claims, instead of actually doing their work. The potential political complexities of the case were so dangerous that the NGO wasn't entirely sure that this was a case they should pursue in America, but they also agreed that there was no moral or ethical way to turn their back on the process at this point. They could feel the invisible wave carrying Zubaida along, and the dominoes in the chain continued to fall, each one toppling the next.

Michael Gray had an additional reason to be glad to see that this case found its way to him—and he would later be one of the people to comment on the happy level of coincidence surrounding this story—because his kid sister,

Rebecca, just happened to be married to surgeon Peter Grossman, who was partnered with his father, surgeon Richard Grossman, at the Grossman Burn Center of Sherman Oaks, near Los Angeles, California.

Gray also knew that his sister Rebecca would listen with special interest, since she had been a magazine columnist and TV commentator on health issues and a successful entrepreneur in medical technology.

"Energy," Gray says of her with a grin, "has never been a problem for Rebecca." He knew that if he could interest his sister in this case, she was likely to grab on to it so hard that she would personally see to it that little Zubaida Hasan got to America for treatment—no matter how thick the bureaucratic red tape might get.

He picked up the phone and called her at home.

As soon as the conversation was over, Rebecca called her husband at work and explained the situation to him. Their level of interest was immediate and intense. The energy wave kept right on moving along the domino chain; the reaction they shared was the same as all the other benefactors the Hasans would never meet, who by this time numbered in the dozens.

❦ ❦

Mohammed Hasan knew almost nothing of the network of people who were rapidly developing an interest in his daughter. He continued to bring her in for her ongoing checkups, and he could see that her infected scar tissue had begun clearing up, but he had no clear understanding of what to expect from the Americans.

They seemed so easily baffled by him.

They would speak his native language of *Dari* through their interpreters, asking him some simple question or other, such as, "When can you bring Zubaida back to Kandahar for another checkup?" But when he promised to return with the full moon, they just looked back at him with empty eyes. Then they made their interpreter speak to him about breaking every single hour into sixty little pieces and then spending each one like a miser with tight fists.

So he followed the Pashtunwali that dominates the land and affects all the Afghan tribes, whether they are part of the Pushtun majority or not. He showed them the respect of speaking back to them in their own fashion, with specific days and hours and tight little minutes. That seemed to make the Americans feel better.

He understood that the Americans were talking about taking Zubaida to the United States for special medical treatment. But the translators also told Hasan that this American medical treatment could consume many months—and since there was no way he could leave his large family without him for so long, this meant that his tiny daughter Zubaida could end up living there alone—among the Others.

He didn't doubt that the Others could conjure all sorts of man-made miracles inside of their own land, but the fact that Zubaida would spend so much time among them was more than he could comprehend.

All alone there, among them. What would it do to her?

While he considered his grim decision, Hasan couldn't help but wonder about the truth of these Americans' medical claims, anyway. What manner of people can replace a body that has been melted away? Who can restore the human face when it is ruined beyond recognition?

He was not the kind of father who could willingly let any small child go away alone, but neither could he rely on his neighbors to continue caring for his wife and children, if he went with her—the pair had already spent so much time away from Farah. His sixteen-year-old son, Daud, was filling in as the man of the house, in proper Afghan fashion, but Hasan knew that in any home that does not have the man of the house around and about, things have a way of spiraling out of control.

Hasan wondered whether he could return home to take care of the family, and send Daud along with Zubaida as her guardian? Daud would be a good choice, as far as his ability to handle the responsibility. And Hasan knew that Daud would be a fierce protector of his sister. Father and son shared names in common with the great hero, Sardar Mohammed Daud, who deposed Afghanistan's king in 1973 and installed, for the first time, a new form of government called a republic. Even though this new thing only lasted for four years before the Soviets invaded and ignited a generation of civil war, Sardar Mohammed Daud's revolution gave the Afghan people a taste of self-government that they had not forgotten.

The fierce spirit of Zubaida's brother was the kind she would need at her side, if she was to be stranded so far away and among so many Others. Hasan's son had a quiet and solid form of strength that would tell people, without words, that they must not think this shrunken girl is unprotected.

Daud might fear making the trip at first, but Hasan didn't doubt that his son would go if told to. And that was about as far as he got with the idea before he realized it was impossible.

The papers were a problem. By the great Ali, the Americans loved to sign papers. They seemed to sign papers for everything. At least when it came to matters of children, the Americans made it clear that it was important for the parents to always sign for the young ones, which at least showed that they had their priorities straight. Still, knowing those things didn't lower his constant amazement at the river of papers.

Unfortunately, even though sixteen-year-old Daud was old enough to marry and old enough to own his own flock and to wander the plains with his wife and children and their herd, if he chose to do so, he was still called a "child" by the Americans. He couldn't sign papers.

And yet, once Daud and Zubaida were far away, in America, alone among the Others, more papers would surely appear, would they not? And what if these Americans did come forward, talking fast to young Daud and waving papers that they might "allow" him to sign—would they be doing that simply to take advantage of a naïve young man?

It was a hard question. Hasan had been dealing with the Americans for several weeks now—but he still couldn't be sure whether they followed any sort of a consistent and reliable Code or not.

No. Daud would have to continue filling his father's shoes at home. If Zubaida was to make this uncertain trip at all, her father had to be the one to go with her, even if he couldn't remain there with her and had to return to their homeland. He could at least see that everything was right.

Hasan had no idea that an American named Michael Gray was back in Washington helping him to secure an emergency visa for himself and his daughter, but he soon felt the result of those efforts on the Afghanistan end. He found himself riding in a military truck next to a Special Forces soldier, with a translator hiding on the floor of the vehicle while they rode through the dangerous streets of the city's ancient section. The possibility of random gunfire was high, but some local authority had decided that this neighborhood was where the visa application office should be located.

So far, the soldiers had been personally generous to Hasan and showered his daughter with kind words and little trinkets. Such things usually seemed to make her happy for a few minutes, at least until something else set her off.

There was always something else.

Hasan felt himself cornered. It was too exhausting to be suspicious of everybody all of the time, so he relaxed into a fatalistic acceptance of the events unfolding around him. There was some measure of peace in knowing that things were quickly moving beyond his control; he had already made up his mind to follow this path, no matter where it led.

❧ ❧

Back in the States, the momentum continued despite inevitable technical difficulties.

The people at the charitable NGO received offers from other hospitals around the country, along with offers of support from the Red Cross and the Shriners and a lot of personal interest from Afghans living in the U.S. or Europe who wanted to know how they could help. The NGO decided to accept the State Department's recommendation of the Grossman Burn Center as the best possible option for Zubaida. Then they began the complicated process of getting all the right signatures on the stacks of papers and permits on their end of the arrangements, in full accordance with Mohammed Hasan's interpretation of the American way of doing things.

Peter and Rebecca Grossman were already so personally interested in the outcome of the case that they both felt delighted and relieved when they learned that a suitable private home for Zubaida's recuperations had been located in Los Angeles. The family was of Middle Eastern origin and spoke Farsi, which is close enough to Zubaida's Dari to permit conversation.

At the same time, Peter and Rebecca felt their first twinge of uncertainty about the complex logistics behind this challenging medical case—even though the NGO had promised to have a "backup family" prepared, in case things went badly in the private home, no one there seemed to be concerned enough to take time away from their stacked obligations to go through the process of finding one. The press of never-ending appeals for help kept every-body on the NGO staff focused on immediate situations and left Zubaida fac-ing the prospect of being ejected from treatment before her body was ready.

The problem was that, like most Non-Government Organizations, the staff perpetually walked the thin line between becoming too "secret" and isolated from their target group and being made so publicly visible that they become overwhelmed with appeals for help. Major portions of their budget would thus be consumed by salaries for people to sift through all the applications, rather than on caseworkers who could create actual results.

For them, the best use of limited time was to hope that all the precautions taken in selecting the host family would ensure success over the long haul. They had countless other hands beating on their doors.

Nevertheless, the lack of a backup location was a special worry for Peter Grossman, as the doctor and surgeon in charge of Zubaida's medical care. The long process that she would have to endure was especially vulnerable to failure if her host situation somehow collapsed in the middle of the months-long pro-cess. Zubaida's father could only remain in the U.S. for the first week, because his large family would be waiting back at home and in need of his support. So Peter knew that it was vital to guarantee her a stable place where she could communicate freely with the adults caring for her—and where her culture would be respected—so that she would remain in the U.S. long enough for him to complete the restorative process that he envisioned for her.

He hit the first hard bump in the road a lot closer to home than he ex-pected, when he brought the news to his father about this powerful medical challenge. Dr. Richard Grossman was less than enthused about the chances of success for such a complex endeavor. Where his son saw great opportunity, the elder surgeon saw overwhelming potential for outside interference. He didn't challenge his son's ability to do the procedures, but had no appetite for trying to press forward with such a complex set of procedures under the constant gaze of bureaucratic supervision.

But Peter Grossman was not to be dissuaded. Old father-son rivalries that had been hanging in the air for years ignited like gasoline fumes. Peter was sur-prised by the passion he felt in opposition to his father's reaction. It struck him as more of a father/son dismissal of Peter's ambitious plan than a serious rejection of the surgical and humanitarian opportunities of the case. Although Peter tended to be even-tempered by nature, when strong emotions were present, his response was to channel them into head-down, eyes-forward determination.

Peter vowed that if he had to carry this case forward on his own, he would do exactly that. He arranged for the facilities of the Grossman Burn Center, part of the nearby Sherman Oaks Hospital, to be there for Zubaida.

Rebecca prompted the Children's Burn Foundation, an organization that raises funds for these types of endeavors, to move quickly. "There are others overseas who'll step in, if you don't," she warned. Then she hammered on the risk of leaving this girl's case to less experienced or less well-equipped surgeons.

At last, the Foundation sent a letter guaranteeing up to $300,000 worth of the many costs behind caring for a child through a year of medical procedures.

There would be a long and complex series of at least twelve operations from a course of treatment that Peter laid out, based on her medical file and the detailed photos of her injuries. Since he couldn't make a final treatment determination until he examined her in person, it was possible that her surgeries could take even more time. She would certainly be in the United States long enough to require schooling, in the meantime. There was even word that her dental situation was abysmal and would require major care, as well.

Red tape began to roll in the door on giant spools.

So far, Zubaida's supporters had managed to slip in under the media radar, still fearing political backlash from jealous other interests, but now that there were Afghan expatriates in the U.S. who got tipped off to the story, there was real worry over the possibility of a rush of angry competitors to the NGO's gates.

There had already been calls, inquiries. . . .

❊ ❊

Zubaida's father explained it to her over and over. He explained it while she raged and appeared not to hear him, and he explained it again when she was calm and seemed able to listen. She heard him every time, but it was impossible for her to believe what she was hearing. Ever since her injury, doctors had meant nothing but pain to her. The American doctors were gentler, and in the past weeks their medicine had healed up most of her infected wounds, but mean-while the scars had kept right on devouring her to the point that she couldn't raise her head at all anymore, and eating didn't seem worth the trouble.

She could tell that the American doctors were trying to say soothing things to her. It didn't help much; everybody said soothing things to her all the time. Then they started poking and scraping and driving her insane again. It was painful to listen to them, anyway. Their strange English language made them sound like they were talking through their noses—blurts of meaningless noise.

If it wasn't for the anger and the fear seething inside of her over this invis-ible monster that was slowly strangling her, she wouldn't be feeling much of anything beyond a dull despair. She was helpless in the world of adults. As the shrunken creature that she had become, she had no control over anything, not even her own body.

So when her father assured her that he would take the initial journey with her, the comfort in that was small—he hadn't been able to do anything to keep the doctors from torturing her in Afghanistan or in Iran, had he? And even though the American doctors didn't hurt her as much, they still insisted on washing her in places where she was hurting, where she wanted to be left untouched.

What could her father actually do, she wondered, if the Americans decided to kill them both? Or what if they decided that Zubaida wasn't worth the effort and it was easier to just kill her? What could her father do?

Even worse, what if the Americans possessed ways to harm Zubaida and her father that neither of them could even imagine—ways that would make them wish for death, instead?

If that happened, how was he going to stop them?

❧ ❧

On June 2, 2002, *The New York Times* published articles stating that the FBI had stumbled in its antiterrorist work so far, and the CIA was publicly ac-knowledging that the successful penetration of tiny, fanatical terrorist cells was virtually impossible. The CIA article contained a photo of former Direc-tor George Tenet at the CIA memorial wall, reaching out to touch a star representing an operative killed in Afghanistan. The war for hearts and minds in Afghanistan was portrayed as a near impossibility.

On that same day, halfway around the world, the same Special Forces sergeant who had accompanied Mohammed Hasan to get his visa was now driving the military truck to ferry Hasan and Zubaida to the transport plane for the trip to Afghanistan's capital of Kabul. From there, they would be administered with a host of vaccinations and Zubaida would have more antibiotic treatment before they flew on to the United States.

In the weeks since Zubaida was taken into the military medical system, the sergeant and his squad had managed to keep a constant supply of small amounts of pocket cash flowing to Hasan and his daughter, making it possible for them to remain in Kandahar while preliminary medical work was done on her. The squad members all knew that their careers were at risk for breaking the list of Perfectly Good Reasons why local civilians should never be taken into the U.S. medical system. The infamously low pay of noncommissioned officers was a further deterrent to discourage the soldiers from pulling money out of personal supplies that were never enough to begin with, and the intensity of commitment required for Special Forces work discourages rule-breaking of any kind.

Nevertheless, the domino chain never failed to move forward yet another notch, every time another combat soldier or military physician had his first actual contact with Zubaida. Whether it was the massive extent of her injuries or the unflinching eyes that stared back from beneath her carapace of scar tissue, the energy wave carrying Zubaida continued to roll ahead.

The unspoken message was somehow conveyed with every individual's reaction to the dilemma that she presented. Whether or not they ever said the words, their actions spoke loud enough.

Screw it. Sometimes the rules just don't fit.

The sergeant pulled the truck next to the military transport plane and noticed that Zubaida appeared to be frightened and depressed. He realized that this was not only her first plane ride, but probably the first time she had ever seen a plane up close. So before they transferred out of the truck, he presented her with a basket of treats that some of the soldiers on base put together for her as a send-off gift.

Her eyes sparkled for a few moments when he surprised her with the basket, but her mood shot straight back down when she realized that the gift didn't mean she was being spared from having to go. From her point of view, everything around her had become unreal and was happening much too fast.

Ever since her accident, any sort of new and strange experience went hand-in-hand with adults who did painful things to her. Now the massive rumbling sounds of the revving airplane engines were far too strange; they seemed to guarantee that there was going to be something awful waiting for her on the other end of this unbelievable trip.

The sergeant backed the truck up to the high door of the transport so that Hasan could walk Zubaida aboard, then he followed them on and helped strap her in her seat. She cried out every time he touched her, and she made it plain that she didn't want to hear any soothing words, either—whether she understood them or not.

Hasan continually spoke to her in their native dialect, and although the American couldn't understand the words, he could see that she obviously didn't take any comfort in whatever her father was saying to her.

What the sergeant had no way of realizing was that from Zubaida's point of view, Mohammed Hasan was allowing the two of them to be taken someplace very far away in return for some vague promise of miracles—as if these Americans had the power to give Zubaida's music back to her, anyway.

She understood that they were going to stop in the capital city of Kabul for a time, while they prepared for the rest of the trip. But she also knew that once they finally reached America, Zubaida and her helpless father were going to be alone, out there among the Others.

3 ⚘

Zubaida and her father were met in Kabul by military physician Mike Smith. He had been coordinating her treatment to get her ready for the long trip, and the more he learned about this case, the more he found that it was beginning to become a thing of personal concern for him. His enthusiasm bubbled up out of him later that evening when he went home and sent an e-mail to Peter Grossman.

> It has been a wonderful day. Our translator arrived at 10:00 A.M., and it turns out she was on the plane with me when we flew from the United States toward Afghanistan, back in January. That's just the first of the many divine coincidences that took place today. Other members of the task force that work at the U.S. Embassy here picked us up and we met Mohammed Hasan and his little daughter, Zubaida, just as they came off the airplane at the Kabul International Airport.
>
> Zubaida could not be more than four feet tall and is very

slender. She said she was very scared on the airplane and I told her I was very nervous the first time I flew on an airplane too....She's afraid of any medical contact. Just talking about putting an emollient on her cracking skin (further contractures are taking place) made her run behind her father and cry.

Hasan states that Zubaida is having nightmares more and more frequently. It doesn't help that she gets reactions in public that are scarring her self-image. I've had to stare down and actually block a few idiots from standing in front of her and making her feel awkward.

My main concern, though, is her adjustment to being a patient. She's terrified at the opening of a pack of gauze and hasn't let me anywhere near her.

After reading the letter, Peter had no doubt that Mike Smith was so involved with her case that somehow or other, he would find the time in his schedule and be just the man they needed to fly to the United States with her—and then accompany her father back home a week later. It was clear that this girl compelled people's help, even though at this point Peter still didn't have any firsthand knowledge of her.

※ ※

As Peter Grossman predicted that he would be, Mike Smith was on the plane with Zubaida and her father on June 10, 2002, when they landed in Los Angeles, nearly a year after the fire. They traveled on the last leg of the journey with the NGO representative and a translator who met them at their London stop and flew in with them. Smith was glad that the public in the U.S. was far less inclined to stare at Zubaida; they made it through the airport without any nastiness. All were driven to the offices of the Grossman Burn Center of Sherman Oaks, in the San Fernando Valley northwest of downtown Los Angeles.

Peter Grossman felt that he must be just as excited as Mohammed Hasan when the two men met for the first time. When he introduced himself to Zubaida, he was heartened to see that although she could not turn her head, she raised her eyes and looked directly at him while he spoke. When he told her his name, she quietly repeated it and made the slight twitch of a smile, all that her face would allow.

His staff liked to avoid confusion in referring to Peter and his father, since simply saying "Dr. Grossman" wasn't helpful. So around the office, the two doctors had long since become "Dr. Richard" and "Dr. Peter." Zubaida quickly picked up on it and began addressing him as Dr. Peter, too.

For his part, he found that the pixilated e-mail photos that he had received months earlier hadn't told the full story of the extent of Zubaida's disfigurements. With the continued growth of scar tissue in the months since they were taken, she now looked much worse. He was presented with a child of ten and a half years, nearly emaciated at sixty pounds, and so badly scarred around her neck and face that she was unable to close her mouth. Even so, when he introduced himself, she said "hello" in memorized English and stuck out her good arm to shake his hand. While her ruined appearance tended to give the illusion that her intelligence might also be affected, such a notion was immediately dispelled by her sharp awareness. Underneath the inevitably hesitant demeanor of a child whose self-esteem has been continually assaulted over the course of an entire year, there was the conspicuous shine of a bright and lively consciousness.

He and his staff found themselves confronted with a girl who was clearly self-conscious about her appearance, but who also made direct eye contact with everyone who dealt with her. When Peter brought in his key support to meet her, anesthesiologist Charles Neal and pediatrician Matt Young, she again stood up and walked across the room on her withered, sixty-pound frame to shake their hands in greeting.

Zubaida presented a striking study in internal conflicts to the whole staff. She was clearly frightened, almost vibrating with fear, and yet they could see with absolute clarity that she was determined to face everything that was happening, eye-to-eye. Throughout the coming many months, their impressions of her would match perfectly with those of the soldiers and doctors who dealt with her back in her homeland—*this is a little spirit whose endurance and determination to live surpasses understanding.*

While it was clear that Zubaida's father doted on her, Mohammed Hasan also appeared thoroughly intimidated by the situation. Only his gaze remained strong. He stared around at everything as if his eyes were sponges. Peter and his staff repeated the basic overview of the procedures that Zubaida needed to have done, just as Mike Smith had already done with the pair back in Kabul. Hasan repeatedly indicated that he understood and was eager to get on with the process before his emergency visa expired. For Zubaida's part, she alternated hovering at her father's side and engaging in brief greetings with each of Peter's staff while they took turns babbling about her in words she couldn't fathom.

Through the interpreter, she repeatedly communicated her concern that the operation might turn out to be an experience on the order of her original, no-anesthesia procedures with the stripping of her burned skin. After repeated assurances about the power of anesthetics and the fact that she would sleep through everything, she began talking about how she felt eager to get started. She had reached the acceptance stage. Now it would be easier to stop talking about it and just get it done. Before they ended the initial consultation, Dr. Grossman kneeled down in front of Zubaida, placed his hand on her shoulder, and spoke to her through the interpreter. "Before she leaves here, I plan on getting her arms free and her neck free. She is going to dance and play and smile again. Everything is going to be good."

On Zubaida's second day in California, she and her father got their first chance to sit down alone together somewhere quiet and talk over the bizarre situation. Just hearing each other's impressions helped to keep it all from dissolving into an unbelievable dream. They found a place at a table in a quiet outdoor visiting area, and she felt herself beginning to settle down. The area was surrounded by a decorative wall, so that the enclosed space held a certain familiarity. Dense, opaque walls keep out strangers, keep you safe within them. The heated summer air was neither as hot nor as dry as her desert home, so the slight June breeze blowing around the area brought a feeling of comfort in the relative coolness of the whispering air. She couldn't see the outside world other than to glimpse a few building tops over the surrounding walls. This American city smelled so much different from her village because of all of the vehicle fumes in the air and practically no animals anywhere to be seen, but in the past few short weeks Zubaida had also been through the cities of Herat,

Kandahar, and Kabul, so she knew that the burned oil smell lingered in the air anyplace that had cars and trucks.

This "Los Angeles" had a newer, almost hollow smell; something about it felt empty. Instead of reeking of ancient occupation beneath the charred fog of modern traffic, underneath the combustion fumes, Los Angeles smelled like nothing. There was no smell from its people at all, so that except for the fumes from the long lines of rumbling engines that rolled along the streets, it felt as if Los Angeles and everything in it had arrived there not long before she and her father did.

She was still in her relaxed little bubble when she saw a smiling woman walk toward her and her father, accompanied by one of the local interpreters. Zubaida studied the woman in fascination. She had seen other Western women who wear no coverings at all in public, no scarf of any kind. The thing that struck her was that this woman's hair was a beautiful honey color, something she had never seen inside her home village. Even in the cities of Afghanistan, very few woman there had light hair to begin with, and even if they did, nearly all kept their heads covered anyway. Zubaida immediately saw that this American woman's hair was a crowning glory that no woman would want to cover up. Zubaida would want to show it to the world, too, if it were hers. In the days before the burns, back when her appearance still mattered in a good way, Zubaida had always been proud of her thick and wavy dark hair. She tried not to stare at the woman, but she had to wonder what it was like to walk around with hair like that all day. Did people stare at her? Did the men ever throw things and tell her to cover herself up?

Speaking through the interpreter, the blond woman introduced herself to Zubaida and her father. "Hello, Zubaida, my name is Rebecca. I am Dr. Peter Grossman's wife. I am so happy to finally meet you. It was my brother who first called us about you several months ago, and we have been waiting a very long time for you to get here." Zubaida walked over to her and shook her hand the way that you do with Americans and looked her straight in the eye because she already knew that you could do that in this place, and because she wanted Rebecca and everybody else to understand that she was there, inside. She was there behind that stiff armor of scar tissue and if they really could carve her face and body back out of the shapeless mass that was slowly consuming her, then she wanted this "Rebecca" to understand that she was someone worthy of their best effort. She didn't know why she felt so worthy of such help any more than she knew why she refused to let go of her life despite the price in physical suffering.

Rebecca went away from the encounter, like many other people before her, distinctly impressed with the amount of charisma that could be generated by any person, and especially any child, who has been physically reduced to such a condition and emotionally assaulted as this waiflike girl had surely been. The father seemed to be a quiet and gentle man, but his eyes flashed with contained emotion. Rebecca had already heard about how quickly he could be provoked into ranting displays if he perceived his daughter's needs to be unappreciated. Today, he had nothing but heartfelt gratitude for this opportunity. He spoke to her as a gentleman, even though he seldom looked at her and didn't seem comfortable in her presence.

But Rebecca had come to the hospital feeling especially eager to meet Zubaida, since the original connection came through her brother, Michael Gray, because of his position in the State Department. She knew that he held that position because of his concern for refugees in that region, particularly the children. She wasn't sure if what was driving her now was the same thing that connected her brother to his work, and she didn't know what name to give the feeling that she carried into that meeting, but she came away with dual sensations of being both satisfied and thrilled.

It didn't matter that she couldn't define what was happening, the wonderful coincidence of having Michael and Peter and her there to attempt to "catch" this girl was made all the more valid to her the moment that she met Zubaida. It was electric, to look into the girl's eyes and realize that this is the little soul who has defied death and endured unimaginable pain, frequently alone in her bed in a hovel in the desert, for an entire year. It was immediately apparent to her that one little girl's hunger for life, supported by her father's unfailing efforts, had reached out to Rebecca through a long chain of other concerned people. Moreover, it reached just about as far from Zubaida's homeland as anyone can go without leaving the planet, in order to touch Rebecca and leave it to her to pass that touch along.

She also knew that this girl was about to embark on many months of surgeries, isolated here in the United States. Even after the many medical hurdles were overcome by Peter and his team, Rebecca was not at all sure that this frail child would find American society at large to be a compatible mix for a girl whose cultural background could be traced all the way back to the Middle Ages.

For Zubaida, Peter's blond wife Rebecca proved to be a pleasant distraction. Her hair color would be a real item of conversation if Zubaida ever got back home again, and the gentle kindness that Rebecca showed gave her a warm feeling.

After she and her father were alone again, excitement and hope battled with fear, and with the kind of deep dread that settles in the pit of the stomach, but she reminded herself that she had already made the journey to this place and survived it, and so far, no monsters had appeared that equaled the Taliban enforcers back home. She and her father had come to this unbelievable place where they were well taken care of, and even though she had seen so little of this American city so far, she could smell the nothingness of it and knew that there was plenty of strangeness all around her. There was some consolation in the momentum that everything had taken on, since it was impossible to predict how things would turn out for them.

There was nothing left to do. She was about to find out whether the Others here in America would actually be able to work any of their famous Western "magic" on her or not.

❧ ❧

Four days later, early on the morning of June 14, Peter Grossman's team prepped Zubaida for surgery at the Grossman Burn Center while her anxious father huddled with the interpreter in the nearby waiting room. She was admitted the day before so that she could acclimate to the place, under the fictitious name of Sarah Lewis to foil media reps and curiosity seekers who were already circling the situation.

By the time she had been in the hospital for a full day, she had already made it a point to meet all of the staff as well as the few other patients who were also being treated there. Peter and his whole staff were impressed by the unusually high degree of adaptability that she displayed. Peter had often been struck by the chameleon-like quality that many children have while their developing brains are still flexible toward change; this young girl was a powerful example of it.

He came to the case prepared with a stellar team to assist him in the complex opening salvo of procedures, and consulted heavily with them before finalizing the day's surgical plan. It was agreed that Peter's father, Dr. Richard, would team up with Dr. Alexander Majidian to focus on freeing Zubaida's frozen left arm. Surgeon Brian Evans would work with Peter on the first of many procedures to Zubaida's face, neck, and chest. Pediatrician Matt Young was there to handle the many pediatric and medical needs associated with extensive surgery on a weakened youngster, and Dr. Charles Neal had the daunting task of handling her anesthesia.

The first complication showed up right away—Dr. Neal was unable to get a breathing tube down Zubaida's throat because of the acute downward angle in which her head was trapped by the scars. He even used the special camera in a fiber optic endoscope to guide the tube, but the degree of contraction was too severe. Zubaida was already sedated, but her airway remained unsupported. There was only a limited amount of time before the IV sedation would begin to suppress her respiratory drive. Then, without an inserted tube for breathing support, she would go into respiratory arrest. And the upshot of her yearlong journey in search of healing would be to die in the American hospital during the very first operation.

Since the body responds much more slowly to an injected drug than to an inhaled gas, it is dangerously easy to overdose a patient with an IV sedative before their physical reactions offer any indicators. On the other hand, too much caution about overdosing could lead to insufficient anesthesia and all its incumbent horrors.

That was the opening round.

The team went forward to race with the clock while the patient hovered under IV sedation. As soon as Dr. Neal had her far enough under, Dr. Grossman made an incision around the chin line to cut through the bands of tightened scar tissue that bound the chin to the chest wall. He encountered a carapace of scar tissue half an inch thick, more like hide than skin.

The first of Zubaida's amazing transformations was almost immediate; as soon as the incision was made around the entire jawline, her head automatically tilted back into a normal supine position. Much of the distortion to her face gave way. With her head in a normal position now, Charles Neal immediately slid the breathing tube down her airway and began a standard gas anesthesia, happy to switch to that far more accurate method of keeping her at the right level of sleep. With the patient's airway secure, the first major hurdle and potential disaster slid by without incident. Like any experienced player, Dr. Peter felt better once the game was on.

Over the course of the next hour and a half, Dr. Peter saw a little girl emerge from under the monstrous mask. He performed two of the most dramatic and challenging surgeries on her at the beginning, the first to release her head and neck from where they were fused to chest, and the second to release her left arm from the binding of the scar tissue that fastened it to her torso.

At that point, one of the near-magical elements of modern medicine came into play. The large open wounds created by the release of the face and neck scars were carefully sprayed with Tisseel Fibrin Sealant, a complex formulation of "glue" created for human surgical needs that seals off tiny points of bleeding and allows a wound to stabilize before the skin grafts are applied. The high level of success in modern skin grafting techniques is due in part to this miraculous substance, and it was especially important in Zubaida's case because she had so little healthy skin available. Every single graft needed to take, and the sealant gave Dr. Peter a head start in that direction before applying the new layer of skin.

No matter what he and his team did, they would be performing under constant video scrutiny in order to document every step of the long and complex series of operations that were only getting started on that day. The video record would be useful in making presentations to teaching institutions all over the world, but he was well aware that if anything went bad under his care, it would also be scrutinized frame by frame.

He made the very first incisions knowing that the Grossman Burn Center's role in this story was one that he had vehemently insisted upon, overriding his father's initial concerns. Thus the full weight of anything that might go wrong rested entirely upon his shoulders, and the Grossman Burn Center as an institution would take the painful hit if he allowed any preventable mistakes. His father had spent years building up the burn center and was already spreading its renown while Peter was still a youngster in school; it would be an untenable disaster for Peter if he failed here. The anguish would be all the more intense because so many people were looking over his shoulder.

On the heels of his original impulse to provide charitable help and surgical expertise for a terribly injured child came the present situation wherein the images recorded in the operating room would also represent the interests of the U.S. State Department, the U.S. Army's Central Command, and an entire NGO community of charitable organizations, plus a sizable number of the Middle Eastern expatriate community in California.

They would all be standing in line to review the tapes if Peter allowed anything to go wrong. In Zubaida's weakened condition, there were plenty of things that could, in this operation or in any of the others that would follow.

On the afternoon of June 14, with the first procedures over, Zubaida began to regain her first flutters of consciousness under the bright fluorescent lights of the surgical recovery room. Her thoughts stuttered like broken bits of film; even the certainty of physical sensations eluded her. She thought that she could feel herself lying on a bed, but she couldn't get a fix on where she was— or on what had happened to her.

It seemed that ghosts hovered all around her, wispy creatures covered in gowns and masks. They talked in an Other language, in quiet, short exchanges. Sometimes the words sounded familiar, like American words, with their smoothed-out throat sounds and their flat, nasal tones. She couldn't be sure.

In between pieces of grayish blur that caused time to jump forward, she was aware that bits of some sort of story were being played out right in front of her. She felt that she should know what the story was, but her brain couldn't put anything together out of the bits.

She wasn't aware of any physical pain, at least anything that came near what she knew from her past, but she began to realize that something was holding her body in one position, as if she were paralyzed. Whenever she was able to focus on the sensations coming from her nerves, she had the feeling of being tightly wrapped in soft blankets, with her arms isolated away from her torso. That impression frightened her, because even in a dream state Zubaida knew that her left arm was fused to her chest.

She could hear a low, constant wailing sound coming from somewhere close by. It was a single voice, crying out in a continuous wail of fear. Zubaida could tell that it was a girl's voice, but the girl didn't try to speak or do anything other than sustain that long, weak, wailing cry.

Zubaida's ingrained social instinct was to leave the girl alone, whoever she was, because one of the finer points of the Afghan tribal code is to show your respect for a stranger who is in a private moment of torment by quietly ignoring them. She could only wait for the cries to stop while she pressed her consciousness to distinguish between dreams and reality—or to even remember what reality was supposed to be.

As quickly as she grasped on to a single clear thought or one convincing bit of memory, a wave of physical nausea rolled through her body and carried all of her thoughts and sensations away with it, leaving her dizzy and confused. She knew from long experience that the realization of a single true thing was enough to anchor her wandering brain and pull it into the world. She had already developed the skill of anchor-hunting, during her long year of escalating nightmares. In the first days and weeks, her worst dreams were pain-induced hallucinations, devilish replays of the fire itself, and she dragged herself out of them like someone crawling from burning wreckage. But before long the worst of her nightmares, waking or sleeping, began to include images of her suffering family. That was where she got the most practice of escaping their grasp.

Most of those dreams took place because Zubaida was aware that the family's ability to survive was being sorely jeopardized by the demands of her burned condition. She had always justified her willful personality by the extra value that she brought to the family with constant willingness to pitch in with whatever needed doing. Her self-declared role as a caretaker in the family gave her a bit of the personal power that it was in her nature to crave. Now the family had not only lost the benefit of her help, but she was well aware that she was draining more of their resources than the rest of them put together.

Once the plans to go to America began to form around her, new nightmares appeared. Her sleep was constantly ruined by dreadful scenarios of her father's torture at the hands of the Others: doctors, soldiers, Americans . . . then it hit her.

This is the American hospital. The ghosts are doctors. This is part of their magic.
I don't hurt now, but I can't move, either. Why can't I move?
As soon as that girl quiets down, I'll ask for my father to come and explain.

❧　❧

Peter Grossman was sure that everything had gone well during Zubaida's opening round of surgery and he knew that her worried father was eager to see evidence of improvement, but immediately following the first operation, he didn't have much more than verbal assurances to offer him—while Zubaida slowly emerged from the anesthesia in the recovery room, all Mohammed Hasan could see was a tiny child swathed in thick cotton pads and countless yards of bandaging.

Speaking through the interpreter, Peter explained that the operation had gone well and assured Hasan that his daughter would quickly be semi-awake and would soon recover. He explained that she would need to stay in the hospital for the next four days, until she had enough strength to go through the second round of surgeries, when grafts from her own healthy skin would be placed over the raw wounds left in her flesh today by the severed and removed scar tissue.

Peter promised Hasan that after the second round of surgeries in another four days, he would be able to remove Zubaida's bandages because then the skin grafts would be safely in place. At that point Hasan could see the effect of the initial surgeries for himself.

For today, once Zubaida was awake and alert, her father could at least explain the progress of her operations to her, himself. When Hasan heard this, he nodded to Peter in gratitude—however his expression made it clear that he was going to have to see these promised results before he agreed to get back on a plane to Afghanistan.

Blood pressures spiked at the State Department. Their absolute worst-case scenario was that Mohammed Hasan would attempt to defect before returning to Afghanistan, creating an impossible political situation and potentially putting an end to Peter's twelve-month treatment plan, long before Zubaida was ready to be safely returned home with any realistic chance for long-term survival.

Two days after those first operations, Rebecca came back to the hospital to see Zubaida again. She was still swaddled in bandages, but spoke readily through the interpreter. She confirmed to Rebecca that her pain was minimal, and that she was happy that Dr. Peter had kept his promise not to hurt her. Rebecca's gentle warmth made her feel comfortable with brief bursts of conversation, but when Rebecca produced a large teddy bear she brought as a bedside companion, Zubaida was so uneasy with the strange object that Rebecca moved it to the other side of the room to let her get used to it slowly. When Zubaida saw the small courtesy extended on behalf of her feelings, she immediately felt a wave of the same warm feeling that Rebecca had hoped the stuffed toy would provide.

Though the Pashtunwali was devised centuries ago, and by elders of a different tribe, the code was so effectively blended into Zubaida's home region that it had melded with her perceptions and her personality. Now, in this new location on the other side of the planet from its point of origin, one of the code's main tenets was activated in Zubaida's mind and in her heart, by a stranger's clear gesture of courtesy. The respect that it conveyed compelled Zubaida to accept the kindness. Because of it, a bewildered and out of place ten-year-old girl, who could only hear American words as a series of bleats and hoots that sounded to her like a herd of sheep with head colds, had her first moment of genuine personal communication with this American woman called Rebecca, with the sun-colored hair and sheep-cream skin. From that moment forward, Rebecca was going to be perceived as having stepped over to Zubaida's side of the campfire. Zubaida's sense of openness with Rebecca would continue to rise up to equal Rebecca's kindness, as long as Rebecca avoided doing anything that could be construed as a threat.

Threats, in the Pashtunwali, are an altogether different matter.

꙳ ꙳

For Zubaida's second round of surgeries, Peter Grossman and his medical team went through the delicate process of harvesting skin grafts from Zubaida's unburned skin, splitting the thickness of some of the grafts to double their surface area, and then stitching each one into place over the large bare areas left by the first round of surgery.

His choices as to whether to use a full graft or a split graft on any given area were determined by the needs of each burn site. A full-thickness graft will allow itself to stretch and mold to the rest of the body while the healing process continues. However, although a split graft will be effective enough to seal a wound with tissue that the body doesn't reject, it won't do much more than that—one of the properties that a graft loses when it is split is the ability to stretch with the surrounding flesh.

For that reason, every moment of Peter Grossman's surgeries on Zubaida actually took place in four dimensions—while the usual three dimensions were enough to define the surgical site on any patient, he was also operating in the fourth dimension of time—in choosing the thickness of each graft and the direction of its placement. He visualized each graft through the dimension of time by including all of the known stages of a body's recovery, as well as the expected patterns of healing along with his surgical considerations for every wound site. While he split skin and sculpted flesh, the real medium of his art was in visualizing and manipulating the healing process over large amounts of time.

He had to look at each burn area and do more than merely see what lay open and brightly lit in front of him; he had to accurately visualize how that wound might look in a week, a month, a year, ten years. He had to visualize each graft's function in its particular location, long after the wound itself had healed. How would the grafted skin move with the body's motion? How would it react while the rest of her continued growing?

Zubaida didn't have enough unburned skin to provide Grossman's preferred level of skin grafting, so he went into the operating room knowing that every square millimeter of each graft was vital to her recovery, both in the short run as a defense against infection and in the long run as an integrated part of her healed flesh.

The list of potential mistakes was nearly endless, as far as those severely limited grafts were concerned. If he allowed any single one of those mistakes to take place, the error would be made under the glare of international attention as well as the critical eye of Zubaida's anxious father.

Meanwhile, Mohammed Hasan waited only a few steps down the hall from the operating room. He was determined to see for himself that everything was all right with his frail daughter. Out of respect for Zubaida's fierce grasp on her life, he had taken her halfway around the planet, but Dr. Peter had made Hasan a promise. And in Hasan's world, a man does not forgive himself for breaking a promise, and he is not easily forgiven by anyone else, either. He knew that if Dr. Peter didn't do what he said he was going to do for Zubaida, Hasan would never agree to return to Afghanistan without her, leaving her here alone in the presence of the Others.

It didn't matter about all the signed papers that the Americans loved to wave around. Those weren't real promises. When a man says to you, I can arrange possible miracles for your suffering child, you just have to sign this paper that promises you will give me your child, you are never expected to follow that insane demand to give your child away. When you have to save your daughter, there can be no honor in anything other than doing or saying whatever had to be done or said in order to secure miracles for her.

Dr. Peter's promises were made directly to Hasan—man to man and eye to eye—the way Hasan knew that a real promise must be done. Dr. Peter was not compelled to operate on Zubaida; he could have walked away and gone back to live in his American castle and dine on the finest foods and anoint himself with whatever kinds of oils that rich Americans smooth across their skin. Instead, he looked Hasan in the eyes and instructed the translator to insist that it was possible to carve the remains of Hasan's daughter out of her suffocating scar mask. It was the kind of promise that a person must always keep, no matter what: the kind that he never had to make in the first place.

And so those American documents were nothing more than pieces of paper with funny scribbling that goes the wrong way across the page. Hasan's signature on those papers was nothing more than ransom forced from a father who cannot walk away from any chance to save his child.

If the American papers burned as well as camel dung, they might be good for feeding a cooking fire. Other than that, they were worthless.

※ ※

All of Dr. Peter's work went according to the treatment plan for the first and second rounds of surgeries. After the second round, Zubaida had enough grafting in place that he was able to unwrap her swaddling bandages, six days after the first surgery began. It would be Hasan's only look at his daughter's transformation before he had to depart for home the following day.

Nothing could have prepared him for that first moment of revelation. He looked on with growing astonishment while Zubaida's dressings were gently removed. Even though it had been carefully explained to him that this was only the beginning of a long process and that Zubaida would undergo such surgeries many more times before she could return home to live again, all of that paled when the bandages were finally off and he saw what Dr. Peter and his team of expert physicians and surgeons had done so far.

His daughter Zubaida sat on the table in front of him, shivering from her body's first exposure to the air. In so many ways she looked dreadful, still bone-thin and sickly, but even though the marks of scarring were still all over her, her face and neck were completely free of the twisted scar tissue. Her normal face was clearly recognizable, and her left arm was free from her torso. Dr. Grossman demonstrated the arm for Hasan as well as Zubaida when he gently took her left arm and extended it all the way out to the side and back again.

Hasan blinked in astonishment. His ancient tribal soul screamed that this was impossible, it was an illusion, it was evil magic. But his real-world eyes welled with tears and his throat seized up. The wonderful truth of it was sitting right there in front of him.

A spark of hopeful surprise shot through Zubaida's eyes. Dr. Peter offered her a small mirror, and when she looked into it, her eyes popped open in wonder. Then she looked up at her father and smiled.

Mohammed Hasan began to cry, touching his hand to his heart in a traditional Afghan gesture of gratitude. He hugged Dr. Peter and heaped thanks onto him without waiting for the interpreter.

Even though Zubaida was still shivering from the removal of the insulating bandages, she continued to look around the room with a happy smile. That first brief gaze into the mirror told her everything she needed to know.

They did magic on her after all. Not perfect magic, but the results astonished her. She looked as if she had been sewn together out of patches—*but she could clearly recognize herself*. The monster was gone.

She could move both of her arms, she could close her eyes, and for the first time since the fire came to punish her for dancing, she could even hear a little bit of the old music. Hundreds of strange sensations inside of her re-carved face and reborn body prevented her from being able to concentrate on the melody in the brief moment that it flashed through her—and she certainly couldn't move to it—but it was there, like an echo from the next valley over.

She kept smiling even though it hurt her to move her stitched-up features. She smiled to welcome back a face that she could finally recognize as her own and because her heart was exploding and she couldn't stop smiling if she tried.

4

Mohammed Hasan was not so foolish as to be blind to the power that he would hold, right up until the instant that he got back on board an airplane. He didn't have to actually do anything so inconceivable as actually defect; all he had to do was realize that they knew he could defect if he really wanted to. These were people it would be effortless to bluff in marketplace dickering—so easy to read. Everybody was always eager, too eager, to answer all of his questions whenever he asked about returning back home. If he could just keep them from getting too comfortable with the idea that he was actually going to walk quietly out of Zubaida's hospital room and return to the airport with them, then they would be eager to keep him happy. And as long as they were, he could squeeze the very best of care for Zubaida out of all of them.

It was the last gift that he could give to her, and it would have to be enough.

A few days after her second set of operations, he quietly gave away his power by cooperating with his hosts, kissing his daughter good-bye, and returning to the airport without any fuss. Dr. Mike Smith accompanied him, and

Hasan had to wonder if that was to strong-arm him if he tried to bolt at the last minute. But Hasan had no such desire. His wife and family needed him, back there in a place that was nothing at all like the playground of indulgence that he glimpsed in this part of America. Those who feared that he would bolt like a donkey and run for sanctuary knew nothing about him.

In his last moments with Zubaida, he could see her fear and uncertainty so clearly in her eyes, but at the same time he saw that her usual air of steady calmness was much stronger, now. Fire couldn't kill her; neither would the Others. She would soak up whatever Western magic that Dr. Peter and his staff performed for her, then return back home and grow up to a life that might come close to something normal. Surely there would be no decent arranged marriage for her, since Dr. Peter made it clear that they could never perfectly restore her features. As damaged goods, she would most likely have to work all her life, probably at some form of manual labor. So it was good that she would now have both hands and that at least her face wouldn't scare people and draw crowds.

Hasan was not from a culture that made him feel ashamed for crying in front of every one of the Americans who were there to help him and Zubaida while he bid them good-bye.

Then with a final hug and a few whispered words of reassurance to his daughter, he went away with Dr. Mike and another translator to begin the seventeen-hour series of flights back home.

For Zubaida, the crash back to cold earth came within hours after her father left, just before she was released to go recuperate with her host family. With all the uncertainty stretching out ahead of her, she was tempted to seize on an overly rosy view of things to make herself feel safe. After all, she had very little postoperative pain, and although the long-term surgical process had been explained to her, when she saw her restored features in the mirror, she seized on the hope that the hard part was over—maybe the rest would simply involve taking a lot of medicine or something.

Denial and gravity are both invisible forces, equally strong. When Dr. Peter broke through hers and made it clear that while everything had gone very well, there were *still* all the other corrective procedures left to do, surgeries and recoveries over and over for many months yet to come—she felt like somebody pushed her off a cliff.

᙭ ᙭

By the time the second set of operations were completed, the first alarms were beginning to be raised by the charitable NGO regarding public knowledge about Zubaida's case. Like Dr. Smith, they not only feared being swamped with desperate people and having their own system clogged by too many numbers, they worried over what sort of acceptable answer they could give irate applicants who might demand to know, "why so much for one girl?"

On June 22, Colonel Joe R. Schroeder at Army Central Command in Florida wrote to Colonel Robert Frame in Kabul trying to answer the question as well. He told him, "This has been a wonderful collaboration of many people from widely varied backgrounds, pulling together toward a common goal. The girl's plight was so compelling that it seemed to enlist all who saw her pictures." Schroeder also wrote to Peter Grossman: "Some I have been told are critical that so much effort was expended on one little girl when there are so many other needy people. There are always critics and there are always people in great need. I am just thankful that we collectively did not turn a blind eye to one so hopeless and that we collectively could do something."

Robert Frame knew what Schroeder was talking about, but he also realized that as true as the words were, they weren't going to be enough to silence the kind of people who revel in righteous outrage. He wrote to Peter and Rebecca Grossman, who had also heard the question, "why so much for one child?" Like everybody else, they couldn't deny that it was a natural concern and that some people—maybe a lot of people—were likely to find cause to object over Zubaida's case.

They already knew that the only true answers anybody could give to the question "why Zubaida?" were: (a) because she happened to be there; (b) because the right other people also happened to be there; and (c) because, most of all, when it is not possible to save all of them, you do the next best thing and save them one at a time.

And somebody will either understand that or they won't.

❧ ❧

In spite of the experience that Mike Smith had already accumulated as a military physician living in Afghanistan, he still found that when he accompanied Mohammed Hasan on the long flight from Los Angeles back to that struggling country, the very act of walking off the plane at the end filled him with the sensation of stepping off a deep drop down into a powerfully different world.

The stepping-off point from Planet West to Planet East began at the long final layover in Dubai, in the United Arab Emirates. There the gaudy metropolis recently constructed over the historic city mixes with some of the most strange and ancient elements of Middle Eastern culture, swirling them among countless concrete and plaster constructs of the multibillion-dollar international establishment. There wasn't much to appreciate here at the intersection of two vastly different cultures, since the sheer power of major oil money had already overwhelmed the core elements of the region. The resulting ambiance always struck him as Las Vegas without the boobs.

The journey was completed and the door slammed behind them at the instant they stepped off the plane in Kabul. There, the effects of fifteen years of internal chaos across the country were evident everywhere he looked. The airport was jammed to overflowing and ringing with the din of hundreds of shouting voices while huge crowds pushed and shoved for every square foot in the place. Guards repeatedly waded into squabbling knots of people just to get them to form into ragged lines.

The presence of all things American was long gone. All of the languages around him were Arabic, Farsi, Pushto, Dari. He heard no English in the clamor. Now it was Mohammed Hasan who was on home turf. He was the one with culture and language squarely on his side. Here, Dr. Mike Smith was merely one of the highly suspicious Western military whose value to the local population had yet to be proven. He knew that he and his few military escorts would be squashed like flies if a crowd chose to turn on them. He thought of the old punchline, "What do you mean 'we,' Kemo Sabe?"

But Hasan's reaction to their arrival surprised him. The man began to cry for his daughter, as if the arrival back into his familiar world somehow punctuated the fact that he had been left with no choice but to leave Zubaida behind.

For Mohammed Hasan, the reason for his heavy emotions was even simpler than that. There was no guaranteeing whether or not her body would adapt to all the surgeries she was yet to face, or if her strength could hold up under so many surgical assaults. At the same time, back in Afghanistan, the post-Taliban rebels now roamed a country where the only real law enforcement was in the few major cities. Hasan and the rest of the family had a host of their own potential dangers surrounding them. Common sense made it clear that there was a very good chance that, one way or the other, he had said good-bye to Zubaida for the last time.

He was provided with enough cash to get all the way back to Farah and still have enough left over to take care of the family's basic needs for a couple of weeks while they figured out their next steps. They had already had a year to adjust to the lack of Zubaida's help around the house with the chores. Now, however, dealing with his daughter's absence would be much more like the way things would have been if she had not been able to shake off Death. That knowledge pushed his stretched emotions still further.

Smith saw to it that Hasan made his next link of transportation to get all the way back out to Farah, hundreds of miles to the southwest. By the following day, he was already writing to Peter Grossman to remind him that he hoped to stay in the loop about Zubaida's condition over time. He mentioned that he had already shown Zubaida's before-and-after photos to a few colleagues, who were universally astonished, and he asked for Peter to forward one particular photo of Zubaida with her father. In it, she is giving him a radiant smile and their expressions seem to capture the heart of their relationship. The image offers something of an answer to the question of where he found the determination to carry out that long and expensive search for help.

Dr. Smith also told Peter and Rebecca about burly Special Forces types who looked over the photos and ended up beaming like kids.

❧ ❧

Zubaida's face-to-face confrontation with American life had been held in suspension while she was in the controlled environment of the hospital. Peter's brother, Jeff, visited her and decorated her room with balloons and hearts, taking on the "Uncle Jeff" role with joy. His kindness, coupled with that of the attentive staff at the center, shielded her from some of the strangeness of her situation. But once she landed in the host family's home, many of the very same measures that the family had taken in order to help Zubaida adjust seemed just as strange to her as the more American elements of the family's life.

She could understand their language, but to her ears it was so heavily accented that while it could convey information, it offered no sense of comfort to her. Alone now in the host family's house, her father's absence suddenly became real to her. She felt the ice-cold realization that he had not stepped away to do some errand; he had climbed back onto the big airplane and gone all the way home—a distance so far she could not comprehend it—to rejoin the rest of her family.

The cultural environment of her hosts' home was strongly influenced by the mother's Afghan heritage, but instead of providing comfort it seemed to be something of a living taunt: close enough to being familiar that it spoke to her, but strange enough to constantly remind her that she was alone in a place where everything was different, down to the tiniest details. The emptiness that she felt all around her seemed to mock her for the absence of any loved ones or anything truly familiar.

Back at the hospital, the room may have been surrounded by the Others, but it was small and tightly controlled and closed to outsiders, so that she felt safe enough from the world there. And so far, Dr. Peter had kept his promise about not hurting her. At least there was some comfort when Dr. Peter was around, making the hospital more appealing for that reason, too.

Now she found herself trapped inside of the home of smiling strangers who seemed eager to be kind to her, but who spoke with such foreign accents and lived such American lives that they barely seemed real to her.

Suddenly the long course of treatments stretching in front of her reached into infinity. She realized that she couldn't do it. Despite all of the strength she had been able to summon in order to survive long enough to reach this place, she now found herself empty of the power to endure another year of this strangeness. The "is, but is not" world of her hosts was a clear example of the kind of hospitality that is coin of the realm among the Afghan people. It should have warmed her heart, but the family's environment was overwhelming, and the intended comforts were no more nourishing to her than lumps of wax that have been molded to look like pieces of fruit.

She was able to move her arms again, but she couldn't do anything with them. She could walk, but there was nowhere to go without supervision. She could talk, but not to anyone she knew or to anyone her own age who spoke her language. She could eat, if they chose to bring her food; she could sleep, if they chose to allow her to sleep. But there was practically nothing that she could do herself.

The wide mood swings started in again, the way that they did during the first weeks after the fire. She found herself feeling all right while she was occupied with some little thing, but then a moment of the smallest frustration would make all the poison come blasting out of her, the same way that her blackened flesh had once forced screams of pain from her throat. Now the pain came in the form of frustration at her state of utter helplessness and the sense of isolation, mixed with a sick dread of suspicion that this chain of events would not be done with her until her entire life was cut up into tiny bits and scattered to the wind.

The only way to exert her will upon the world was with shrieking explosions of temper. She learned that the sudden emotional outbursts struck most people so hard that they frequently did whatever it was that she wanted at the moment, just to make her stop. The power was similar to that of an infant lying in a crib, trying to get attention, and her will to live had already proven itself ready to grasp at anything that might help her.

While the slow summer days drifted by, whether she was in her isolation in the host family's home or in their structured outings among the Others, Zubaida found that even this humble form of infantile power was better than having none and being an invisible pawn among these strangers.

Once again, it was good to make them see her.

And so it was a familiar thing to Zubaida when the host parents began to step away into a corner and discuss her in whispers. She sometimes managed to catch enough that she felt like she had a pretty clear idea of what was going on. She recognized it from the whispered conversations of desperation that she had often heard from her mother and father back when all she could do was to lie in her burn bed, trying to hold still, trying not to cry out and to keep silent, and not being able to do any of it.

It was clear to her: They were asking themselves how badly the accident had damaged her—and whether it might even have affected her mind.

They were wondering if she was crazy.

❧ ❧

By July 3, 2002, Zubaida had completed three weeks of recovery following her first two sets of operations. So early that morning, she was prepped for her third round of surgery, then placed under anesthesia while Peter Grossman and his team prepared to take her to the next step.

At the same time, over on Zubaida's home side of the planet, the Afghanistan countryside that has played unwilling host to centuries of marauding hordes and a number of modern-day armies was embroiled in a subtler war of hard-fought propaganda. The day's leading story was about forty innocent civilians who had been killed in central Afghanistan by U.S. military forces. Army representatives reported that Special Forces observers who were out scouting for Taliban resistance had been fired on from a nearby residence, so in accordance with their rules of conduct they called in powerful flying gunships onto the source of the fire, resulting in the local casualties.

Representatives of the families claimed that the people who were attacked were only gathered there on the occasion of a wedding—and that the victims were merely firing random, celebratory gunfire into the air in accordance with accepted local customs. The complaints offered up the event as a clear case of deliberate mass murder by the U.S. Army.

However, the American commander pointed out that the gunfire that the Special Forces soldiers originally responded to was not "random" at all, but it was directed straight at the soldiers and was focused for accuracy. He also pointed out that the night before, the American gunships had already been in the area to fire on several gun posts there that were presenting a continued threat.

Everybody involved insisted that everybody else was lying.

❧ ❧

When Peter Grossman entered the operating room that day, his confidence in Zubaida's case was beginning to rise. So far, all of her grafts were healing well, and her pain had been kept to a minimum. He felt especially thankful for that; these early stages of the entire procedure would not be an acceptable time for his credibility with her to falter. He knew that of all of the many people now involved in Zubaida's case and in her story, he was the literal point man of the mission. The hopes of Zubaida and everyone in her family, as well as her growing roster of supporters, Non-Government Organizations, government sponsors, and military personnel who dared to endanger themselves by trusting her father and allowing them into the unprotected and vulnerable interiors of the American bases and medical facilities there, would come to a focal point as sharp as the scalpel's edge that carved and shaped her.

Today's procedures were to prepare her for a series of much more subtle operations that would be designed to smooth out her re-carved features. The first thing to do was perform a complete change of all of her dressings, under anesthesia. Then the cleaned wounds would be sealed for healing using homografts, donor skin taken from cadavers and processed so that a patient's body won't reject it. Their vital function was to keep her wounds protected from infection, but to allow them to "breathe" naturally through the porous structure of the donor grafts. They were a temporary part of the overall process, but their role in protecting her was vital in helping her to remain strong enough to complete the entire long list of surgeries. The less energy that her body had to expend in fighting infection, the more it could retain for the long uphill journey.

Dr. Peter worked on his sedated little patient like a custom tailor slowly building a full bodysuit out of living fabric. Now when the procedures went on to become much more focused and delicate in their nature, the permanent grafts could then be taken from her own body and blended into the surrounding skin. The living pieces of the suit would have to do much more than fit and function; they would have to move through every day and night together, stretching, pulling, flexing as much like the old born-on suit as possible. As time moved on, they would have to grow with the rest of her and not betray her by going out of control like her own scar tissue had done.

Once again, Peter Grossman spent the morning occupying the fourth dimension, while every slice and stitch that he made took place with one eye on
the present moment and the other on the possible repercussions to every one
of his medical choices and surgical actions, as they were going to spread out
over time.

Zubaida awoke after the third session feeling much stronger than she had
after the first two. There was a big difference in the size of the areas being
worked on this time, and the assault on her body had been of a much lesser degree. Now was the time when her past experiences of unmedicated agony
helped to make her strong in the present moment. The level of discomfort was
so pale compared to how she had spent many endless days and nights that she
might have felt positively cheerful about the whole thing, now—except for
the fact that Dr. Peter or somebody had apparently wrapped her up in padding
and bandages to the point that she could barely move.

It didn't matter that she had nowhere to go, or that she was too connected
to tubes and wires to move around. For her, the intolerable problem was that
she couldn't move at all, even though the lack of pain from the operations and
the low level of physical shock left her feeling so cheerful that little bits of her
old music actually floated through her. They went at her like breezes across the
hairs on the back of her neck. They flitted through her head in little frag-
ments, teasing her by appearing and disappearing.

Now Zubaida didn't simply want to move to the music, she *needed* to feel its
energy moving through her, allowing her to have something of herself back.
She knew from experience that every move she made with her arms, her legs,
her body, had always confirmed Zubaida's identity to herself and the rest of the
world. In the days before the flaming orange teeth devoured her, dancing had
always left her feeling stronger afterward. So she was certain that even the
smallest musical movement could move more energy through her and help to
speed her healing, but at the moment she was so tightly bound that all she
could do was wiggle her muscles beneath them. It was barely more than
clenching and unclenching, in time to the beat. It brought her close to what
she craved, but her abilities just weren't up to her desire; the tiny muscle-
clenching movements would never be enough to free her, or to pump healing
energy through her.

Now the nightmares that had been steadily increasing since she boarded the plane to America leaped ahead in strength. She lay drifting in and out of sleep from a world no more real to her than the imagined scenarios. Faces of people who had once jeered at her reeled again in front of her mind's eye; they stared down at her melted countenance as if she were something under a rock. She tried to run from them, tried to strike out at them, but her legs melted out from under her and her arms stuck to her body.

When her recovery progressed enough for her to move around the halls, she visited one teenage boy whose legs were badly burned. Using gestures, she encouraged him, saying "look at me," knowing that by simply standing next to him and smiling, she was letting him know that he could cope with all of this, too; that he would get past it.

The problem was that she couldn't hold on to the good feelings. Once her dressings were lightened, she was able to make up little dances while sitting up in her bed, causing the nurses to watch her and laugh, and although the attention felt good, some little thing always seemed to go wrong. It never mattered what it was exactly, all that mattered was that whatever went wrong was strong enough to kill the good feelings and to instantly turn her world back into a thing of pain and frustration.

The result was that her rages got people's attention even better than her attempts to dance. It made her feel embarrassed and angry for the same nurses who had looked at her with admiration to blink at her in surprise and concern. But the thought that she had let them down made her feel even worse, as if poison were running in her veins and spilling into her thoughts.

She heard them conversing just outside her door in the bleating nasal tones of the American language, and it seemed plain that what they were doing was asking one another the same question. It was a question that Zubaida had already heard spoken about her, in other places: *Has this girl lost her mind?*

She wanted very badly to know the answer herself.

5 🌿

Rebecca Grossman found that her few visits with Zubaida had
touched her in a way that no other patient at the burn center ever had. The
language barrier was frustrating, but she found that it actually served to facili-
tate the awareness of all the other nonverbal aspects of communication.
Zubaida's body language, as well as her own, delivered meaning when words
could not. Nonverbal sounds, voice tone, facial expression, and, most of all,
eye contact were the primary tools that she and the girl had available. Even
within those limitations, Rebecca found that she got a palpable sense of
Zubaida's iron will as well as her playful spirit, but that the moments of insight
into the girl were fleeting. It seemed clear to her that there was a firestorm of
activity inside the girl's brain that was sure to have had few opportunities for
expression.

After Zubaida had a couple of weeks to recover from the July surgeries, Rebecca called the host family and arranged for Zubaida to come for a visit over
the weekend. Zubaida was initially tentative, but she quickly warmed up and
began exploring around the property. She was unsure about the swimming

pool, coming from a place where there was no such thing and where few people ever learned to swim. She allowed Rebecca to coax her into the water and splash around for a little while, but she was not at all sure how people could relax when they were up to their necks in water.

The Grossman's menagerie of animals didn't seem to charm her much. In her country, animals were beasts of burden or walking items of food. Any value in the idea of keeping them for pleasure and feeding them with resources that could keep another human being alive seemed lost on her. The two horses in the barn behind the house lived in quarters the size of her family's home, and there was another entire house back there that was explained to her as a place for relatives and visitors to stay. That idea fit into her background, with her culture's emphasis on family and hospitality, but only the local warlords had the resources to keep up desirable, empty houses on their land.

One of the strangest new things about this American-style castle, to her, was that instead of using the beautiful kitchen inside of the house, her host explained that in this country the people often cook outdoors over open flames *for amusement.* They do this even when they have kitchens outfitted with a host of devices, which Zubaida had witnessed for herself as they performed amazing tricks in preparing food with hardly any work at all.

She didn't understand some of the kitchen appliances yet, but at her host family's house she saw how fast and easy such things made the preparing of a meal. And yet out there behind Peter and Rebecca's house, right next to the pool and the horse barn, there was a whole area dedicated to cooking and eating outdoors—right next to all the animals—instead of indoors where it was cool and clean and quiet.

And the dogs, four of them, huge animals. How much would four dogs that size eat, without doing any work in return? They seemed too friendly to be guard dogs, too big to go inside the house. Everybody was always telling them to go away. What were they for?

Strangest of all, while much of an Afghan's time is spent trying to avoid the desert's summer sun and staying out of the worst of the heat; here in this place called California, people seemed to spend a lot of time outdoors lying around in the blazing sun *voluntarily.* She saw that Peter and Rebecca had special chairs for that very purpose, even though the chairs looked so perfectly new that it seemed as if nobody used them.

Since Zubaida had only learned a handful of English words, her reverie was unbroken while she toured around the home with Rebecca and her host mother. From time to time, she could tell that the two women were talking about her, but since she had been the focal point of adult attention for the past year, she had long since learned to tune it out. The women's animated conversation receded in Zubaida's awareness and dissolved into a blur made up of the flat vowels and strange consonants that Zubaida now knew to be typical of the American language.

Rebecca listened with surprise and concern to the stories she was hearing from the host mother. Peter was still at the hospital for the day, but she knew that he would also want to know the things that she was being told. The host family expressed the pride that they felt in taking care of this Afghan girl and had the admiration and support of a number of their friends, many of whom could also speak Zubaida's Dari or the closely related Farsi language. The family's sense of personal and ethnic pride weighed heavily on them in this task, as well as their social standing among the Afghan community, who was now largely aware that the family was hosting Zubaida. They seemed to have some degree of personal warmth for Zubaida as an individual, too—all the characteristics that the charitable NGO had looked for in a host family. But the good news ended there.

Rebecca listened with mounting discomfort to a series of events that supposedly had taken place with Zubaida in the brief time that she had been with the family. As Zubaida grew stronger after the hospitalization, her personality apparently grew stronger, as well. Much of the time, that seemed to mean that she was in a state of conflict with one of the family members—sometimes with the household in general.

At night, Zubaida seemed terrified of being alone in the dark and suffered from such horrific nightmares that she woke up the entire family by crying out. Even a simple afternoon nap on the sofa was likely to end with Zubaida making some huge jerking movement that was so powerful, it woke her with a loud gasp.

She was described as having mood swings so rapid and so severe that nobody ever knew which version of Zubaida they were going to be dealing with
from one moment to the next. Her behavior was described as flipping from
gentle teasing to confrontational torment to black moods of isolation that left
her unreachable. Any discussion about her family back home sent her into
such a strong funk that she seemed, to the hosts, to be capable of violence.
They admitted that they hadn't actually seen that from her, but insisted that
they felt more concern than they had expected regarding the safety of their
own child in Zubaida's presence.

After all, the mother explained, she and her husband had only taken on
the task of hosting Zubaida because they were moved by the story of her
plight. They felt proud to step forward to help someone from a civilization that
they had long since left behind themselves. Now, with the first rosy blush faded
from the situation, the colder realities of attempting to make a severely damaged child feel at home in an utterly foreign situation were revealing themselves to be far more strenuous than anticipated.

The host mother described moments when Zubaida appeared to be gripped
by manic energy so strong that she could not sit still. In those moods, she
seemed to take some special delight in pulling mischievous little pranks and
annoyances. She pressed them long past the point that they were funny or
even tolerable, and any attempt to prevent the behavior would send her into a
fury.

It was the fury that frightened them. How deep did such anger run inside of
this girl? How far would her fury carry her in destructive behavior? Had
Zubaida ever been a violent child before her accident? Did anyone know the
answer to that? Had anyone even checked? Because after what they had seen
of Zubaida's behavior inside of their home, they felt forced to stop and ask
themselves, just as they were now asking Rebecca—do you know how deeply
disturbed this child might actually be? Did anyone know if she had a violent
past? The fact that Zubaida seemed so comfortable with her expressions of
anger made them wonder why that was so.

How could they not ask themselves whether they and their child, a toddler,
were safe with Zubaida in their home? How could she not ask that of the
Grossmans, now?

For Zubaida's benefit, Rebecca made a conscious effort to keep a pleasant expression on her face while she took in the grim report. Conflicting emotions ran through her without bringing any idea of what she could do with this depressing news. She felt eager for the chance to talk it over with Peter after he got home in the evening, but in the meantime, she could only hope that this woman was having a hard day or something—perhaps she was presenting the situation in terms more bleak than real. Because otherwise, whether Rebecca was hearing an accurate and fair version of things or not, it was clear that feelings at the host home were running to such a negative place within these first few weeks that it didn't seem possible for Zubaida to ride out a year with the family.

Later that night, after Rebecca had a chance to repeat what she had been told to Peter, they decided that the only way to get more insight into what was going on with Zubaida would be to invite her to come and stay with them for a weekend. It would give her hosts a little break, which they seemed to need, and provide a fairly relaxed and natural way for the Grossmans to spend some private personal time with her and try to get a handle on the truth.

Zubaida's next round of surgeries was scheduled for August 13, still a couple of weeks away, so they called and made arrangements for her to come and spend the next weekend with them at their home, without the hosts, without the NGO reps, and without any interpreters. It would just be Peter, Rebecca, Zubaida, and their small zoo of domestic animals. Rebecca didn't have any idea whether or not she would have any answers once she came out the other side of the experience, but everything that she had already seen of the strength inside of the child served to convince her that she couldn't listen to the kind of report that had been brought to them without getting personally involved in the search for the truth.

On the day that Zubaida arrived for the weekend, carrying her little tote bag, she was sullen in the host mother's presence and acted as if she was at Peter and Rebecca's because she had been expelled from her hosts' home. But Rebecca noticed that as soon as they were alone together, Zubaida's mood brightened considerably. For the rest of her stay, she remained well behaved.

And so Rebecca had to be struck by how different Zubaida was while she visited with them, compared to the sort of descriptions that came from the host family. She had noticed Zubaida's spark on other occasions, but now she got the chance to form a clear impression of her personality. It didn't take long. Within a few hours of arriving, Zubaida felt safe enough to drop her sullen defenses. Their lack of ability to converse seemed to make touch even more important to her, and she soon became affectionate with both Peter and Rebecca and was clearly eager to feel close.

Peter and Rebecca both found that they reveled in their brief role as foster parents to her. They had been talking about having children of their own for quite some time, but had not yet been able to get pregnant. They both felt like their house had a very nice full feeling when Zubaida was around. Her need for constant attention and reinforcement also played into their desire to care for a child, and both of them discovered that they loved the way that it felt.

Zubaida herself had no prior experience in dealing with a blonde, but before that first weekend was over she realized that they are more or less like regular people. As for everything else about her time with her American doctor and his wife, she felt a certain relief in being away from the almost-but-not-quite Afghan environment of her hosts' home. In a purely American environment, the uniform strangeness of everything was somehow reassuring. It was honest; it didn't try to make her feel that she was not among the Others. At the Grossmans' place, with no common language and few common rituals to force closeness upon them, Zubaida found it easier to accept the kindnesses shown to her, instead of the resistance that she felt at the host family's house where she felt like she was expected to behave as if their lives were not impossibly strange to her.

Once she was back there with them after the visit with Peter and Rebecca, she withdrew and plunged into isolation and boredom. There wasn't much else to do but wait for her body to be ready for the next set of operations. After those first good feelings that she was able to share with Peter and Rebecca, she rejected what she perceived to be the negative attitudes that she felt directed toward her in the home of her hosts. She began to make her resentments clearly known.

Life in that house continued in this manner right up until the time for her next procedures of reconstructive surgery and continued skin grafting. Four separate rounds of operations were to be scheduled throughout the month of August, with the first one beginning early on the morning of August 13.

Zubaida's life throughout the month of August took place mostly inside of the hospital. She complained that it seemed like as soon as she recovered enough to be sent back to the host family's home for a few days, she was picked up and whisked back to the hospital. No one could argue. The first procedure of the month was when Peter Grossman carved away the constrictive tissue around her right ear and reconstructed what was left into a near-normal appendage. In that operation and in the rest of that month's surgeries, part of the process was to inject large amounts of steroids into her burn scars, gradually shrinking them.

On August 16, three days after Zubaida's first set of procedures, Peter did a series of new skin grafts. Some were the full thickness grafts that can stretch and grow with the rest of the body; others were split-thickness grafts whose temporary function was mostly to seal the wounds and allow them to heal.

On August 22, he replaced some infected skin grafts around her underarm area and on her trunk.

On the twenty-sixth, he had to repeat the last skin grafting procedure to replace some of the grafts that didn't take. So borrowing from the precious few square inches of unburned skin on her back, Dr. Peter mined the limited resource for new sections of pliable tissue to seal the tracks left by the burn scars.

But while the month progressed, the physical toll on Zubaida came to be matched by the emotional toll that the combination of the surgeries and the strangeness of her life was taking on her. Confrontations with her host family became daily or even hourly occurrences. Sometimes they seemed to be nearly constant—which had to be true for everybody involved.

※ ※

Within a couple of weeks after Zubaida's release from the hospital following her final operations for the month of August, Rebecca answered the phone one day to hear one of the NGO officers tell her that the host family was becoming overwhelmed by the emotional problems that they were having with Zubaida. She relayed these concerns to Peter, but beyond absorbing the additional anxiety over the complaints, there was little they could do besides hope that the hosts would continue to understand that Zubaida's behavior couldn't realistically be held to ordinary standards.

It was an especially volatile situation for everyone concerned, since at this point she was only halfway through the surgical plan. A host family was vital to the terms of her presence in the country; the State Department was firm in only allowing her to remain in the United States under specific conditions. Without a host family she would quickly be whisked back to Afghanistan and left to take her chances with the village healers. Worse, the NGO that initially sponsored her was so overwhelmed with work that nobody ever got around to finding a properly qualified backup family in anticipation of something like the current situation. That alone carried the potential to derail everything. They had been left with no alternatives.

The plan was for Zubaida to have the last week of August, the entire month of September, and the first week of October away from the hospital, to help get her strength back up for the second half of the process. Since that gave her more than six weeks for physical and psychological recovery, Peter and Rebecca hoped that things would naturally calm down. Maybe peace at home would be possible once Zubaida had a chance to remain comfortable for days at a time without being hauled back into surgery.

But over the following days, Peter and Rebecca both repeatedly heard from the concerned NGO officer. The stories about Zubaida that were now coming back from the host family had reached alarming levels. Some of her behavior was innocent enough on the surface of it. For example, she displayed a continuing habit of wandering away from the house and going for long walks without telling anyone, since the ability to walk again was a joy to her and it was her lifelong independent habit of walking alone through the ruins of Farah that made the appeal of long walks so strong to her now. After so much extreme confinement, it felt so good to be free, to walk and walk and walk and not have to answer anybody's questions.

The practice got no support from the people responsible for her well-being. More ominous, they told of times when Zubaida would become so inconsolably upset that she would grab one of the kitchen knives and threaten to kill herself, sometimes in defiance of some ordinary point of typical domestic disagreements.

At that point neither Peter nor Rebecca could stay out of the picture any longer. They invited the host family to bring Zubaida over for another weekend stay, to try to see for themselves what the situation really was with her.

Their offer was met with receptive ears. Zubaida was there the next weekend. The moment she and her host mother arrived, it was clear to Rebecca that the tensions were high between the pair; the air between them felt brittle. The woman made no effort to conceal her relief to have a couple of days off. Zubaida appeared so glum and closed down in the host mother's presence that Rebecca felt a sudden rush of concern over what she was getting herself into.

It was a great relief for her to see how much Zubaida relaxed once the host mother was finally gone. The change was almost immediate. By the time that Peter got home from the hospital, the two were getting along well. Zubaida had learned a very few words of English, but not enough to be useful in conversation. Without an interpreter, they made a game out of communicating with the same sorts of gestures and nonverbal sounds that everybody uses when they don't share a language but need to make themselves understood. The process allowed Zubaida as much self-expression as she wanted to use. That seemed to suit her well. The extra energy involved in the most basic acts of communication helped to focus the flighty energies of a girl who was alternately timid and defiant.

For their first outing together, they took her bowling, since the simple sport doesn't require much conversation. Zubaida was only mildly interested in the challenge of rolling the ball down the wooden lane, but seemed very impressed by the echoing sounds of multiple bowlers rolling out their games and by the mechanical pin changers working like robots. It was her first opportunity to interact with an American pastime in a uniquely Western setting, but the lesson for the couple was that hands-on experience was good for her. In an environment of people who sounded to her like they had motors in their mouths, chugging out whole clouds of nonsense syllables, she clearly took a real pleasure in just grabbing a big, heavy ball in her hands and rolling it down a long, flat lane to try to knock over some wooden pins.

Zubaida knew for certain that the Taliban would hate to see her out in public playing this big, silly game—plus, she had already turned ten years of age and so was expected to spend most of her life hiding indoors from now on, and this knowledge gave any noisy public sport a lot of extra appeal to her.

The next day, Peter and Rebecca drove her out to a small public beach set inside of a Malibu cove, to play in the waves that break on the curved spit of sand that forms the horseshoe-shaped beach. Zubaida seemed to open up and drink in the environment. She splashed in the surf and ran around in the sand with Peter and Rebecca, who delighted in seeing her come to life and jump around like any other kid.

The sheer physicality of the activity was so good for her after the long convalescence, it was like watching an entire section of her healing process taking place in a single afternoon, as if some strong force had been invisibly accumulating inside of her and only needed something that was in the waves or the seashore air in order to be released. Watching her run and twist and leap on the sand, it was easy to forget for a second or two that the little girl they were playing with was unlike any other.

By the end of that day, though, Rebecca was already beginning to pick up a number of disturbing signs—little things—clues to what might have been going on at the host family's house. The more comfortable that Zubaida became in their presence, the more that the pleasant artifice of manners tended to occasionally slip for a moment or two. A simple point of conflict such as, "Can we walk in this direction?" "No, we need to go the other way," could be greeted with the same sort of petulant face and slump in body language that would be typical for a lot of girls her age, but it was hard not to notice that for some time following any point of minor conflict, Zubaida seemed to be struck by a whole series of little inspirations about how to best provoke annoyance in anyone who happened to be around. Little bits of mischief began to stream out of her, and were frequently pushed a few notches too far.

There was nothing endearing about it. Passive hostility became the main presence in the room. It wasn't enough to lessen Rebecca's desire to spend more time with Zubaida, but it was easy to imagine how destructive such generally defiant behavior could be—especially if it got ramped up a few more levels, the way the hosts had described it.

That didn't change the fact that Peter and Rebecca were both surprised by how satisfying they found the brief experience as surrogate parents. Their frustration in trying to have a child of their own sharpened their appreciation for having a child around. Both realized that Zubaida's visits had likely been just as good for them as for her.

All of that made it a much more daunting prospect to have to sit by idly and pray that things didn't blow up over at the host family's house. They had seen her capacity for asserting her will by provoking annoyed reactions, but they were unaware of anything that appeared to be genuinely dangerous to her or anyone else.

They wondered, if the hosts weren't exaggerating Zubaida's extreme levels of behavior, could it be that they had somehow provoked these responses from Zubaida themselves, perhaps without even realizing it?

As usual when so many different points of view are involved, it was important to determine the truth and nearly impossible to find it.

6 🌾

Zubaida's first surgery for the month of October was on Monday, the seventh. Peter Grossman began the surgical session with a series of multiple steroid injections throughout Zubaida's face, neck, and both sides of her body, to help break down existing scar tissue and to prevent it from thickening the way it had done in those first months after her burn.

There was a sizable, tight scar remaining under one side of Zubaida's jaw that was still preventing full movement. When he cut the binding scar tissue away from her neck, the open wound that remained required sixty square centimeters of skin to seal it. The area would be temporarily covered with a homograft, made from processed cadaver skin. The Grossman's clinic routinely carries quantities sufficient to completely graft a large male adult. But since these grafts can't take life in the patient's body, they are only good as temporary measures to allow the patient to recover some strength before enduring the process of donating their own skin. The same sixty square centimeters of homograft that the skin bank could easily supply from its stock would soon have to be replaced with an identically sized piece of living tissue from one of the few unscarred areas still left on her body.

The subtlety of the day's work culminated in the work to her chin, underneath the vermilion border of the lip on both the left and right sides. He carefully traced the outlines of each lip, cutting away any binding scarification, then reconstructed the tissue using a "Z-plasty," one of the powerfully effective tools of reconstructive surgery.

Since any cut leaves a straight scar whose stiffness will resist stretching from both sides, a Z-plasty allows that principle to cancel itself out by re-cutting the line of a scar into a relaxed Z shape. In this way the natural pull from the skin will be distributed all along the Z, allowing much more natural movement of the surrounding flesh. The depth, the angle, and the size of the "Z" have everything to do with what that living surface will look like in six months, in a year, in ten years. Errors in such choices would be measured in millimeters.

Everything went as hoped and expected that day, so Zubaida stayed at the hospital; she was scheduled to be back for the second round of this set of procedures in three days. It was much easier to assure that the dressings were maintained in a sealed and clean condition under constant care. Dr. Peter had noticed that since Zubaida's last procedures, she seemed to be filled with a nearly compulsive need to hum or sometimes sing out loud and even dance her body around despite her limited range of movement, so he made it a point to wrap her with extra thick gauze and asked the nurses to do whatever they could to keep her still so that the grafts stayed clean.

That afternoon, after Zubaida was awake enough for a conversation in the recovery room, he gave her the same caution about not wiggling around to music and stretching her new skin grafts, using simple words and gestures to make his point. Her gaze detached from his and fixed on some point far away while she murmured a generic "okay" that could have meant anything.

On October 10, 2002, Zubaida went back under general anesthesia so that Grossman and his team could replace the cadaver skin temporary grafts with an equal amount of full-thickness grafts from the inside of her thigh. There was enough unscarred skin there to get the needed sixty square centimeters of donor skin, but since the donor site's skin would also have to be replaced, the surgical wound would be covered by a split-thickness graft from her own body, so that it could incorporate into her skin even though it would never stretch like the surrounding tissue. He swabbed the finalized surgical wounds with a mesh dressing impregnated with a solution called Scarlet Red.

Scarlet Red is a user-friendly name for a synthesized organic dye that Dr. Peter would be applying liberally on Zubaida's donor graft sites. Scarlet Red has been in widespread use for more than fifty years by the mainstream medical community as a topical antiseptic and for its known power to speed healing for many types of burns, even though no one is sure exactly how—or even why—the bright red organic dye works the way that it does.

Experiments on the thin red liquid have shown it to have the power to stimulate the proliferation of new cells in an injured area, and it has also been used to enhance the speed of wound healing. Since Scarlet Red shares most of its chemical makeup with more than half of the world's commercial dyes, the understanding of why it should work when other colors don't is a dissertation topic looking for a doctoral student.

Scarlet Red is also picky about where it spreads its power—a different kind of organic dye will have the same antiseptic and healing effect on a slightly different type of wound. Medical dictionaries can list the various shades of organic dye one after another, noting the particular types of injuries for which each one is prescribed, with no specific explanation as to how Scarlet Red or any of the other dyes work.

The concept of using an organic dye as a wound-healing substance may go back much, much further than the fifty years it has been recognized in mainstream medicine. And so it was in that bright red topical elixir that modern Western medicine touched fingertips for a moment with the impoverished clinics of an ancient nomad culture—who also rub their patients' wounds with ointments whose power they can't explain.

❧ ❧

The cultural laws mixed into Zubaida's blood and impressed onto her view of the world were clear in telling her that adults around her represented the Law. Of course, that wasn't supposed to hold true with the Others, but she was alone among them now and they seemed to be in charge of every aspect of her existence, so whether it was right or wrong, the adults around her also represented some sort of law. It was law because they had authority and she did not.

They explained things to her, so many things, over and over again, as if the words of their own laws had any meaning to her other than as the pronouncements that the adults made about what was to happen to her next. Her hosts could communicate with her in a language that she could now understand fairly well, but which still sounded foreign to her ears. In the hospital or at her hosts' home, most of what was said to her didn't seem to mean anything, whether it was perfectly translated or not. All the adults around her, all of the cold and impersonal adults, tried so hard to be friendly and only succeeded in looking like strangers trying hard to appear friendly. It was consoling sometimes, but other times sent a cold shiver of warning up her back.

She couldn't really tell why the same sorts of actions might strike her as pleasant one time and make her skin crawl at another. It was as if she had two separate sets of nerve endings, which the world randomly selected every time any part of it touched her. Sometimes, when her skin felt crawly inside, she could jump and shout and run around until she burned enough nervous energy to smooth herself back out. But other times, her changeable nerves reacted to the world by overloading, burying her under more sensation and information than she could bear to take in. Then it didn't matter to her if it was coming from her hosts in her language or from the Others in the American language. It meant nothing to her; it was like listening to people gargling a mouthful of gravel.

When that happened, she liked to crawl under a table and roll herself into a ball. She tried to pretend that she was in a little hole in a bank of cool sand and that she could pull the sand over her and disappear, safe from any further disturbance from the world and its sensations.

Sometimes that sent the people around her into various states of upset, which was good, since it allowed her to feel her willpower reaching out into the world and having some measure of effect, even though she generally felt invisible and unheard. At other times, she could hear adults talking about teaching her a lesson and not giving in to her manipulations. That was good, too, because then they left her alone and safely curled up under the heavy table, in a state that was sort of like peace.

Other times, though, the adults seemed to need to provoke her. It felt as if they only existed to push her first one direction and then the next, with no clear reason to any of it. It was all just a series of instructions, explanations, orders. Doctors and nurses poked at her during her checkups at the hospital, the host parents poked at her while they checked her dressings, and through it all the carefully translated words made it abundantly clear that these things were all for Zubaida's benefit. She was beginning to lose track of what her "benefit" was even supposed to mean.

She understood, as far as any ten-year-old understands the idea of immediate sacrifice for a long-term gain. But on deeper and more primal levels she shared the trait with most other humans of hating the feeling of being poked and prodded. The infuriating messages of helplessness that went along with every push and pull and poke and jab were far worse than whatever physical discomfort might be involved.

Sometimes the adults were so sure that what they were doing was for her own good that it seemed to her as if they didn't even realize she was a living thing. Then she had to stop them in their tracks—wake them up—make them see her. Make them listen to her. More than once, when their continual orders seemed specifically intended to drive her insane, she exploded and grabbed a kitchen knife, swearing that she would cut herself or anyone who came near her. It took that much to make them snap out of their adult trances and to actually see her as she was, standing in front of them. The pause never lasted for more than a few moments, but it was good to make them see her. And as time went by and the host family tended to forget, she kept having to make them see her again.

❦ ❦

The charitable Non-Government Organization that handled Zubaida's case from Afghanistan to California was like any other NGO, in the sense that its interest in her remained strong even after arrangements for the trip and the surgery were completed. Throughout the month of October, however, the ordinary interest morphed into real concern. Peter and Rebecca began getting calls and e-mails from the NGO representatives with news of behavioral episodes involving Zubaida with her host family. The parents had grown worried about the unknown depth of Zubaida's levels of emotional disturbance. Now their questions took on a real sense of immediate alarm. How extreme might her behavior become? Was their own family in danger?

The hosts wanted reassurance, but who could give them such a thing with confidence? Could the NGO who sponsored her, the hosts now wanted to know, offer any guarantee of Zubaida's mental stability?

When that question came in, the NGO reps contacted Peter at the hospital and asked him what they should tell the family. Were the hosts in any danger? Could Peter and the NGO offer any guarantee at all that anyone was safe in this girl's presence?

And it wasn't her overt emotional scenes and melodramatic threats that upset them most; they could see through those manipulative sorts of behavior. Their greatest concern was over the increasing inability to get any cooperation out of her at all. It was as if Zubaida had somehow dismissed their credibility and was now detaching herself from them and from their authority, across the board.

When they challenged her solo foot trips, she explained that back in her village of Farah, she made it a habit to work off her considerable nervous energy with long walks through the ancient city walls. Even the strict local customs allowed such petty freedoms to a little girl. Now here in Los Angeles, Zubaida was firmly insisting that since there were no Taliban around to enforce their code of driving all girls inside the home after their tenth birthday, she intended to keep up her very Zubaida-ish habits of long walks filled with flights of imagination. The big problem was that she tended to disappear for these long walks at odd hours without announcing that she was leaving or giving any indication where she was going or when she would return.

However, the hosts knew her customs well enough to understand that such disrespect for household rules would never be tolerated inside of her own home; the implied message of contempt was difficult to miss. They complained of their utter inability to gain any cooperation from her about it at all. In fact, once Zubaida saw how much this sort of thing rattled them, she appeared to step up the behavior.

What were they supposed to do?

Peter was baffled by the situation and wondered how he was supposed to be able to solve their dilemma. Most of Zubaida's time with him was on a medical patient basis; these other issues just never came up at the hospital. There Zubaida seemed to clearly understand that maximum cooperation was her most reliable route to a comfortable process and the best possible outcome. Even though the nursing staff maintained a family atmosphere among the patients on the ward, and despite the fact that Zubaida fondly referred to Helena San Marco, one of the older nurses, as Grandma, there were really no family-type confrontations there. Sometimes Zubaida would try to negotiate for a little more recovery time before her next procedure, but other than that—and her tendency to wiggle and dance whether or not she needed to be still and let her stitches heal—she had never presented him with such irrational behavior.

Still the calls and e-mails continued. Her behavior, according to the host family, was eroding so rapidly that they no longer felt safe in the house with her. They wanted to be replaced—they demanded to be replaced—and they wanted Zubaida out of their home as quickly as possible.

Peter's heart sank the moment that he heard that. This was the nightmare scenario that he hoped to sneak past, because he already knew that the charitable NGO had never followed through on securing a backup family—their own stockpile of obligations siphoned away enough of their work time that nobody ever got around to it.

He urged everyone to find some sort of compromise. The surgical process with Zubaida was nowhere near completion. Her original treatment plan already compacted three years' worth of surgery into a single year, so there was just no acceptable way to speed that timeline up any more. It would only deny her fragile body the already limited recovery time that she was getting now.

He made sure that everybody involved in the decision-making process understood that if Zubaida had to return to her village at this stage, much of her current progress would eventually be lost while her body continued to grow and the unresolved scars pulled harder and harder against the rest of her. Both her appearance and her mobility would be heavily affected if essential work on her chest and torso was left undone.

But no matter who he dealt with at the NGO, the same answer came back: They had already done everything that they could to secure housing and care for her. How could they ask another host family, even if they found an acceptable one, to take on a child that the original host family was afraid of? Aside from the moral issues, who could begin to unravel the legal implications of such a thing if indeed a second home was established but the situation there turned out even worse? What if it involved violence?

Who would answer for it, among all of them: the soldiers who first encountered her, the medics and doctors who cared for her, the State Department, the NGO, the Sherman Oaks Hospital, the Grossman Burn Center, or even Peter Grossman, himself—the doctor who first insisted that the burn center take this case on in spite of its many risks—who would answer for such a disaster, if it happened?

Who would have the power to fix that one?

⚹ ⚹

The ancient and instinctive animal drive to avoid torment is imprinted in the bones and the blood. Nothing that lives and moves will tolerate poking and prodding without attempting to move out of the way. Sufficiently provoked, it will strike out like a deadly predator. Within human interactions, civilizations teach various methods of learning to delay that response and to tolerate a certain amount of poking and prodding as the inevitable consequence of life in the community. But the veneer of civility is known to be thin. Poke anybody a few too many times, and even the most bland personality will erupt in anger. Further provoked, they will rise to the level of rage where violence not only becomes possible, but is likely, even guaranteed.

For any human being, the best thing about freedom is the power that it bestows to be able to walk away from something that is poking you, so that you don't have to wait until it causes you to explode and beat it to death.

Then you get to live in peace.

Zubaida knew that her lack of freedom was only the product of the massive efforts to help her recover from the damage left by the teeth of the orange monster, but understanding her lack of freedom didn't help her tolerate the inability to get away from the poking and prodding. It went much further than medical examinations; she was continually poked and prodded from the inside by her feelings.

Her culture is built upon the life of the extended family and one's place in it. In this country, she felt strangely naked a lot of the time. The pangs of separation prodded beneath her stomach and her feelings of guilt poked her with reminders of how much she had cost her family by carelessly dancing into the teeth of the orange monster.

In this country, the constant strangeness of the language jabbed at her ears, whether it was the flat-sounding American English or the accented Dari spoken by her hosts. In both cases, the odd sounds of the words scraped over her sense of hearing like dull blades. Everything about America was impossibly foreign, and even though she had spent most of her time indoors, the weekend trips with the Grossmans helped impress upon her that nothing about this place resembled her homeland or her people's way of living. Here she was amidst abundance such as she could never imagine, while her family remained behind in Farah in circumstances more destitute than before she fell into the fire. And now they were less able to keep up their home life, because of the lack of Zubaida's constant help with all the unending chores of group family living.

The harsh realities of all that made for too much poking and prodding to endure. She felt like she had been enveloped by a cloud of invisible bees. The needling stings came at her from every direction.

She needed to release little bits of that pressure by exploding in frustration and rage, and that need was becoming just as compelling as the need to scream away the pain of the burns had once been. She knew all about the civilized reactions that were expected from one who receives help and hospitality, but the need to either flee or to strike out was stronger, stamped into the cells of her bones and her blood. And since there was nowhere to run, somebody close by was sure to encounter a girl who was being driven half mad by swarms of unseen bees.

That wasn't the way Peter Grossman heard it, when he got the doomsday call from the NGO. What he heard was that the experiment was over; it had failed.

Zubaida was going back to Afghanistan.

The host family was now demanding that Zubaida be immediately removed from their home. They were no longer listening to entreaties.

"What?" he barked into the phone. "She's not finished! You're telling me about what her hosts want, but what about the patient? Are we just going to throw her away?"

Maybe, they gamely tried to assure him, she can eventually make her way up to Turkey with her father. Some of the hospitals there were known to be pretty good. Maybe the Turks would offer up the facilities, the expertise, the desire to show deep charity to a foreign patient who cannot pay.

Oh yeah, Peter thought. *And maybe she'll find a magic lamp and wish it all away.*

It's helpful at this point to get a clearer picture of who was receiving that news. Peter was born in 1963, just a year before his father finished his surgical training. He was still only a year and a half old when the family moved to Los Angeles. His father, Richard Grossman, went to work for a Beverly Hills medical firm for a few years, then opened the first incarnation of the Grossman Burn Center. Peter's parents were divorced when he was thirteen, and he lived from age fourteen through age sixteen with his father, whom he idolized.

From the time Peter was seven years old, Richard Grossman had been taking his son to the hospital with him from time to time, to follow him on medical rounds. The good life and the solid private school education that Richard Grossman's work had provided to his son were alluring, but Peter's sense of his father's expertise was always the thing that he admired most.

It was that admiration that propelled him through Chicago Medical School and a four-year residency at Cedar-Sinai Medical Center in Beverly Hills. When he joined his father's practice and began his own career down the same road, he felt a mixture of privilege at the opportunity and challenge to not allow his own identity to be swallowed by the many years of considerable achievement that his father had already accumulated. And this case of the burned girl from Afghanistan was, more than anything else had ever been, something that was his alone. Better yet, it was Peter's case all right, but it was now fully supported by his father, even though he had once opposed their involvement.

This was the man, not yet forty, who sat on the other end of the connection with the NGO and listened to them tell him that it had all been a very nice try, but that now it was time to cut their losses and pack it all in. Zubaida was going back to Afghanistan.

By the time Peter got home from his office that evening, his mood was so low that Rebecca saw the change in him as soon as he walked in. He sat her down to break the news—they're sending her back, he told her in dismay. They're going to pull the plug on everything, all because they never arranged for a backup family like they promised to do in the first place, and now they're afraid to look for one.

He shook his head. *We were so close.*

It's helpful at this point, as well, to get a clearer picture of who was sitting next to Peter and listening to him deliver this grim news. To all appearances she was an attractive and poised woman residing in a beautifully decorated luxury home, and it would be easy for an observer to underestimate her as some Beverly Hills beauty whose life had been velvet coated. But she was born Rebecca Gray in Odessa, Texas, and grew up in Irving, just outside Dallas, in a household where her parents had also divorced. In her case, they split up before she was even born, so that her mother had raised Rebecca and her brothers, Michael and Steven, alone on her salary as an executive at Continental Airlines. Rebecca's childhood ensured that she and Peter shared a fierce devotion to the idea of drawing a family unit together, as opposed to standing by and allowing it to be split apart.

She and Peter were born the same year, and while he was in Los Angeles enduring his parents' divorce at the age of thirteen, Rebecca was in Texas while her mother struggled with bouts of depression and turned to alcohol when faced with the financial burdens and emotional challenges that come with parenting three teenagers alone.

At thirteen, Rebecca began to pitch in more and more to keep things functioning at home, on top of working outside of school for spending money while participating in a full roster of school activities. She replaced an uncomfortable home life with a happier social life, and through her combination of beauty, brains, and ambition she rose among her peers as an enthusiastic leader

with a refined ability to make friends. She carried those traits into an early career as an airline flight attendant, then went on to become a successful entrepreneur in the medical equipment field, making her way as a single woman in
that male-dominated industry.

She was also no stranger to the world's misery, since her mother's airline
position gave them the opportunity to fly all over the planet for very low rates.
Her mother saw to it that they were exposed to many different cultures in
Asia, Africa, and Europe.

And so, by this point in Rebecca's life, she had become so adept at over-
coming emotional adversity that the idea of standing by and allowing
Zubaida's medical recovery to be slashed in half, simply because nobody in Los
Angeles was willing to ride the emotional roller coaster, was a notion that fell
squarely on her list of things that can never be permitted to happen.

She and Peter sat up talking for a long time that night. The upshot was that
neither one found the situation tolerable. The way they reasoned it out, they
were young and healthy, they wished for a child of their own, and until that
happened, they had a place in their hearts and home for temporary custody of
Zubaida, and they had the financial wherewithal to make the necessary
arrangements and absorb the considerable costs.

The next day, they contacted the charitable NGO and announced their intention to gain official approval as Zubaida's new host family, then made sure
that the current host family knew that relief was on the way. They also prepared to overcome any potential objections from official corners by asking the
court to declare them to be Zubaida's new legal guardians. The complex process, which could easily consume months of legal maneuvering, was accepted
as an emergency hearing and took place in days instead.

On the first of November, by the time that the presiding judge heard all the
arguments and got the full picture about what Rebecca and Peter were agree-
ing to do, on top of what they had already done to restore Zubaida's life, he
ruled in favor of granting them custody while the rest of her treatment was
completed, noting that she would be staying inside of a home where she would
be guaranteed dignity and respect in addition to the necessities of survival. He
ended the proceedings by smiling at them and saying, "God bless you."

* * *

Two days later, Zubaida was dropped off at their house carrying a couple of small bags and a burning resentment, in a state of complete turmoil about whatever was happening to her. Somehow, she had arrived at a firm conclusion that the host family did *not* want her to leave, and that Rebecca and Peter had mysteriously used their influence to "steal" Zubaida away from them and to bring her into their own home—all against the host family's wishes.

But it was done. And she was there, and their rocky road as a family was about to begin. Three people now lived in the Grossman household, even though so far, only two of them considered that to be a good thing.

7

For Zubaida, the only response that made sense in the middle of this crumbling situation was to cover herself with a thick shell of glum attitude and stay hidden underneath it. She could tell that everything was falling apart around her, but she couldn't make any sense out of whatever it was that the Others were planning to do with her. It seemed pretty clear that the host family was afraid of her because of her temper, or maybe that they were mad because she didn't like to listen to them. Or maybe somebody was even punishing her for going out and walking around, finding out a little something about freedom. She knew that under the Taliban, she was now past the age of being allowed to walk long distances by herself. The thing that the American adults did not seem to appreciate was that every step that she took alone out there on the American streets was a dance of freedom. The dance defied the black-turbaned overseers who had somehow managed to travel halfway around the world inside of her brain so that they could generate this torment inside of her.

So while the adults talked in the living room, she made her way through the huge house and into the kitchen, where she crawled under the dining table and curled up into a space that was like a little cave. Her head was packed with conflicting stories about whether her hosts insisted on getting rid of her or not. Either her host family had decided that the answer to the question of whether the Afghan girl had lost her mind was "yes," and they were forcing her out of their home—or else they still wanted her to live with them, but Dr. Peter and Rebecca had done some mysterious things that she didn't know about. And whatever those things were, the result was that now she had to live with them instead.

At that moment Zubaida had nothing more to grasp on to than the fact that Dr. Peter had helped her so much—even though the surgeries always scared her and the recoveries still hurt, no matter how much better the American doctors might be—and the fact that Rebecca was so friendly with her on the two weekends that they spent together.

That didn't mean that things were all right. She already knew that the doctors and nurses only told her a little piece of the truth about whatever they were doing. They acted like they thought she wouldn't understand it, but what else weren't they telling her?

She knew that the Others were the same as her own people in one sense; they really didn't like it when she got extremely upset. She had been getting extremely upset a lot lately, so could they be taking her to Dr. Peter's house so that he could operate on her even more? Was everybody just not telling her, so she wouldn't get extremely upset?

It was as if everyone and everything around her were all individual cogs of some giant and unseen Other machine, grinding away and pulling her through its mechanical innards whether she struggled against it or not. Her sense of danger came more from the idea that no matter how much certain people were trying to help her, she was in danger of being consumed and disappearing inside of the invisible Other machine—never to come out.

And if so, what would anyone do? What would her father do, back there in their homeland, so remote that they couldn't even speak on the phone? It struck her, then, that her family couldn't possibly know whether she was even alive at the moment. So how would they know if things went bad here? How would they find out?

Her dark musings were cut short when the front door of the house closed.

The former host family was gone. That was it, then. On one hand, she felt like a new snake crawling out of an old skin. Now they couldn't make her do things as if they were her mother and father anymore. Even though their Dari was rough on Zubaida's ear, there was still enough common language for conversation, which meant that she had to endure their endless suggestions.

But now she was alone in the home of her doctor and his wife, and there was no common language between them at all except for a handful of random words she had picked up at the hospital and around the host family's house. Maybe that wouldn't be so bad. Without language, it would be a lot harder to boss her around. People would have to leave her alone. As for Dr. Peter, he would surely be gone at the hospital all day, so he couldn't boss her around except when she was there for treatment, and as for Rebecca—she was so smiley and pleasant all the time—it seemed pretty certain there would be no trouble from her. Zubaida only wanted to concentrate on getting through this whole experience and making it back home alive. She didn't need anything else from these people. She still had her attitude shell for protection, thicker than the scars had once been. In fact, she felt pretty sure that she would be able to get Rebecca to leave her alone and to let her do whatever she wanted, just to keep things smiley and pleasant. She had already figured out that Rebecca liked it that way.

It was a fair assumption to make, since she couldn't know how different Rebecca's background was from the way she assumed it to be. She couldn't have any idea of the fire in Rebecca's belly, as real as the heat that seared Zubaida's face. They shared a kinship in more ways than one.

⚹ ⚹

Zubaida wished that she hadn't paid attention to the TV show about birds, because the one they called a woodpecker in English was a perfect picture of the way that Rebecca dealt with her. And she never expected to have to cope with something like that. Rebecca didn't yell at her or make threats or worst of all start to cry just to get her way. She just kept being very polite and then repeating what she wanted, over and over. It completely took Zubaida off guard the first time she encountered it and she really hadn't come up with any effective response since then. Now there was an image to go with it—Rebecca was the woodpecker and Zubaida was the tree. As far as she knew, there weren't any such creatures around her homeland. Now she lived with one.

With her father, Zubaida had long since learned that while he loved to shout and throw his arms around, all she had to do was stand there like in a strong wind, and after a while he got tired or distracted and gave up. Sometimes he even walked away, but then came back later and gave in anyway. And her mother was prone to lapse into deep bouts of the silent treatment to express her anger or disapproval. It could make an entire room a pretty unpleasant place, although Zubaida had learned how to ignore it fairly well. Her mother always seemed to sense Zubaida's personal strength and usually gave her a wide berth.

But this Rebecca person was proving to be a lot more difficult than she expected. Where was all that willpower during their two weekends together? Everything was easy, then. Now, if Zubaida was refusing to eat or refusing to come inside when she was called or refusing to turn off the TV that she loved so much and which she drank from in much the same way that a desert traveler drinks from an oasis, here would come Rebecca, asking over and over, not going crazy like her father or turning cold like her mother would do.

No, she was a smiling American woodpecker who went rat-tat-tat on Zubaida's head like she was trying to make a hole and wouldn't stop until Zubaida came to the table, or took her bath, or turned off the TV. How was she supposed to fight a woodpecker?

Even though Rebecca was a fancy American woman who should be weak and helpless without her money, when Zubaida resorted to getting big and very loud and making herself look too strong to stop, Rebecca didn't back away from her at all. She just somehow made herself get big, too, and she turned into some kind of solid statue that you couldn't move with a donkey.

Zubaida tried everything she could think of, but as far as she was concerned, Rebecca was managing to get her to do what she wanted far too much of the time.

Peter was just as hard to deal with. She wasn't even going to call him Dr. Peter anymore, since now he got to tell her what to do whether they were at the hospital or not. As a doctor, he simply had too much authority and power over her for her to be able to stand up to him. Peter wasn't around as much as

Rebecca, so he didn't try to make her do as much as Rebecca did, but even so, it was easier to feel like she had a choice in the matter when a name didn't begin with "doctor."

He didn't yell like the village men, either, and it was maddening. He just stood there like a tree, refusing to give up and go away, and explaining in simple words and gestures what he wanted from her. When she ignored him, he just kept staying there like he was made of stone. Then he would repeat whatever he wanted, using new words and gestures, calmly, quietly, over and over until she wanted to scream.

And against the two of them together, forget it. They were like huge mud-brick walls, blocking her path, forcing her to turn this way and that until she arrived wherever they were making her go. Only crazy people argue with walls, and when other people see that, they leave the crazy people alone and let them go back to whatever crazy thing they were doing. But when Zubaida let herself go crazy, screaming with rage and stomping her feet, Peter and Rebecca just kept right on being these silent walls, blocking her from running off on her own, turning her this way and that, taking her to some place that only they knew and understood.

From the beginning, Peter and Rebecca relied on their next-door neighbor, Patty Moayer, who could translate for them when they needed to communicate complex thoughts to Zubaida. Patty was raised in Iran, where she worked for years as a nurse, and since immigrating to the United States in 1979, she continued to work as a special education school nurse. Her ongoing compassion and desire to help children was a perfect match for the situation. That relationship was another of the happy coincidences that already surrounded the story. Only a few days before, on Halloween, Patty's two teenage daughters, Mona and Nina, came by Peter and Rebecca's house to do a little early trick-or-treating and to introduce themselves to the couple, since the Grossmans had recently moved into the home where the girls' close friends used to live. Mona and Nina had heard that the new neighbor next door was a handsome young doctor, so Halloween was a good excuse to go over to say hello and get a peek.

They were making a little conversation with Rebecca at the door and hoping that Peter might happen by, when Rebecca asked—half in jest—if they had any friends who spoke Dari and could help by occasionally "baby-sitting" with a ten-year-old visiting Afghan girl who was going to be staying with them.

Both girls grinned. *Sure we speak Dari—or Farsi, actually, but the two languages are so close that people who speak either one of them can understand some of the other.* So it went with the continuing "divine coincidences" that Mike Smith had already noticed in Zubaida's story: next door, not one potential baby-sitter, but two of them, and nice girls, too.

Mona and Nina, along with their mother, Patty, were the main language link between them all, and anything that Rebecca and Peter couldn't communicate to Zubaida with pantomime was translated through them. The attention of older teenagers who could talk to Zubaida made her feel so important that she kept herself under control most of the time when they were around, eager to win their approval. The usual admiration of a young girl for older teenage girls crossed the cultural boundaries without any trouble at all.

Four days after Zubaida moved in, Peter and Rebecca gratefully thanked the girls for their help and gladly promised to continue including them at their house. They had managed to find an experienced nanny who spoke Farsi. After that, the nanny took care of Zubaida's moment-to-moment needs, while Rebecca walked Zubaida through the final steps toward getting admitted to a special learning program in a local public school. At the age of ten, this would be the first time that she had ever entered a classroom. Rebecca also completed the arrangements for her to attend classes in reading and writing her own language, knowledge that the Taliban had denied to her entire generation of girls. Zubaida's frenetic energy was best controlled by keeping her busy with activities. She appeared to love structured time and a routine of any kind appeared to help her keep from falling into bouts of depression.

Zubaida was starting to feel the warmth from the fire in Rebecca's belly.

Rebecca's work ethic was strong, going back to her first jobs as a kid, and her personal energy was high, both as a born-in attribute and as a product of her long dedication to healthy living. That energy was now put to work on Zubaida's behalf in ways that hadn't been possible before she came to live with them. Rebecca felt a sense of relief; she was tired of being appalled at the girl's condition and feeling helpless to do anything about it.

She sent a flurry of phone calls and e-mails to the State Department and the military to arrange for Mohammed to be taken to the nearest landline for a planned phone call with his daughter. It would be the first direct contact between them since he had left. The Grossmans asked Patty Moayer to listen in on an extension and translate the conversation for them to make sure that Mohammed's instructions to his daughter didn't raise her level of conflict even higher.

What Patty heard and relayed back was the excitement and delight between both of them at hearing each other's voices. When Mohammed asked Zubaida to tell him how she was doing, she complained that she didn't like all the surgery, but that everyone was taking care of her. She complained of missing the family badly and wanting to return home. Mohammed was loving and gentle with her, but he also remained firm that she should drink up every aspect of this experience. When Zubaida told him that Rebecca was enrolling her in public school as well as in private Dari classes, he shouted with joy and urged her to pay sharp attention during every moment of schooling. "Learn everything you can," he implored. "Soak up everything you can learn and come back here to teach it to your brothers and sisters! This is an opportunity such as no one here can even imagine. You have to do the best you can for everyone here, Zubaida!"

After the satellite contact was broken and the call ended, she was quiet and withdrawn for a long time. They left her to mull things over by herself. Later, when she finally rejoined them, things weren't instantly better, but Peter and Rebecca agreed that they saw an improvement.

Zubaida began to make eye contact more often, and to hold it for longer periods of time. She began to go easy on shooting those dirty looks at them for any passing trivial reason. Most of all, it seemed that being given a firm "mission" directly from her father had restored some feeling of control to her.

Now she wouldn't be going to school just because Rebecca and Peter thought it was a good idea and she had nothing else to do; she was on a mission for the family who had been so depleted by her injuries. She was going to learn to speak English and to read and write in her native language. With that sim-ple, giant task, she was going to do something that none of the women she had ever known and none of the women that those women had ever known would ever imagine possible.

The power of this order from her father, made on the entire family's behalf, sank its hook into the fundamental images and sensations of her life, as deeply as they went. This order compelled her to lift her thoughts away from what-ever direction that they might stray in, and consistently direct them back to the mission of learning everything she could and of bringing the knowledge back home to share with her clan.

She wasn't a helpless bundle of flesh, anymore; she was a spy for her family. She was a student of all things American.

Her father and the rest of her family were going to be expecting a lot from her when she got back to them. More than ever, more than she could possibly have done before the accident, she was going to be a vital personality in the family. She was going to bring them all kinds of American knowledge and in-formation and abilities. Her active and contributing place in the family order would be restored beyond her dreams.

What Peter and Rebecca both noticed at that point was that Zubaida started to become less prone to fits of antagonistic behavior. Her father had given her a way to see herself as someone far more powerful than she could have imagined before all of this happened to her, let alone in the long days since the fire. And as soon as she began to see herself in a form that she recognized—as Zubaida—she also felt a little less need to force other people to see her.

It was one of those times when the release actually felt like a physical weight being lifted off her. When it was gone, it left her with extra lung space, so that she was able to draw a stronger breath.

❆ ❆

Twenty-eight-year-old Kerrie Benson was in her fifth year of teaching at the Round Meadow Elementary School in the fall of 2002 when, during Staff De-velopment Day, Principal Rose Dunn took her aside in the hallway to give her important news. Dunn had carried out a number of conversations with a local woman named Rebecca Grossman, who had recently gained custody of an Afghan girl. The girl was ten, but had never been to school, and was recovering from a series of operations to restore her after massive burn damage. She would not only require special classes in remedial schooling for the rudiments of alphabet and language, but her classroom teacher was going to be expected to "mainstream" the girl in with the rest of the class and find some way to keep her involved with lessons that were years ahead of her education level.

Kerrie Benson, it had been decided, was the best teacher for the task. Her third grade class of eight-year-olds was close enough in age, in social terms, for ten-year-old Zubaida. Bensen's careful presentation of lessons and patience with her children had already convinced Principal Dunn that her personal style was suited to the range of challenges that this situation was sure to produce. As for those more advanced lessons that can only be expected for children with a couple of years of schooling under their belts, they would be replaced, for Zubaida, with equal time in a smaller special education class, where the more basic lessons were highly visual and hands-on, clear enough to cross all language barriers.

So in a few days, Kerrie Benson would be getting a new enrollee, and she might want to start preparing herself to receive a ten-year-old girl who had never been to school at all, who spoke very little English, and who was only in the area in the first place because she was in the process of enduring a full year of surgeries to restore features that had been obliterated by a fire in her home country of Afghanistan.

It was pointed out to Benson that tremendous behind-the-scenes interest was focused on this girl's development, and that it was very desirable for this experiment in late-stage basic education to demonstrate positive results.

Benson threw herself into preparation. She, as the main classroom teacher, would handle the task of including Zubaida with the rest of the students during those activities where Zubaida could reasonably be expected to understand and participate. Benson would also coordinate her class time with special education teacher Kendra Kreutzer, who took Zubaida into her special education classroom to work on filling in the pre–third grade schooling that she lacked.

In Benson's classroom, while she presented the regular third grade lessons, she took care that Zubaida's fundamentals would be constantly reinforced by a number of simple techniques. An old-fashioned alphabet chart was taped to her desk, and she would be provided with a picture book of alphabet letters. To complement and reinforce those learning tools, Benson also hunted down a set of soft, molded rubber cut-outs of each letter, coated in sand. These would be among Zubaida's regular daily tools, so that she could not only see and draw each letter the way any other child learns to do it, but she would also have the tactile stimulation of handling each letter in 3-D, as well as trace her fingers over the roughened face of each letter, a process designed to help bury the knowledge of this letter deep into her mind.

Zubaida would be kept within the social structure of the overall class, but would also be provided with constant activities that focused on using "manipulatives," as Benson called them—items she could touch and feel to reinforce a lesson through a number of senses at the same time. Every lesson would be fed to her through a variety of sensory stimuli, so that lack of common language was never a reason for her to become disconnected from the ongoing lessons.

A key part of Benson's classroom plan for her newest student was to provide a constant level of activity that would provide Zubaida with enough moment-to-moment satisfaction to keep the process an engaging one, but would also challenge her enough to prevent boredom from sneaking in. Benson already knew from years of experience that in order to communicate with kids that age in any meaningful way, you have to keep their attention consistently engaged. Any time that Zubaida might spend being either bored and underchallenged or confused and frustrated would only end up as wasted opportunity within the small amount of time that the medical situation allowed them. Those wasted minutes and added-up hours would ultimately spoil the tremendous work that lay ahead: playing catch-up to several years of schooling with a student who spoke no English and had no American cultural background.

"But what an opportunity!" Benson later enthused. "And not just for Zubaida, either. Imagine the educational value to a classroom full of American third-graders who have never had contact with a girl from Afghanistan to begin with, let alone one whose appearance supposedly had a somewhat shocking effect, even though she'd already been through several surgeries."

The trick would lie in how the class was prepared for her arrival. Benson knew that children that age are capable of both casual cruelty and equally strong gentleness and devotion. The devotion usually appeared to be activated when something caused them to empathize instead of judge. She immediately went to her class and began to prepare them, letting them know that there was going to be a late enrolling student joining them in a few days. The student was a girl from a country called Afghanistan, and she had never been to school before because in her country girls are not allowed to go to school. Benson looked around at all of her girls and let that one sink in.

"Just think if all the girls here had to go home right now, and *never come back?* They would never be allowed to learn anything more about the outside world." She elaborated on the description, constantly checking the kids' eyes to make sure that the class was visualizing the situation.

Then she broke the touchy part. "Now, this girl had a terrible accident last year. She fell into a big fire and got burned, very badly. She barely made it through alive, and after it was over, the scars from the burns were so bad that she had to come to America for a whole year of operations to help her get better."

Benson asked how many of them had ever been in a hospital and counted a few hands. "This girl has been in hospitals all over the world, but she couldn't get the right help until she came here. She's had a whole lot of operations just in the last few months, over and over and over. And she has to have more of them, too.

"So when she comes here, you're going to see a girl whose features are still scarred, even though she looks better now, and she is going to have to leave school sometimes, to go back and have those next operations."

Benson asked her class to try to imagine being far, far away from everybody they ever knew, without their family or any friends. She actually saw a couple of faces blanch at the thought.

"What we need to do is more than just help her to learn things. We need to sort of be like her family and friends, because that's what we would want other people to do for us." That one hit home; she saw the impact on them, on all those faces that were already so full of the world but still innocent enough to easily accept such ideas. Benson went home feeling sure that the right tone had been struck.

Within a few days, the only thing left to do was to meet with the girl. She arranged for Zubaida to come in on an off day, so that Benson could get her acclimated to the classroom without the pressure of staring eyes.

When Zubaida arrived, Kerrie Benson's first impression was that she was about as timid as any kid would be in such strange surroundings—but that at least she didn't shrink back into herself, the way that so many children do at such times. She appeared to be fiercely alert and seemed eager to understand what was being communicated to her, paying close attention while Benson showed her to her desk and then pointed out the various classroom displays while doing her best to communicate something about the purpose of each one.

She felt good to see that Zubaida paid sharp attention even when she probably had no idea what Benson was talking about. For Benson, this was a process that was all about tone of voice and level of spoken volume, and eye contact, and of letting the warmth show in her eyes. The real lesson was not in the words or the class displays; it was in the very fact that Benson was spending this special, one-on-one time with her.

Taliban had imposed their worldview upon Zubaida and her people all of her life. Under their dark judgment, an American adult like Kerrie Benson whose job it was to fill the heads of young girls with skills of reading and writing and with knowledge of the world was a living example of one of the unacceptable Others. But instead, here she was speaking privately with Zubaida and addressing her in terms of gentleness and respect that were the most important messages which Benson had for her new pupil, on that first orientation day.

Benson was relieved to see that by this point in Zubaida's surgical progress, her appearance was not grotesque at all, so that her third-graders handled the situation without any destructive drama. The grafted scars were obvious, but Zubaida's features were balanced at this point and Benson had been told that Zubaida was not nearly as distorted as she used to be. She hadn't seen the photos of Zubaida's condition when she first arrived, but she had been told that the situation at that time was very grim. Now, at least, there was a girl standing right here who was restored enough to go to school and learn, even though she was alone in a foreign country.

She introduced Zubaida to her alphabet book and pointed from the letters in the book to the letters on her desk chart to the letters on the wall. Zubaida's face lit up. Once she grasped that she was looking at the basic pieces of written English, she stared at the book and pored over the letters as if she were running gold coins through her hands.

They spent a while playing a version of the Helen Keller story, while Benson pointed to various objects and worked with Zubaida on the pronunciations. When she produced a drawing pad and suggested that Zubaida draw a picture of the two of them, Zubaida happily went to work at producing recognizable sketches of each of them. The best thing about the sketches was that Zubaida had shown both of them with normal features.

Benson immediately saw it—this girl was more than ready and willing, she was eager to learn. No, Benson thought, *she's more than eager, she's hungry. She's already soaking it up.*

Kerrie Benson felt her pulse rate jump. A child who is hungry to learn and devours every morsel of learning is the dream student of any good teacher; Benson was no exception. That was the primary image that she had in mind when she decided to become a teacher in the first place.

❧ ❧

Over the week of November 19, 2002, The Los Angeles Times *reported on a rash of self-immolations by young women in Afghanistan who were distressed with their complete lack of social freedom under the residual pockets of Taliban influence. More than a hundred of these self-inflicted burn victims had appeared at various Afghan hospitals up to that point in the year, which told nothing about how many uncounted others there may have been throughout the country's sprawling, isolated regions. With the lack of burn care and treatment in that part of the world, these severely burned women, almost all of whom would go on to die, were cited as over-burdening Afghanistan's few existing burn hospital facilities—which was used as justification for the implied prospect of turning them away in the future so that others could be saved. After all, they did it to themselves.*

The quandary for the doctors and clinics grew out of the need to show mercy and care to these agonized women, but it was also noted that this same care was wasted when it was given to someone with self-inflicted wounds who, realistically, was certain to be tomorrow's problem for the grave digger. In that way, the region's few resources were expended on these losing cases, creating a financial sinkhole in the impoverished national medical services.

But what graphs and charts fail to quantify is the tremendous level of despair that was attacking the region's female population. These women, within their own recent memories, had been painted into smaller and smaller corners. It was done first by the Soviet invaders, then by the opportunistic regional warlords, and finally by the Taliban enforcers, who brought with them their violent interpretations of Islam. Now the country's women found themselves driven backward onto a tiny slice of the floor in each room's darkest corner. More and more of these women were finding intolerable the prospect of a life spent on tiptoe in an imaginary corner so tiny that she couldn't take a deep breath for fear of losing her balance and stepping out of her allowed space—with the dire consequences that could ensue.

Some of the self-immolating women were fully aflame before onlookers could extinguish the fires and carry the victims to the nearest aid. Those died quickly, trapped inside physical systems so heavily assaulted that they struggled to continue functioning from one moment to the next. Others were burned at about the same level of injury that struck Zubaida. Most of them would die, too, although it usually took them longer to succumb than the ones with full body burns.

A lucky few were burned to a much lesser extent when passers-by jumped in and smothered the flames. But while those sorts of injuries shouldn't have been life threatening, it was the infections that frequently set in after a burn that tended to finish the job. Even after word circulated all along the gossip trees of the villages and towns about the awful deaths that the desperate young women brought upon themselves, such a terrible means of ending their lives remained—for the most despairing among them—preferable to the thought of enduring a continued existence of repression and enforced ignorance. And it was the only way they could think of to express their rage.

8 ❦

If there was any doubt in Kerrie Benson's mind about her students' ability to embrace Zubaida, it was gone by the end of her first day in school. When Benson brought Zubaida up before the class to be introduced, she appeared a little shy, but just as she did when she first met Benson, she didn't shrink away from the situation, either. Benson gave her the same introduction she would have done for any incoming student, then got everybody focused and back to work.

Benson assigned a rotating roster of students to partner with Zubaida each day, making sure to show her around and demonstrate how things work. The kids argued over the chance to spend time with her and pick up some of the reflected attention, so Zubaida rose to the occasion. Her cultural background placed such a high value on family and clan relationships that the ability to see the importance of relating to other people kept Zubaida in a responsive attitude with the kids in the class. Once the students had a chance to see that this new girl might look different but that she was easy to relate to, even without language, her new place in the class was formed.

Kerrie Benson later spoke of being struck by Zubaida's eagerness to learn her school lessons as well as her determination to relate to the other kids. She readily joined in on games and activities, and within days she was already beginning to use assorted English words and phrases that she picked up from the other kids. The result was that at the same time she was working on the difference between the words "I" and "me," and learning not to use phrases such as *me no want to*, in place of *I don't want to*, she also absorbed language from the other girls even more quickly, so that she rapidly absorbed their knowledge of what was and wasn't considered "cool."

Her natural self-consciousness was frequently overridden by bouts of insatiable curiosity. She seemed to find the most difficult lesson to be the one about always raising your hand and not shouting out your answer just because you're excited that you know it. Before long, several girls in the class began to show a level of interest in her beyond anything that they had been asked to do. And in spite of Zubaida's rudimentary English, she managed to communicate with the others well enough that she was soon fully enmeshed in the class, as well as the girls' social group after school.

Benson knew that Zubaida's life had completely lacked any regular form of daily mental discipline, which made it a concern as to how well she would fit into the structure of classroom life. Another personality with a background like Zubaida's might find that the social challenge of entering school as a cold plunge would be more overwhelming than the lessons themselves. Zubaida thrived under the daily structure. One game that made her blossom was the point system that Benson used with all of her students, letting them win starstickers next to their name on the name board.

Although Zubaida lacked all of the rudimentary skills, Benson was impressed by her native intelligence and by her natural abilities with social behavior. The high regard that she had come to feel for Zubaida's inner strength was cemented in place when she saw how Zubaida related to Emily, one of the other girls in the class. Emily had been attacked by a dog some time before, and had a scar across her forehead that made her self-conscious about her appearance. She worked to keep it covered with her hair as well as she could.

Benson didn't know just when Zubaida spotted Emily's scar, but she watched her go over to Emily and put her arm around her. Zubaida's manner of relating to Emily expressed what her language wasn't developed enough to do, making it clear that Emily didn't have to fear any sort of judgment from her— and that she knew all about what it means to be afraid to look in the mirror.

And so it went for the foreign girl who had been assigned to Kerrie Benson in the hope that Benson could find a way to help her adapt to an American schoolroom and avoid being a social outcast. Zubaida proved eager to learn, and went on to make it a point to take one of the other girls under her own protective wing. Zubaida and Emily became inseparable friends.

※ ※

In a world that was strange to her on almost every level, Zubaida fell into camaraderie with the ease of long practice. The idea of an extended group of trusted friends was a principal concept of her culture and her family background, and the interdependence of her family and their neighbors was so thoroughly interwoven, so essential to their survival, that it was her solitary existence in America that presented the strangest part of her journey.

No matter how well-meaning the adults around her might be, they were all authority figures who had the power to force any sort of awful experience on her, whenever they wanted. However, when Zubaida was in the company of other children close to her age, and those children were accepting and supportive of her, she got a sense of safety in numbers. The feeling had been missing from her life ever since the day of the fire, after which she was left to those long months of existence alone behind closed doors, living as a burned thing made of pain.

Not only did the class kids step into Zubaida's safety zone with her, but Benson too was included inside of this bubble of familiarity, even though she was an authority figure. To Zubaida, the things that Kerrie asked her to do didn't feel like useless chores, instead they felt like she was being given exactly what she needed, water in the desert. Her father had left a large hole inside of her with his instructions for her to learn all she could and to bring the knowledge back home to her sisters, who might never see the inside of a classroom. Now, every time she mastered another English phrase, she helped to fill that hole back up with the very knowledge she'd been instructed to bring home.

She was, in a way that she clearly understood, building her own future place in the family. After the crushing experience of watching herself go from being a real asset to the family's daily survival to being a heavy drag on the chances of survival for all of them, she could happily picture herself occupying a valued position as a contributing member of the family. Every time she thought of it, the very idea soothed her like a kiss on the forehead.

The real problems were at home, away from school. She valued the company of other children so highly that she was able to keep the turmoil stuffed inside of herself, most of the time. School only lasted a few hours each day, which meant that if something was really bothering her badly, she only had to hold it in until later in the day.

Then, sometimes, the turmoil insisted on boiling up out of her. It felt like millions of needle points poking her from the inside while her chest grew tight, and it got hard to take in a deep breath. Sometimes she was spurred into manic fits of energy, running around the yard and banging through the house. She tried to burn it away just as she once tried to scream away the pain. That didn't work this time, either.

Sooner or later, she had to go back inside the house and deal with people. They would start bothering her with something or other, which then made it feel like the needle pokes were coming from outside and inside at the same time. When that happened, anything could set her off. The last needle could be tiny—insignificant, in the course of her day—but it wouldn't matter. That last little poke would be just enough to set off the explosion and then all of the accumulated rage blew out of her at once.

Peter and Rebecca never exploded back at her, but that didn't fool her. She could sense their recoil when she burst into tears, screaming and wailing in drawn-out fits. It was the same with them as it was back at home—no matter how calm they remained, she could sense their concern over her behavior. Nobody could hide a thing like that from her. She could practically feel them asking themselves, *Is this girl losing her mind?*

She asked Rebecca to call the former host family and arrange for Zubaida to spend the weekend with them. It bothered her to have left the hosts' home under strained circumstances, so she felt happy when Rebecca came back later and told her that it had been arranged. Whether or not the family was seeing her merely out of guilt, Zubaida was doing so well at stuffing the turmoil during school hours that she felt confident she could keep it up for a couple of days of visiting.

🌸 🌸

Peter and Rebecca were both stymied by her state of mind after the weekend visit was over. She came home acting more distant and volatile than she had ever been up to this point. She refused to take part in any activity around the house with Rebecca, or to acknowledge Peter's presence when he came home from work in the evenings. Both of them could feel the anxiety radiating from her, and the fact that they couldn't identify the source or figure out how to relieve her emotions caused the anxiety to infect them, as well.

Since Rebecca was at home with her far more than Peter was, Rebecca decided to enter into family counseling to try to sort out her own feelings about the strained situation, hoping to take home some measure of insight that would guide her on how to handle things. The sessions consoled her and helped to restore her confidence in the daunting task of caring for this traumatized girl, but it soon became clear that there was a limit to the amount of progress that could be made unless Zubaida was able to get into counseling and unburden some of the load that appeared to be crushing her from within.

Rebecca searched out a family counselor in Los Angeles who spoke Farsi and could appreciate the cultural subtleties involved in earning the trust of an Afghan child who was so emotionally loaded down. Zubaida barely agreed to attend the sessions and sulked on the way to the doctor's office, but she didn't refuse to go, and even though the idea of hiring a strange woman as a personal counselor was utterly foreign to her, Rebecca noticed that on some level Zubaida seemed to understand that the process itself was helpful to her. Here was a place where she could display any emotion or mindset that she wanted to, without being condemned or punished for it. She seemed to come home feeling a little lighter inside, but she remained so aloof that neither Rebecca nor Peter could guess at what was going on inside of her.

The answer came before long—the charitable NGO representatives called to tell them that they had received a very disturbing letter from the host family, claiming that not only was Zubaida emotionally unstable during her entire visit with them, but also that they were convinced that she was suicidal.

That came as a heavy blow to both of them, since they were familiar with her mood swings but had never witnessed anything that indicated a suicidal state of mind on her part. The hosts' letter went on to say that they no longer wanted Zubaida in their home at all, not even for brief visits, and strongly suggested that she be sent back to Afghanistan. What the letter didn't do was say whatever it was that they thought Zubaida was supposed to do once she got back, with her surgical process still incomplete. Would the rage and despair that she displayed be anything other than a perfectly appropriate reaction to the prospects that would face her then?

One aspect of the mystery was solved by the letter, however, when the hosts implied that it was Peter and Rebecca who were actually alienating Zubaida from the hosts, and that this was only one more reason why she should be returned to her people. There was no suggestion as to what she was supposed to do, back among her people, with the combination of her interrupted education and her still-flawed appearance. There was no schooling for girls in Afghanistan, especially in the remote villages where there were not enough learned people to conduct secret reading groups.

By the time the phone call about the host family's letter ended, Peter and Rebecca felt that they finally had an insight into Zubaida's hostility ever since her visit with the hosts. She came back with the idea that Peter and Rebecca had not only snatched her from the host family, but that they had been deliberately keeping her from them. She didn't seem to know anything about the hosts' reactions to her behavior or their insistence that she ought to be sent home right away.

It gave Peter and Rebecca a place to start, but the road ahead looked even longer, now. Rebecca responded by stepping up the amount of cultural activities for Zubaida that would be familiar to her from her homeland. Through their neighbors, the Moayers, they connected with enough of the Afghan and expatriate community to provide a list of parties and social gatherings that would embrace as much of her background as possible.

Slowly, as the days drifted by, Rebecca began to see some positive change in Zubaida again. Her forced aloofness began to lighten up and she allowed herself to smile and laugh with them once in a while. It felt like dialing back the hands of a clock and starting all over again, but at least Rebecca could see progress during the daytime, and Peter began to get warmer reactions from her when he arrived home at night.

But by now, neither one of them had any illusions that this situation was going to suddenly become smooth and easy. They knew that they were blazing a path with this child, one that had no precedent. Beyond a certain point, the only counsel available to them was going to be their own. They spent a lot of evenings quietly going over hopes and plans for Zubaida's time with them, while Peter struggled to stay awake, knowing that he had to rise at 4:30 in the mornings to be at the hospital.

⚘ ⚘

After the last host family visit, Zubaida spent most nights tossing her way into the early morning hours with nightmares chasing her. She refused to sleep in the dark anymore, and spent much of her sleep time unconsciously clinging to the large stuffed doll that Rebecca had given her. The bedroom light and the stuffed doll helped to calm her a little, but the renewed upset over her sense of rejection by the host family remained, even after she accepted that Peter and Rebecca had never done anything except try to help her.

All the old images of turmoil that had haunted her during the months of searching for medical help had returned in force. Tortured plots about suffering family members, about her own postburn agonies, and of wandering lost and alone in forbidding and dangerous places all ran unfettered through her sleeping mind. She woke up feeling relieved that the night was over, even as she could feel that what her body needed was to lay back down and get some rest.

Even so, her new peer group at school remained so important to her—and the process of learning to speak English and to absorb the rudiments of reading and writing remained so exciting to her—that she was able to keep stuffing the turmoil down inside of herself. Everything usually went smoothly during school hours. It was only when she felt the ominous weight of another round of surgery approaching that her emotional load became too heavy to conceal in class.

On Friday, November 22, Kerrie Benson noticed that Zubaida seemed more distant and detached, both from her lessons and her classmates. Benson knew that Zubaida was scheduled for another surgery on the coming Monday, but couldn't tell if that was what was bothering her or not. The day ended and Zubaida went home before she had a chance to talk with her about it. Benson decided that if the depressed attitude remained after Zubaida returned to school, she would press to get to the bottom of it.

On Monday, November 25, Peter Grossman and his team prepped Zubaida for surgery early in the morning. Once Charles Neal placed her under anesthesia again, Dr. Peter administered a series of some eighty steroid injections to the scar tissue on the front and rear sections of her torso to help break down the scars. Then he went to work on fine-tuning the balance of Zubaida's facial features. While Zubaida wandered the dreamless terrain of sedation, Dr. Peter entered back into his operative state in the fourth dimension of time, making every surgical choice and move with an eye toward its effect on the patient today, next month, and next year.

He made an incision along the lower eyelid to release the area of tension there. Once that was done, he made an incision near the upper eyelid and worked on the nearby tendon to improve the placement and function of the eyelid. Then he carefully grafted a full-thickness graft to the open area under the eyelid, covering about three square centimeters. Next the left eyelid was adjusted for symmetry with the right. With a Z-plasty to her torso to reduce the scarification there, he cut away another two and a half square centimeters of scarred flesh, then placed a patch over her eye and applied the postsurgical dressings to each of the areas.

Her recovery in the hospital was unusually quick this time, spurred on by visits from Emily and her mom, and get-well cards from the kids in her class. Zubaida was still enduring her long transformation in the land of the Others, but she no longer felt alone among them.

꽃 꽃

At the same time that Zubaida was undergoing her surgery, November 25 was also declared as an international day of protest against violence toward women. It was noted that "honor killings," forced female circumcisions, and public stoning, even in such modern times, were still active forces of destruction in the world. Neither the world's governing bodies nor the leaders of the

Zubaida with her best friend, Emily

This is how she looked when she arrived in Los Angeles.

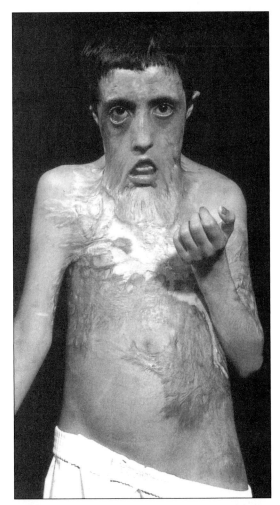

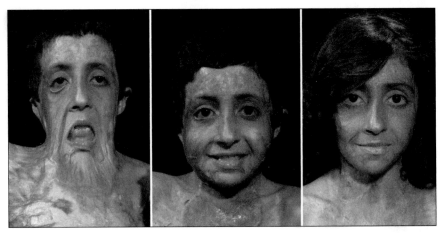

The amazing transformation

Zubaida and her friend with
Rebecca Grossman and
a secret admirer.

꙳

The Father-Daughter dance at
school cemented her relationship
with Peter Grossman as "Dad."

Friends at a sleepover

Zubaida and the Grossmans on the streets of New York

Hear no evil, see no evil, speak no evil, and shut up.

Embraced by American friends from school

Robert Frame (in black vest) helps Mohammed, Zubaida's father, deal with the Americans' baffling love for signing pieces of paper.

Zubaida with her parents, Bador and Mohammed, in Kabul just before the family returned to their desert village

You can't be charming all the time.

❦

First day of school in Herat,
with her two younger sisters

پروژه مرکز تربیوی کهکشان برای طبقه اناث
FEMALE GALAXY TRAINING CENTER
(FGTC)

Back with her family in their new home,
bought with donations from hundreds of Americans

major religions seemed to have any idea of how to combat the constantly re-
curring instances of inhumanity flaring all over the globe.

※ ※

Three days later, Zubaida joined Peter and Rebecca at the home of Richard
Grossman and his wife at their ranch in Hidden Valley, California. Rebecca
marveled at Zubaida's studied coolness while she took in the luxury of the
sprawling ranch house and grounds. She had watched Zubaida do it often
enough that she recognized it as one of Zubaida's main coping mechanisms.
Zubaida seemed to feel in some way that for her to express amazement or to
show that she was in any way impressed by American luxuries was demeaning
to her. She made it a point to pretend that there was nothing going on around
her that she hadn't seen before, whether or not that was true.

She still wore a patch over her right eye after Peter's latest work on her, but
the concern shown by her classmates while she was in the hospital had soft-
ened her attitude quite a bit. Peter's father made it a special point to dote on
her with grandfatherly concern, and Peter and Rebecca both watched with relief while Zubaida warmed up to the attention.

But whenever people's attention turned away from her for a few minutes,
she seemed to fall into some invisible pit. She was still only three days out
from her latest surgery and much of the time her mood remained bleak. Even
though an occasional spark came into her eyes at one moment or another, she
spent most of that day in an increasing funk that the food and festivities
couldn't alleviate. There was little of the lighthearted happiness that she had
begun to show any time she went to school. She had been out of class since
the Friday before, and knew that she would be out until the coming week.
The long days before she would see her new friends again stretched out in
front of her.

Her father's clear directive was that she should contribute to her family's future by learning everything she possibly could in America, so that she could
come back and teach them, and that was powerful enough to keep her motivated for school. But at home with Peter and Rebecca, or at Grandpa Richard's
home, it was safe to let her guard down. For much of that Thanksgiving Day,

the anger and frustration that she usually managed to keep to herself in class kept leaking out. By the end of the day, Rebecca was eager for Zubaida to return to school so that she could enjoy a few hours of happiness—and everyone else could take a deep breath.

9 🐦

Zubaida's sister Nacima had already married and was living away from home by the time Zubaida was flown to America. Nacima and her husband had been driven from their home by the U.S.-led war on the Taliban into an Iranian refugee camp near the Afghanistan border in the town of Zabol. They were the only members of Zubaida's family who lived there, but Nacima's hometown of Farah was so remote that it was actually easier to communicate with someone inside the camp than in Farah. Zabol was enough of a city to have some small municipal services and a few telephone lines that functioned sporadically amid the ebb and flow of insurgent combat.

The town is located alongside the ancient caravan roads winding through the region. Only about a third of its residents have running water or electricity, and farming and grazing are difficult to sustain there because of the lack of available water. The presence of huge rock surfaces on the ground prevents farming and drilling, but at least the camp was relatively safe from military battles, even though the existence for the refugees there was as bare-bones as it can get.

In the month of December 2002, Peter and Rebecca used a telephone number that Mohammed Hasan had given Zubaida during their first telephone call for reaching Nacima inside the camp. They helped Zubaida to call her sister once every week. Although the results were always hit or miss with the unreliable satellite connections and spotty local phone service, sometimes the calls actually got all the way through. The number would ring at one of the permanent homes in the area, so when someone answered, Zubaida would speak to them in Dari and explain enough of her situation to enlist their help and persuade them to help locate her sister in the camp. That person would then run down the street and fetch Nacima back to the house so that Zubaida could call again later that same day and speak with her. It was the only direct contact that she ever had with anyone in her family except for those rare phone calls that her father was able to place to Peter and Rebecca's home from the UN office in Kandahar.

Nacima, however, left the camp to visit the family home in Farah often enough that she could occasionally relay messages from them back to Zubaida, helping to provide her with some sense of still being in touch with her family. At first, the calls had a visibly positive effect on Zubaida and lightened her spirits like few other things could. But when Nacima heard that there had been a custody dispute over Zubaida and that she had left the host family's home under cloudy circumstances, Nacima also took the position that Zubaida should return to Afghanistan right away without finishing the surgeries. To her, the whole impossible enterprise that was going on over in America seemed doomed to fail. Nacima's hardscrabble experience and barren view of the world undoubtedly made it seem as if Zubaida was trapped in some kind of highly unreliable and potentially dangerous situation. She had seen enough of her little sister's suffering and didn't want to allow anything else to happen to her.

At first, Nacima's position only raised Zubaida's level of internal conflict even higher. So both Peter and Rebecca were relieved when Nacima made a trip to Farah and informed her father that she had been telling Zubaida that she should come home. Mohammed Hasan immediately took a hard stand against that idea and sent Nacima back to the camp with a stern message and his orders to relay that message back to Zubaida. He had no desire for her to end the stay in America before the surgeries were complete. Most of all, he reiterated his strong desire for Zubaida to soak up every bit of learning in school that she possibly could during her time in America. Speaking to her through Nacima, he assured Zubaida that what she was doing was not only right for her but was going to be vitally important to the rest of her family, as well.

It was those words from her father that did the trick. Not only did Zubaida have the cultural desire to honor the wishes of the man of the house, but also this advice was coming to her from a father who had dedicated a year of his life and bankrupted the family in order to seek help for her. She knew without having to think about it that she was only alive because of his dogged persistence. He not only commanded great authority over her view of the world, so that his desire to see her remain in America held great sway over her, but his assurances that she was in the process of learning things that would prove vital to her entire family helped to raise her sense of herself back up to a tolerable level.

So it was that a single indirect message relayed to Zubaida by her eldest sister had the power to do for her what no one else could. After that, Peter and Rebecca began to see a slow and steady upward arc to Zubaida's levels of tolerance and an equally steady lowering of her need to explode over ordinary annoyances.

It was as if, after a long period of time when there were only occasional glimpses of sunlight in an otherwise dark world, a consistent source of light had finally entered her heart. They greeted the change with great relief, which was only temporarily dampened when they got the word that because of the NGO's concerns over Zubaida's fate, there was going to be a visit to their home from a social worker who would evaluate Zubaida's situation and who had the power to force them to return her to Afghanistan if the social worker came away with the impression that Zubaida's interests weren't being served.

But after the months of hearing their actions criticized and their motives suspected, their confidence that they were doing the right thing and that anyone who looked at the situation with unprejudiced eyes would see it the same way was finally validated. The social worker left convinced that Zubaida should stay right where she was until Peter Grossman declared her surgical process to be complete, and furthermore, that the loving and supportive home into which they had brought her was not merely a luxurious environment, but a healthy and healing place for her to be.

Peter and Rebecca both breathed a long sigh of relief. This entire enterprise had been forced to exist on a day-to-day extension of temporary permissions from the various agencies who held authority over Zubaida's immigration status. This official recognition of the positive power of their work on Zubaida's behalf—as well as Mohammed Hasan's unwavering commitment to making sure that Zubaida took absolutely everything from this adventure that she possibly could—finally gave them the luxury of knowing that their quest to give Zubaida a viable future was not going to be prematurely interrupted.

This was just before the holiday season got underway. It was the best present that either of them would receive that year. The noticeable rise in Zubaida's spirits and her willingness to be cooperative, as well as her tendency to display affection toward them, took a welcome turn for the better.

※ ※

The mundane problems were as important as the larger ones—Zubaida's many months of being unable to close her mouth or eat properly before Peter began his work had left her baby teeth in extensive decay. So Rebecca took her in for a full round of dental work and paid for it herself, just as she and Peter were doing with Zubaida's personal therapy. It was simpler than working to gain permission to fund the work through the Children's Burn Foundation, which had already provided hundreds of thousands of dollars.

The worst of the baby teeth were eventually pulled so that the healthy adult teeth could grow in later, while the others were drilled and filled until the large areas of tooth decay were completely removed. When it was done, Zubaida found that the added comfort of a healthy bite and of teeth that didn't hurt anymore gave her relief from the nagging background pain in her jaws. The ache had become such a constant presence in her life that most of the time she no longer noticed it. With that pain gone and a normal bite restored, a general wave of relaxation spread through the rest of her body. It felt good to be able to bite down and clench her teeth together, hard. It made the rest of her body feel stronger.

Now her increasing sense of coming back to life matched her father's support for her long journey as well as Peter and Rebecca's gentle, firm, and unrelenting support as her surrogate family. It all began to sink in, with the result that more and more time was spent with Zubaida as the girl they knew and were growing to love, and less time with her spontaneous displays of anger or aloofness.

Even though Zubaida still had no answer to the haunting question of whether or not the fire had burned away her ability to control her thoughts and her behavior, most of the time she was too busy with school and a mix of afterschool activities to remember the question at all. Whatever squabbles she got into with the other girls were typical of their age and background, so that no one seemed concerned about it. Broken friendships re-formed within days, and she began to rely more heavily upon the telephone to keep her in after-hours touch with the other girls, wrapped up as they were in the daily drama of why Amber was so mean to Tiffany out on the playground that day.

Her language was still awkward, verb conjugation was hit or miss, but her learning didn't proceed on an even line. She spent more time talking with the other girls than she did in class itself, so that her growth in certain areas often leaped ahead of the rest of her progress. Even though she still stumbled over when to use "I" and when to use "me," she was already mastering a rapidly growing command of special Southern Californian English via her peer group.

Her existing mastery was already strong over the range of interpretation that can be given to a certain word through pronunciation. She quickly absorbed the considerable knowledge required to pronounce the word *yeah* in the appropriate tone of voice, and to employ its conversationally powerful nuances across a range of agreements whose intensity could be adjusted from cautiously affirmative to wildly enthusiastic.

Most powerfully, she learned to use the proper tones of *yeah* for personal commentary, satirical mockery of an agreement that not only negated the opposite opinion but also simultaneously discouraged any prospective opponent from wanting to appear so thick in the skull and slow in the wits that he/she would even pursue an argument in the first place.

Throughout the experience of her life, Zubaida had only known herself as a dominant personality. Except for the time she spent imprisoned in the scar jacket, she had always gravitated toward ways of influencing current events among the group. Now, with mastery of the Southern Californian American English *yeah*, Zubaida was able to snuggle in a little tighter with her circle of local girls. Then, according to her established nature and without requiring any real planning on her part, she began to take a leadership role among them. The change wasn't dramatic. It was just that more and more often, the girls got together to do any given activity because Zubaida seemed convinced that it was a good idea.

The next major step occurred quietly enough, during that same holiday season. Peter Grossman later said that while he couldn't recall the exact time that it took place, he would never forget the sensations that washed through him the first time that Zubaida spontaneously switched from calling him Peter to calling him Dad. Little hairs stood up at the base of his neck while a smile inched its way across his face. He watched her for some change of expression, or for any other acknowledgment that she realized what she had said, but Zubaida just went right on chattering as if nothing had happened.

That didn't answer the question for him, though. He knew that she tended to play her way through any emotionally charged situation with a poker face. Only afterward did she seem to process her feelings about whatever went on, and only then did she form her response—if she formed one at all. Peter couldn't tell at that moment whether her fear of a potential rejection from him prevented her from acknowledging it, or whether "Dad" just slipped out in some unconscious way, but he appreciated that the small shift in her name for him revealed a tremendous deepening of her personal trust, far beyond the medical trust that she otherwise had to place in him.

Peter felt the weight of that, and it hit him at a level that he could never have predicted back when he first saw her terrible medical photos and agreed to help her. However, he had learned from experience that to push her about any emotional topic usually resulted in getting back a silent and sullen response. She seemed to do best when she could sort things out at her own pace and then work up her confidence in a response. That particular coping mechanism was far more likely to be effective in a society that operates at the pace of her small desert village. But the saturated sensations of an ordinary day in affluent America can stimulate more nerve endings than might occur in a month back where most of her life had been spent.

Peter saw her proud way of carrying herself and her sometimes haughty behavior as components of her emotional mask, thicker than her scars, and when the pressure on her became too much, after days or hours or sometimes only minutes of forcing a nonchalant attitude amid these new and unfamiliar environments of constant stimuli, something had to go. The occasional outbursts that detonated inside of her with no apparent cause may have simply revealed her survival instinct in action, dumping another overflow of accumulated emotions.

So on the day that she called him Dad for the first time, he focused on the challenge of following her rambling conversation through a thicket of grammar breaks and mispronunciations—and let the rest of it pass by.

The moment was just too nice to jeopardize by pushing it.

Even though Zubaida was still a nine-year-old when her outdoor life effectively ended, she had already become familiar with the ways of the public marketplace. She grasped the entire process of shopping carefully, bargaining for the best price, and bringing home something to show for your efforts at the end of the day. Of necessity, the primary rules are always the same for every tribe who gathers at every town bazaar or roving outdoor marketplace.

No one is trusted. It makes no difference if you have seen them before, it makes no difference if you have had good dealings with them before, it makes no difference if you know their name and their cousin's name and you have helped them to clean up after their camels. Be certain that your own camel is tied down and keep your eyes on the other person's hands at every moment. It is understood; in the marketplace, one takes care of oneself first, while always remaining alert for someone who doesn't know that.

The marketplace may not even be there tomorrow. Even if it is there tomorrow, this person may not be there tomorrow. This person may never be seen by you again. But even if that person is there tomorrow and even if you accost them, the fact that you are not allowed to kill or injure them means that your privilege, in such a case, is nothing more than to yell and wave your arms around until you get tired of wasting your time.

Therefore no one is trusted.

Zubaida already had a clear, if limited, picture of the adult world as a place of constant tricks and slippery negotiations that never ended until both parties walked away feeling like happy thieves. Even within her familiar culture, surrounded by native speakers of her language, she had felt the strangely foreign power of the marketplace. She would never be allowed to compete with the men in such a place, never match her own wits up against their sly traps and cool deceptions. The foreignness did not come from the ways of the marketplace; it came from the knowledge that she would never be permitted to join in the fascinating and never-ending game. It came as an invisible dream crusher, leaving behind an energy drain that was the sure sign of contact with the Others. She was aware that, as a nine-year-old, she was being permitted to freely observe this marketplace in a blunt way that she would no longer be able to do after she turned ten. It was a place where she would one day be expected to walk with her face covered and her head down. It was, by and large, a place of men.

She knew all the stories that her mother's generation told about their way of life in the days before the reign of the Taliban. Just out of reach from Zubaida's living memory, there had been plenty of Afghan women occupied with honorable trades of buying and selling in the marketplace. Of course such things had been forbidden ever since she was old enough to recall, although a woman who had an old and familiar clientele might dare to continue working on the black market. If she did, she took a life-endangering risk, so that the work was most often taken up by widowed or abandoned mothers, women facing the daily reality of feeding hungry little ones, women who have exhausted all other alternatives.

The Taliban were supposed to bring peace after stopping the feuding warlords, but they were just another army with a new list of people to kill.

No one is to be trusted.

It is widely known among students of human nature that it is far easier to develop a suspicious attitude than to get rid of one. Learning how and when to lower her guard was a task as difficult and frustrating as any other. The natural longing of a young girl to feel affirmation and closeness made her feel hungry for more of Rebecca's attention and approval, and for more good-natured Dad time with Peter. She found herself in close moments with each of them, without realizing how they got started, then suddenly at a loss for her next response. It was like running into a blind alley in a strange city in a bad dream.

Sometimes it was all she could do to stuff everything inside and shut herself down and keep her face blank. It would happen like the pull-away reaction that everybody gets when they touch a fire; suddenly she was off the floor, out of the spotlight, tucked back inside of herself and covered in a giant tortoise shell where nobody had the power to touch her in any way. In a place like that, it's safe to brood long and hard on the nagging feeling that somebody is to blame for all of this. Yes, these Americans were trying to help her, working on her in the hospital for free and then pouring all this time and money into her after taking her into their home. Her culture respects the value of generosity and hospitality, and so did she. She also knew that all of it was highly dangerous because she had no control over events and that you never look to make friends in the bazaar, or trust anybody inside of a marketplace.

But America is the Land of the Marketplace. Everybody knows that. You have to keep your eyes on their hands all the time. The lonely girl couldn't help needing the closeness that Rebecca and Peter offered, but sometimes the wide-eyed and alert little girl still living inside of her also remembered the subtle and sometimes elaborate profit games of the marketplace, where you never trust anybody. Whenever she thought of that, the scary pulling-back-from-a-flame reaction would go off inside of her and she was instantly back down inside the shell again, the thick one that nobody could see.

❧ ❧

By the time that the 2002 Christmas holidays approached, Zubaida was able to flip herself up into a good feeling and be with people without feeling anxious or afraid at all. She couldn't hold it for long, but sometimes for hours at a time, it felt as if some invisible weight had lifted from her shoulders and all of her Perfectly Good Reasons to be suspicious vanished.

That was when it became the most fun with the other girls. Zubaida's growing vocabulary gave her more opportunities to interact with other girls in more personal ways, and the passing bursts of light heart and easy spirit somehow gave her the power to make people fall in love with her and have fun doing it.

This was the perfect time for her torments to ease, with the natural procession of family gatherings and parties with friends. It was easy to take her eyes off everybody's hands and let herself take a good look around at things.

She danced without caring what people thought or what they might say. She did it because she could make her body do what she wanted again.

When Zubaida got into spats with the other girls, they seemed to pass quickly, with feelings somehow smoothed over. She was eager to work at making the other girls like her—she could see a good reflection of herself so clearly in it, whenever she pulled people into her orbit. Sometimes when Rebecca studied her from some quiet corner, it seemed as if what Zubaida really wanted was to watch things stop in one place and start up again in another place, for no other reason than that she had wished it to be that way. Because whenever she could make that actually happen—without needing any imagination or fantasy to help it along—it became the most powerful mirror that she knew of, in anyone's world.

And then there would be her beautiful reflection, for just a little while.

In that state, she could meet the wonderful strangeness of the season and the very generous customs and the frequent displays of too much food with open joy. But her delight was usually followed by a quick imitation of somebody who had been there and done that a hundred times already. Any American ritual that looked like fun was fine with her and she didn't care what anything meant; all she had to do was let Peter and Rebecca make sure that everything got taken care of while she let herself roll with the situation.

The game where the girls took turns standing in front of the rest and then closing their eyes and falling backward, trusting the others to catch them, struck her as particularly funny and made her jump up and down while she laughed.

So when Rebecca offered to put together a slumber party with some of Zubaida's best friends, she jumped at the idea. Within a few days, Zubaida and four of her friends from school were there for the night. The girls talked and shrieked their way through the evening until darkness fell and everyone was in their pajamas.

Then Rebecca sat them on the floor and filled the girls in on a little something that she suspected was missing from their childhoods. "I know that Halloween is over, but back in Texas when I was a girl, there was a Halloween tradition that we had, and the secret of that tradition is that you don't have to wait for Halloween to do it. You can do it any time! You always want to do it after dark, though, because whatever you do, *you never want to let them catch you!*"

She had their attention now. They were five schoolgirls, giddy from hours of near-hysteria, pleasantly full after dinner and comfortably sloppy for the night. They caught Rebecca's drift right away—something big was coming. Something secret. They were all going to be in on it. The very charge hanging in the air set them to giggling and trying not to look each other in the eye because then they would explode and they knew that they weren't supposed to do that while the adult in the room was talking. And after all, it was very interesting when she described to them the proper technique for executing the noble tradition of toilet papering somebody's yard.

Zubaida understood—sort of. She had played around with pulling long sheets off of a toilet paper roll, so she could picture the idea of holding onto the paper while you throw the roll over the top of a tree. The concept struck her as so utterly foreign and bizarre that at first she didn't feel much of a reaction to the thought at all.

You hold one end and throw the roll over a tree or a bush. As soon as the roll hits the ground, you pick it up and hold the paper again and throw the roll back over the tree or bush. You repeat this as many times as you can, or until another target appears.

If a team of five girls is assisted by an unapologetically regressed Texas girl and everybody works with genuine cooperation, Rebecca guessed that much of an entire front yard could be majestically draped in just a few minutes.

When Rebecca began teasing the girls about how they should each take a roll and go around the corner to a friend's house and strike, Zubaida giggled along with the other girls. Nobody actually thought that she meant it, but they seemed to get the humor and their giggling was contagious. The idea itself still wasn't doing much for Zubaida. She hated being the outsider and tried to get in on the joke, but when she made a mental picture of throwing perfectly good paper around in the air, it all just seemed pointless.

Still, the excitement kept making her giggle while she hurried along in the dark with Rebecca and the other girls, running across people's front yards and around the corner, to the victim's house. She played along with the other girls at first, just imitating what they were doing with the paper rolls, even though she began to get the idea as soon as her friend Caitlin threw the first roll and everybody watched it land. After a while she realized that it was pretty funny after all, just to be in this impossible dreamworld where she and these other girls could run through the night and do this foolish wasting of paper. Pretty soon everyone was staggering around snorting with laughter that they attempted to suppress with varying levels of failure. She tossed her roll until her arm got tired.

What she didn't realize was that Rebecca had saved the game's real trigger, and that she planned to pull it just as soon as the paper streaks were thoroughly laced over the tops of everything in the front yard. Just when the girls began to run out of paper and the yard was thoroughly whitened, Rebecca let out a long, high whoop that scared the girls in the first instant and sent them into riotous laughter in the next.

When they saw her jump onto the porch and ring the doorbell, they didn't have to be told to take off running and sprint back around the corner. By the time the shrieking girls made it back to Peter and Rebecca's house, Zubaida was laughing so hard that she could barely stay on her feet. She tried to run but mostly just staggered along laughing harder than she could remember doing in a long time, maybe harder than she had ever done. Within her realm of permitted existence, this level of excitement and girlish play simply didn't exist.

The girls tumbled into Rebecca's living room half crazed with excitement and completely elated. None of the other girls had actually done this before, so for Zubaida as well as the others, this was their first chance in this life to deliberately create a great big sloppy mess and purposely draw attention to it—and then openly flee the adult authority before they can come barreling down onto you.

It was the high point of the sleepover and would require some explaining to the other parents, but it was a powerful blast of pure adrenaline and girlhood camaraderie that Zubaida and each of the others were unlikely to ever forget. Since it was an arranged strike and Rebecca had tipped off their "victim" that afternoon, the girls were spared the possible consequence of an outraged neighbor hammering at their door at night. Instead they spent the next couple of hours rehashing the experience and slowly drifting back down to earth.

Zubaida fell asleep easily with the rest of them. It felt the same way that it did back home when there was a houseful of visiting family members who sometimes stopped by and always had to be entertained, no matter how meager the fare might be. Experience had sharpened Zubaida's ability to sense the presence of the other people in the house, even after the lights were out and everyone finally grew quiet.

It was almost as if she could feel the space that they occupied in the air. There was a solidness to the clannish feeling that the sleepover gave her; it was a familiar one. She pulled it up around herself like a warm blanket and took long breaths of the air that was filled by the other girls.

Behind her eyelids, now, whether she was awake or dreaming, the music was playing away inside of her for minutes or even hours at a time. Something always snapped it off, sooner or later, but then the music always rebounded to help vitalize her during the daylight hours and accompany her through the worst of her dreams at night. Even when her music came out timed to surreal scenes of her own destruction or images of her family's demise, its very presence wrapped her in the welcome familiarity of something that she recognized about herself. The music kept her in touch with the Zubaida who would not let herself be forever haunted by evil dreams or waking suspicions.

Peter already knew about Rebecca's taste in mischief, and later recalled specifically telling her "no TP-ing at the slumber party." His mistake was that he left it at that, and then fell for it when he went along with being granted the night off to go see friends while Rebecca and the girls took over the house.

When he returned home that night, nothing appeared to be amiss and they were all peacefully asleep. It was only the next morning at breakfast with Rebecca and the girls that he began hearing little digs from his wife about how he was a stick in the mud—and he noticed that the girls all seemed to think that Rebecca's comments were hysterical. Before long the whole group was too goofy for him to get any sense out of them at all.

He got up from the table and walked outside, then went around the corner to check his hunch about where the victim's house might be, and there was the crime scene. Their friends were lighthearted enough to play along with a gag like that, but when he looked at the intricate web of paper streaks covering most of the yard's surfaces, he could also see that the joke would wear thin fast if he didn't get it cleaned up.

He weighed the idea of going back and telling the girls that they'd had their fun, and now the responsible thing to do was to go back there and clean it all up. It was the mature thing. It was the big kid thing to do. He spent a few seconds visualizing the chore of organizing and enforcing a girly yard cleanup.

A good hour later, Peter had most of the yard finished and had spent so much time climbing around in the tree branches that he knew it would be okay to skip his workout at the gym. The science of the operating room was far more predictable than the art of the long-term relationship, but he already knew that with Rebecca, a little bit of willingness to spontaneously compromise was a workable peacekeeping skill.

10 🌿

Bador: A Mother's Point of View

Bador had eight other children at the time of Zubaida's accident, seven of them at home. They ranged in age from her married eldest daughter, Raima, who was not with Bador when the fire struck Zubaida, down to her youngest toddler. Zubaida had always been her trusted middle child. But while Zubaida was so far away in America, Bador seldom indulged in the luxury of allowing her heart to ache for her daughter. The fears that she imagined on her daughter's behalf would, if she let them, multiply until they were like a cloud of locusts swirling all around her.

Bador was accepting of her culture's patriarchal conception of the adult female as household caretaker, but under Taliban rule she was also a physical prisoner inside her home, in that she could never leave it without a male chaperone. She was fortunate that her husband, Mohammed, despite his first name, had never been a religious zealot and didn't bother to impose strict behavioral codes upon her. The cultural restrictions had been tight enough without that ever since the fundamentalist Taliban takeover.

In her brief years of growing up, Bador never heard of something called a "Taliban," but she already lived amid an invisible thicket of traditions and peer expectations. One such custom required girls to submit to being traded as a family asset via arranged marriages, despite the modern era's accepted custom. These forced unions were consummated late in the bride's childhood, in a practice still found in various civilizations around the globe.

Women in the cities lived less restrictive lives, but the time-honored family ways of the Afghan tribes left most women of the primarily rural population mired for want of education in the traditional household role. More recently, the holy regime of the Taliban clerics had cut off every other alternative for the nation's female population. They sealed the exits and violent public retribution was inflicted upon any and all transgressors.

However, at the end of 2002, right about the time that Zubaida was off in America learning how to fit into the local holiday celebrations of the equally foreign Christmas and Chanukah, the U.S. military and a coalition of supporting nations forcibly ejected the Taliban rulers from power in Afghanistan. The remaining resistance was driven north toward Kabul, away from the central core of the country where Zubaida's home village of Farah is located. Throughout most of the country, the Taliban's fundamentalist control over Afghanistan's government was shattered. But during their five years in power from 1996 to 2001, the Taliban set back the cause of women in Afghanistan to a place more backward and misogynistic than any nation in history.

While the extreme fundamentalist rule of the country was enforced in the name of Islam, the actual practice was completely at odds with Islam's teachings. Ever since the fourteenth century, Islam has declared the equality of women in all matters, at home and in the marketplace. It is specifically written in the Koran that women are permitted to buy and sell in the marketplace as readily as males, and entitled to enjoy the protections of society at large from teachings of deadly antifemale bias.

Men shall have a benefit from what they earn,
and women shall have a benefit from what they earn.

Koran, 4:32

However, the reality of the lives that faced Bador's daughters under the Taliban's years of control proved that the Taliban clerics were not dedicated to these particular precepts of Islam. Many civilizations have failed to respect the rights of women, but nowhere else in history has there been such systematic abuse of half of an entire population.

Perhaps such levels of repression can only take root under the guise of religious piety—they immediately began to lose their strength at the moment that the Taliban rulers fell from power. *Voice of America* released a report on the various effects upon Afghanistan's women resulting from the repressive restrictions during the Taliban years. There was a dramatic rise in major depression, chronic anxiety, and posttraumatic stress disorder among women, who were universally denied almost all forms of healthcare.

Bador found that this not only affected herself and her other daughters, but also had a negative impact on her sons when she was too sick to run the household in her husband's absence. Treatment for illness was almost always of the home remedy variety. All of the female doctors had been driven from the profession, and many were so financially paralyzed by lack of opportunity that they were reduced to begging and prostitution. Male doctors were only allowed to examine women with another male family member present, and they couldn't examine them under their clothing at all. It didn't matter much—even if the doctor found a need for surgery, he wouldn't be permitted to operate on a female, anyway.

In what turned out to be a holocaust imposed on the entire female population of a country of more than twenty-five million people, medical, dental, and reproductive health deteriorated severely among all of Afghanistan's women. The process was begun in the time of the anti-Soviet war of the 1980s, which destroyed the country's fragile infrastructure, then continued through the 1990s while the regional warlords fought for pieces of what the Soviets had shattered. The final clampdown came when control was seized by the army of the murderous Taliban regime.

After that, results were typical. Totalitarian governments that smash all opposing voices are known to be highly efficient means of controlling society; once the Taliban seized control from the local warlords, anarchy ended and order was imposed.

It was a quiet order, and strange.

Since the Taliban banned women from work, and there were fifty to sixty thousand widowed women in the city of Kabul alone, children became the only breadwinners for many of those widowed families. Under the Taliban rule, boys and girls as young as eight and nine begged and sold their bodies in the street in the attempt to provide enough food for their families. During that same period, there was also a long list of forced marriages upon girls as young as eight or nine years of age—often to those same members of the Taliban militia who had installed themselves in power in the name of bringing the heavenly ways of Allah to the nation's people.

According to sources such as Doctors Without Borders, UNICEF, and the World Health Organization, throughout the time of Taliban rule there were increasing numbers of women in Afghanistan who suffered not only depression, but also major bouts of neurosis. Further, many of them suffered much more severe forms of mental illness such as deep breaks into schizophrenia and psychosis.

During the initial takeover by the Taliban in Afghanistan's capital city of Kabul, almost all of the children witnessed acts of violence, while two-thirds of them saw dead bodies or parts of bodies. Nearly half reported seeing many people killed at one time during the rocket and artillery attacks.

Ninety percent of the children interviewed believed that they were going to die at the time of those attacks.

Bador was still in her thirties when her daughter Zubaida fell into the fire, and already the physical struggle of her daily life had left her gaunt in the face and tired in her body. Pains of age filled her movements; tweaks and stabs pierced her in this or that joint whenever she had to move around much. Nevertheless, that daily chase after her large family's needs was based upon her children—the only source of hope that she could have for living into old age with any security at all.

There was no such thing as any form of governmental relief for elderly citizens in a land where the infrastructure had long since been shattered, and the mosques were too poor to help the throngs of needy ones. She and her husband had to fill the house with children and do their best to raise them all the way up to adulthood because the future held nothing else for them. Their younger generation was an expression of hope by the parents for a living insurance plan against the miseries and infirmities of an impoverished old age.

But Bador felt herself aging far ahead of the calendar throughout Zubaida's long spell at home before they sent her to America. During those months, she discovered that everyone in the family already pulled so much of her strength out of her each day that the extra time and energy demanded by Zubaida's condition was draining Bador down to the bone. The exhaustion left her in such an empty state that migraine headaches began to plague her and arthritis taunted her joints.

She didn't have to exaggerate her symptoms to convince anybody in the household that she was ailing; everyone saw that she worked from morning until night and that she did her best to take care of them, even if she was beginning to let certain things pile up a little too often. Sometimes people took the hint and catered to Bador a little bit; other times they clucked their sympathy without bothering to actually pitch in and do anything for her.

As a woman who must serve, Bador wasn't particularly offended by their failure to help carry her load for her. To take offense, she would first need to hold the expectation that such a thing was ever going to happen in the first place. She knew better. But she also knew that there could be some measure of security in a position of service, since many of the ones served possessed no such skills. That was important to her. If the served ever learned to do for themselves, Bador would become expendable.

If that happened, her status could slide downward from being an indispensable family head to that of a mere convenience who does a few chores around the house. From there, it was a short slip to general uselessness, and then the smallest of steps to the status of a full-time family burden, one who only awaits death.

Even Bador's damaged daughter held a higher spot on the scale than that. Zubaida was refusing to wait for death. She clung to life with an iron grip and fought back the prospect of death every day that she survived. Bador took inspiration from her daughter.

Even though no one willingly occupies the place of the family burden, Bador could feel herself being pushed toward that grim place. A woman who must serve is frightened when her body, tall and broad-shouldered and strong as a tree root, begins to fight with her all of the time, raising painful objections to tasks that were once undertaken with ease. Not only is her physical strength her solace in life, but the services that her strength allows her to offer to the world justifies her very existence.

When she felt frost in her bones, creeping up inside of her even under the thick desert heat, she had no choice but to wonder whether she could manage to raise enough of her offspring up to adulthood before her aching body lay itself down in the road like a sick animal. Her only consolation against that dismal prospect was simply that dying young and worn out would still be better than dying in poverty without children.

The thing that Bador grasped with an iron grip as strong as her daughter's hold on life was the simple goal of never becoming useless to the family, never becoming an empty ghost of a person who had once filled her days with the products of her skills but who now waits only to be cleaned and fed.

A woman who must serve is seldom given the necessary level of simple consideration throughout her usual day, such as that which silently assures other people of their basic human worth while they go about their lives. Instead, she must stand resolute under the continual inner torment of knowing that there is something almost sacrilegious about becoming so self-absorbed that she causes others to be unduly concerned about her.

She can even speak of suicide in front of the family and express a longing for her own death, in order to attempt to communicate something of her distress. Such talk rises from a long custom—so long as it is done in a style so melodramatic that everyone understands that she is exaggerating and doesn't really intend to cause her own demise. In this way, to shout something like "I want to die!" is accepted as her expression of general distress—while ignored at the same time as any actual announcement of her intentions. Such a woman knows, and her audience knows as well, that what she is describing with such a statement is merely her level of feeling, not an intention. Her audience also knows that they have the privilege of either acknowledging her feelings or ignoring them altogether, without being concerned that anyone will actually trip over her body later.

Therefore, as a woman who must serve, Bador was a juggler, of a sort. She had to continually balance the fact that her only guaranteed means of temporary relief from her daily burden was to be too sick to work—or at least too sick to work at full capacity—against the reality that she could only have so many symptoms before she slipped in her social rank and began the dreaded downward slide, steadily closing the distance between herself and uselessness.

Mohammed: A Father's Point of View

One of the men in the bazaar who did not know Mohammed Hasan asked him how a father could stoop so low as to take his burned and scarred little daughter through the marketplaces of the cities that they travel to for medical help, just so she might be used to gain sympathy from others and gather a few coins from their pity. Sometimes Hasan answered the challenges, stiff in his defiance. Most other times, he kept the wise things that he had learned to himself.

When it is God's will—Enshallah—that your young dancing daughter is forced to exist inside of a melted shell of burned flesh, her face destroyed and her arms nearly useless, one look at her will assure you that it must also be Enshallah that she survives.

And yet you know that in the eyes of others, the very fact that she remains impossibly alive and aware within her tormented and agonized state is a direct reflection on you—perhaps Allah has elected to inflict some extra degree of punishment in addition to the flames themselves?

And you understand that the misery of this thing is never going to be done with you and with your family, if you allow anyone to assume that this terrible thing happened to your daughter because one of the Hasan household somehow offended Allah.

Perhaps it was your daughter?

Perhaps it was you.

When you say to the world that you are a laborer, but there is no labor to consume you, and when it is God's will that your wife and children plus your daughter who no longer dances must still eat every day or starve, then you are a weakling and a coward and a deserter of your own family unless you fend for your wife and for all those whom you have created. You will do whatever you must, to be certain that your family survives. You will respect your obligations by seizing upon any opportunity, no matter how small or how daunting it may appear to be. You will do this continually, day to day, month to month.

It does not matter if your grief for your daughter who once danced like a butterfly is raining upon you. You only pray that whatever you have to do, whatever stories you may have to invent in order to pull your family through one more day, they will not be unforgivable things.

And you will certainly never dare to point out to God or to any of his clerics here on Earth—rather you will simply ruminate within your own mind—that it was His will which thrust this situation upon you and *made your extreme behavior necessary in the first place.*

Even if Zubaida has become a blight upon the face that you show to the world, she is still your dancing daughter. You can still paint her face back onto her skull with your mind and you can see her there in front of you, buried under her prison of melted flesh. In that moment, your very bone marrow feels the truth that if you had to kill a man with your bare hands to keep him from taunting your daughter, from ever again tormenting anyone in the family by implying that Zubaida somehow deserved her fate—you could do it in an instant.

And why not? God willing, when a civilized man attacks a mongrel, it is the civilized man who walks away.

So you fight to survive every single day. Make it known in the marketplace that you will take any job at all. Anything. Then you roll with the motion of Allah's curse upon your daughter like a good rider rolls with the motion of the camel saddle. You make sure that everyone knows: if they allow Mohammed Hasan to suffer hunger, they will be condemning his burned daughter Zubaida to the same fate.

Enshallah, their hard hearts will be moved by the unbelievable sight of a small human being who still lives, hideously melted, months after the flash fire that devoured her—and for her sake, they will perhaps offer work opportunities to you that might otherwise go to others.

If you get a bad feeling in your stomach about doing something like that, or if you get a tight feeling of guilt in the back of your head, then you simply call up the picture of the doctors at the hospitals who sent your dancing daughter back home to you and who told you that there was nothing else to do but to *pray for her to die*. With that memory, you let the anger fuel you.

And because you know that you will never have an opportunity to flush that anger away, all at one time, by throttling the arrogant stink of a doctor until his neck bones break like the neck of a hen, you will hold the anger close instead, deep inside of your heart, and allow it to smolder. You will also allow its power to make you bold while you move into the marketplace and when you stand up and demand special consideration, even from among so many other desperate men.

When you feel weak and cursed, you will release the power of your hidden anger and feel it lift up your jaw and stiffen your spine. It will make you so determined that even if some would rise up to taunt you and imply that you have drawn this terrible thing down upon yourself, nevertheless you will remain bold among them and you will overcome any resistance that they present.

You will do it every day for the rest of your life, if you have to, because you cannot bring home a bagful of excuses for Bador to feed to the children. It was never the family's fault that their meager resources should be consumed by the needs of your damaged daughter, just as it was not hers.

Is the blame yours, then? It does not matter. You were not made a beggar by the power of guilt; you were made a beggar by your daughter's tragedy. Therefore you will beg for work, when there is work, and you will simply beg when there is no work to be had. You will do that, because you are a man and this is your family.

You will gather your strength from your sense of manhood and stand before anyone who might be able to help you and then you will grovel until they do just that. You will cry like a child, if that is what it takes to move their help in your direction, so that you can go home to your family with your hands full, one more time. Your primary allegiance is to them, even before your allegiance to the clan—and the clan would have little to do with a man who failed to make every possible effort to care for his own.

You may be mocked for debasing yourself, but you would be shunned if you failed your family and you would be cursed if you failed your daughter.

And so it shall be for you, Enshallah.

11 ❧

One of the big topics of the season for Zubaida was the concept of Santa Claus. She had no trouble at all in sharing her classmates' excitement over a special day where you get things for free just because you have been a good girl. She didn't like the fact that Santa looked like a fat religious cleric to her with his long beard and red suit, since religious clerics had never brought good news to her hometown or to her family. But once she realized that you don't have to be a Christian to buy into the Santa Claus story and that the myth of Santa doesn't have him rewarding children on a religious basis, she had no reason not to join in with the other girls' anticipation. She especially liked the part about Santa having some kind of magical powers, and wondered if they might include the ability to grant wishes.

She gave it her best try, in a note that she had a friend help her write because she was old enough to suspect that it might work better if it was written in English. Rebecca found it just before Christmas:

Dear Santa Clause,

　　Dear Santa please make my wishes come true, that my Mom gets well soon and my family be well and blessed. Please help me get well soon so I can go back to my country. Please God give Rebecca and Peter four children 2 boys and 2 girls.

Love,

Zubaida

❦　❦

On February 6, 2003, Zubaida steeled herself to go back under the knife, marking her return to the operating table after a ten-week break for physical and psychological recovery.

The time between had mostly been occupied by what she came to know as the American holiday season, where people seemed eager to make her understand that a variety of different religious faiths all existed in American society and that most of them celebrated one holy day or another during that season, and that there didn't seem to be any problem about that, in this place.

She grasped the concept before they finished the explanation, but it all seemed to her like the latest news from the land of the Others and it didn't really matter much. She knew, without even thinking about it, that life would never be anything like that back at home.

It was still very early in the morning when Dr. Charles Neal took her deep under anesthesia in preparation for a series of major operations to the muscle and skin of her chest and both sides of her torso. During the day's set of procedures, Peter Grossman and the burn team would excise burn scar contractions on the left and right side of her chest, then reconstruct the destroyed flesh of her chest wall by splitting off a section of her back muscle, the *latissimus dorsi*, and pulling it underneath the flesh of her armpit area and then back out onto the chest wall area, giving her a set of working chest muscles.

Hours later, with that long and difficult procedure finished, Dr. Peter turned his attention to her right lower eyelid, where he did some fine-tuning to the scar damage, relieving a slight downward pull on the lower eye area. This left her wrapped in bandages around the right side of her face and all around her torso.

When Zubaida came out of anesthesia and felt herself being rolled into the recovery room, she could tell that she was once again completely swathed in the familiar "mummy" wrappings. They had her trapped.

As far as Dr. Peter was concerned, there was no need for Zubaida to know how much of the wrapping was actually required by the surgery itself and how much was just added on in hopes of getting her through the first couple of days without having her trying to dance and pulling out the new stitches.

❧ ❧

The days following that February 6 series of operations made for one of Zubaida's toughest recoveries. The difficulties only began in the physical realm; they landed with a thud in her emotional life. At first, her bound-up body felt trapped again, almost the same way it once felt when the ropes of scar tissue bound her. Even after Dr. Peter removed the bandages—it never occurred to her to call him "Dad" at the hospital—the flashes of pain and soreness from the large carved areas of her torso made almost any movement painful.

It was as if one of the superstitious old crones back in her village had laid a curse on her that forced the missing pain back into her awareness and stole away the new joy of living that had begun to form inside. In the weeks after that day's operations, long after the need for drugs was gone and she could go back to walking and feeding herself and even going back to school, the surprise bursts of hot knife pain continued to shoot through her at random moments throughout the day. The cruel, unseen force was trying to train her, through pain, not to move at all. If allowed to go further, it would eventually force her to hold herself so perfectly still and quiet that she would vanish and become nothing at all.

The feeling of confinement was abhorrent to her. It didn't help her to remind herself that the burn pain had been worse. Dr. Peter kept telling her that the pain would go away pretty soon, but when her own body taunted her so unpredictably, it was hard to listen to his words. Even though she now understood most of what was said to her in English, those words added up to nonsense. They felt like sand scrubbed across her raw skin. At such times, it didn't matter that everybody wanted to help her and that they were kind to her. It didn't matter that Rebecca and Peter tried to make her feel loved. With the pain nipping at her and her captive spirit silently raging against renewed imprisonment, she couldn't feel anybody's love at all.

What she needed was to swat away the invisible scorpions that stung her when she stood, sat, bent, reached, stretched, walked, or stumbled. Instead she was tossed back into that dark dungeon where she had no control over anything, not the people around her, not her own body. They could tell her over and over that her loss of motion was temporary, but words don't speak with the force of pain. With the eyes of a ten-year-old, she could no longer see an end to this journey. All she knew for certain was that after this latest set of operations, something as natural as the shortest little dance was an invitation to a stabbing.

Now, more than any other time since the flames consumed her, the sum total of the conflicts inside and all around her was enough to drive her completely through the looking glass—just like the "Alice in Wonderland" character in one of the American books at school.

On the other side of the mirror, there was her father, giving her orders that she must learn everything she possibly could, even as he vanished into nothing more than a grin carried over the satellite phone. She felt the need to please him, but she also knew that most of what she was learning in America was forbidden in her country, anyway. The Taliban enforcers were said to have fallen, but what was to stop them from coming back? And either way, what would really change for Zubaida, as far as her future prospects back in the village of Farah?

She understood that the girls in her class at school were all being raised to be *good for something* in a land of many choices, but she also knew that she faced the prospect of being trained to be good for something and then sent back to a country that Zubaida had never known as being anything other than a prison for its women, where the very knowledge that was beginning to open her imagination to countless possibilities would have no more value than to sit unused inside her head and add to the torment of her life as a woman who must serve.

Since she was through the looking glass, it was strange to give her back her face so that she could go back to Farah and spend the rest of her life hiding it.

It was strange to know how to read books that women back home were not allowed to have, and it was even more strange to be able to go back home and not read such books in both English and her native Dari.

Rebecca and Peter made sure to fill her with all sorts of unbelievable experiences that opened her eyes to untold amazements—things she was probably never going to see again and that people back home weren't likely to believe or to even comprehend if she tried to tell them, anyway. So what was there that she could bring back home to her father and her family about all of that?

Everything was good/bad, up/down, black/white. Here in America, the difference between right and wrong seemed to simply mean "don't hurt anybody else." In the Afghanistan that she had always known, the same issues of right and wrong could get you killed in a hundred different ways.

And there was her father, calling to her on the satellite phone and telling her that everyone in the family was counting on her to come back and teach them all a bunch of skills that Zubaida was old enough to know could wind up getting all of them thrown in prison. And all of that was apparently a *good thing*.

She needed to regain some sense of control over her life, or at least over her immediate situation, and some escape from the terrible pressure constricting her from all directions. But since Zubaida's lifetime of experience outweighed the relatively small measure of free days that she had spent in America, her coping mechanisms mostly consisted of the ones that her mother and her aunts had modeled for her over the years. They were the ways of the women who must serve. And the message for Zubaida was that her only source of power was to raise the veil on her emotions.

That much, at least, she could do.

※ ※

Mahnaz, the nanny hired by the Grossmans, sat alone with Rebecca speaking in urgent tones while Zubaida played by herself off in another room. Mahnaz told her story to Rebecca in halting terms, as if she feared that Rebecca would refuse to accept what she had to tell her. But she had to let it out anyway. There was too much to hold back.

According to Mahnaz, even though Zubaida's teacher Kerrie Benson was reporting that Zubaida continued to make a real effort to fit in and to get along at school, she appeared to be saving up her most hostile urges to inflict upon

Mahnaz after classes each day. A pattern of difficult behavior had developed that Mahnaz was having to endure nearly every day when she picked Zubaida up from school. On this day, everything had taken a grim step backward.

She told of how they were riding home on the highway that afternoon, when Zubaida began to tease her by joking that she was going to jump out of the car and kill herself. She faked opening the door several times, ignoring Mahnaz when she insisted that she stop.

Mahnaz had grown up in Iran before immigrating to the United States, so she knew the tendency of many Middle Eastern women to employ melodrama for others' benefit. At first, she didn't react to the threats other than to question why Zubaida would even mention such a thing as suicide when so many people were working to restore her life to her. Zubaida ignored the appeal to her reason and again pretended to open the car door as if she was about to jump. She laughed when Mahnaz shouted in fear.

"They will blame you, Mahnaz!" Zubaida laughed. "They will say it's your fault!"

Mahnaz tried to describe the way that Zubaida's face looked to her at that moment, her voice, her attitude—it was hard to get across. She said that the momentary change in Zubaida was so dramatic that it seemed as if she was looking at a girl who was possessed.

Rebecca thanked her and confided that she was also seeing more episodes of troubling behavior, although this was a distressing new low point. She shivered at the thought of a child toying with an adult's fears by threatening to commit suicide in such a way that it would frame them for the act.

She and Peter had noticed so many instances of similar although less intense behavior that they had already started her in therapy. They were also attending counseling as a family to learn the best ways of coping with these stresses. This news, however, was going to force them into more immediate action. She thanked Mahnaz for telling her.

But the problem went deeper. Mahnaz no longer felt safe with Zubaida. She wasn't afraid of being hurt, herself, but she feared that even a child's game about suicide could have unpredictable results. Mahnaz knew that no one would blame her if Zubaida actually went through with an act of self-destruction, but she also knew that she wouldn't be able to forgive herself for not stopping it. Something in what she was seeing in Zubaida's demeanor made it impossible to dismiss such threats as overstatements. Even the smallest chance that there would be some merit to them was too much for her to bear.

She gave notice and drove home for the last time.

Rebecca and Peter sat up late that night looking for answers. The situation with Mahnaz came as no surprise to them. In recent days Zubaida had been subject to such manic fits of behavior that she would repeatedly run up behind one of them and shout in their ears, then run off laughing. At the slightest angry tone of voice in response to her actions, she could fall into a deep funk that might last the rest of the day. With Peter, she alternated between hot and cold, calling him Dad and wanting to sit on his lap at one moment, while refusing to acknowledge him when he walked in the door after work, in another.

Sometimes there was an apparent cause to her outbursts, usually an ordinary passing nuisance. Other times, there was no sign of any external reason for a radical shift in her behavior. She could be equally fierce whether the cause was obvious or not.

Peter felt sure that some of the manic behavior and the rapid mood swings that they were seeing in Zubaida could be the result of a form of Attention Deficit Hyperactivity Disorder. He spoke to Matt Young, the burn unit's pediatrician, and together they decided to try her on a long-acting form of Ritalin called Concerta. If he could get her brain chemistry balanced out it would be a lot easier to evaluate what they were actually dealing with, as far as her long-term state of mind and her overall mental health.

Individuals who have taken Ritalin report that their subjective experience of the drug was very subtle. They were not particularly conscious of feeling different under its effects; rather, the vast improvements in their behavior, both for themselves and for those around them, came as a result of feeling that the ongoing din of distraction that ordinarily blasts inside of them all day long has suddenly been quieted.

The downward pull of despair that has kept them so manic in their attempts to resist its power simply dissipates. The new powers of concentration and focus experienced by the patient seem to come as a result of finally being provided with a mental background quiet enough to let them concentrate.

With Zubaida showing signs of being overwhelmed, the only way of knowing for sure if her behavior had a brain chemistry imbalance to it or if it simply came from the aggregate of her suffering over the last year and a half was to try the chemical approach and look for the changes in behavior. They sometimes come before the patient is even aware of anything being different, because the drug is fast-acting and doesn't need to accumulate a therapeutic dose over time. The desired effects are a mixture of quietness and alert behavior, and will usually begin to show up on the first day.

The American Psychiatric Association lists fourteen symptoms of Attention Deficit Hyperactivity Disorder that must be present for a child to be diagnosed with it:

1. Often fidgeting with hands or feet, or squirming while seated;
2. Having difficulty remaining seated;
3. Being easily distracted by extraneous stimuli;
4. Having difficulty awaiting turn in games or group activities;
5. Often blurting out answers before questions are completed;
6. Having difficulty in following instructions;
7. Having difficulty sustaining attention in tasks or play activities;
8. Often shifting from one uncompleted task to another;
9. Having difficulty playing quietly;
10. Often talking excessively;
11. Often interrupting or intruding on others;
12. Often not listening to what is being said;
13. Often forgetting things necessary for tasks or activities; and
14. Often engaging in physically dangerous activities without considering consequences.

Zubaida's behavior at that point in time included at least ten of those signs.

Here Peter's double position as her physician and as her personal guardian gave him a depth of doctor-patient insight as well as an opportunity to keep a watch on her at a level that few doctors ever experience. With Zubaida under his and Rebecca's constant access, it was as safe a situation as there could be for attempting to expand the range of her medical intervention, and sending some support to places where the scalpel doesn't go. He decided to begin a course of treatment for ADHD the following day.

On the home front, Rebecca needed more. She worked harder at the skills she gained from counseling, hoping to make sure that her reactions to the behavior issues were the right ones for both of them. She found that watching Zubaida try to bluff her way through so many struggles at the same time also managed to press old buttons deep inside of Rebecca. Feelings emerged of being trapped and frustrated, going all the way back to her own past as the latchkey child of a single working woman who struggled with depression and with the alcohol she used to battle it. Whatever choices that Rebecca made now on Zubaida's behalf, she promised herself that they would come from her best consideration, not as a reaction to some old score of her own.

※ ※

Back in Afghanistan, Colonel Robert Frame placed a call over to the Ninety-sixth Special Forces Unit, instructing a small detail of soldiers who were operating out near the village of Farah to look up Mr. Mohammed Hasan. They were to inform Mr. Hasan that there had been a phone call from his daughter. Then they were to drive him directly to the UN office there so that the call could be put through on the more reliable land line.

The local villagers didn't mind the intrusion of a couple of jeeps, since the soldiers kept their weapons stowed, but it must have made a mighty impression upon everyone who witnessed it—armed American soldiers show up and seek out Hasan, who is smiling when he gets in their vehicles with them and rides away. Since it is clear to the villagers that Hasan is not being taken captive, and furthermore that he *desires* to go with them, then it stands to reason that the mighty American military was there to help him with his daughter. So much of what Hasan told the villagers in recent months had been dismissed as his own wishful thinking, but now it was apparent—as sure as pulling their own beards—there had to be some truth to it.

But how much?

And in a village crushed by the political whimsy of dueling rulers, a population of struggling husbands and fathers stood numb with confusion while

they all asked the same question that any human being who stood in their san-
dals would ask:

How has he done this thing?

What could such a fellow as their neighbor Mohammed Hasan, aging now,
past his chance to break out of poverty in this life, possibly say to a military
force such as the American army that would cause them to send warriors out to
escort him back? *And he departs with them while the joy is plain upon his face?*

Because if their longtime neighbor and close friend Mohammed Hasan has
made himself a man of such interest and importance to the Americans, then is
it not abundantly clear that Hasan knows something that they themselves
must also learn?

His friends and neighbors of day in and day out all knew from personal experience that with all due respect to Mohammed Hasan, he deserved nothing
more in this world than what any one of them might also claim, if only someone cared to listen. And yet he had made the Americans listen, at a time when
the villagers were not yet even sure whether or not the Americans were in
their country simply to be the new conquerors there.

How has he done this thing?

He had to know something, some magic, some clever piece of something
that made him of value to the Others. Logic alone assured all who knew Hasan
and who had lived in this world with him over the years that he could never
simply present a burned young daughter to invading soldiers and get them to
do his bidding. What was there to compel them? She was a girl child of a
crowded family, who lived on the edge of survival along with many others.
Even if the child were male, it would still only be one child of one poor desert
family.

When, the villagers asked themselves, do soldiers come for the father of
such a child, bearing mysterious news that causes that father to go away with
them grinning like a happy fool? When has anyone here ever seen such a
thing? *When has anyone ever even heard of such a thing?*

Before long, gossip floated out of the Hasan house on the wings of talkative
visitors. The story quickly circulated about Hasan going off somewhere to
place a phone call to America to his daughter. The answer gave them nothing
but more questions.

After all, the landscape of Afghanistan was littered with millions of land mines and had been since the days of the Soviet invasion. Thus horribly injured and burned children were familiar to everyone in the country. Afghanistan, the battlefield, had given birth to a generation of amputees. Yet in the town of Farah, far from any of the cities or the important places in their country, one burned child had somehow caused the Americans to shelter her in their country, as Hasan has described it to them. And then, most unbelievably, their army had come here to summon him—just so he could speak to her?

Their suspicions were a glove-tight fit with their lifelong experience, in a land where invasions have washed back and forth across the landscape like desert tidal waves for so many years. It left the other villagers with a clear mission: to get some of whatever Hasan was getting. Their old friend Hasan was going to share his bounty with them, anyway, they could be assured; peaceful existence among them was impossible for any man if the rest were collectively unhappy with him. But they also didn't doubt that Hasan already knew that.

Logically then, Hasan already planned to be generous with his treasured friends and loved ones who have shared the laughter and sorrow of life with him in good times and in bad. This alone was cause for celebration. But there was also much left unsaid, and which did not need to be spoken in order to remain true.

These, after all, were men of the marketplace, existing in a broken village filled with farmers without land and craftsmen without materials. They haggled away their days over tiny pieces of a dwindling pile, and for any one of the men, the failure to perceive an opportunity for material benefit not only was a potential invitation to his family's starvation, but also showed an unforgivable level of irresponsibility to his place as head of the household.

For these eagle-eyed husbands and fathers, the smell of enhanced opportunity wafted from every pore of this mysterious situation with Mohammed Hasan. But surely, they reasoned, this opportunity for Hasan must be far greater than the undoubtedly generous level of opportunity which he was no doubt already contemplating for them. Men of the marketplace know that a man who will pay you fifty has one hundred and fifty more in reserve, if you can separate him from it. The same is true for a gift. To the wise receiver of any gift, there is always a second gift available, just waiting to be gently pried loose from the giver.

Each of them knew that the first step in such a situation is to smother the giver with gratitude, like that of a man who has just been given his heart's desire and ten extra years of life to enjoy it. Praise the giver as you would praise anything short of the Holy realms. Refuse to do anything but cry out to the giver and to all the witnessing world that the giver has saved your life and all of your family's lives and restored your hope for the future.

Whet his appetite for a well-slathered tongue forking until he is so sated and pleased with himself and with his lovely life that he is as tender as a well-cooked lamb. Make sure that he is publicly recognized as a saint of generosity to the point that he has very little left to do but *follow up with another gift that will live up to his exalted image.*

If he is like most others, he will go along with you the whole way, protesting that he knows what you are up to and that it isn't going to work, even as he reaches for his purse.

That was just what they were going to have to do to Mohammed Hasan.

The sweet smell swirling up from every aspect of the Americans' appearance in Farah grew stronger while the village men stepped back and thought about things. There was much to consider, and Hasan had only just left with the Americans. Gossip indicated that he was expected to return on the following afternoon. He would have more to tell them, then.

Hasan would also have much more to tell them than he actually intended to, they realized. That only made the possibilities more fascinating. In a land where possibilities had become as rare as desert rivers, the village men had plenty of free time to mull the main question from many different angles—how could each one of them attach himself to whatever it was that was flowing toward Hasan's household, whom they all knew to be no more deserving than their own families, after all?

When Mohammed Hasan was returned home the next day by the same military escort, he made it a point to go straight inside his house and told Bador to keep visitors away and to have the children leave him in peace. He sat and savored the unbelievable experience of spending twenty-four hours under military guard while being treated with respect and allowed to move around—and fed well, too.

He relished knowing that the quiet village observers who had watched him arrive with eagle eyes wouldn't tolerate waiting for the full story for very much longer, before they started getting angry. They were wondering how to get in on it themselves, of course, just as he would do in their place.

The trick for Hasan, it seemed obvious, was to be as mysterious about everything as he possibly could, while hiding most of the facts. If he only fed them tidbits, they might not notice that he himself had no idea what was really going on, as far as the American soldiers and their willingness to come all the way out here for him. If the villagers found out that he didn't really know himself, he was sure to lose prestige, but if he hung on to that prestige, perhaps bolstered it a bit, it became social currency that could create repeated opportunities to end a workday with full hands. Men of the marketplace know that if they are going to execute a true bait-and-switch maneuver, they must always create a distraction strong enough to get the buyer to look away for an instant, while the seller switches a decoy with the real merchandise. The most reliable distraction available to Hasan then was the power of the other men's greed and imagination. Instead of allowing them to focus on finding out everything about what was going on between Hasan and the Americans, he decided to mention a few of the small things that he might do for his loyal friends— perhaps some additional ways in which he could thank the people who had loaned him the money for his many trips with Zubaida. Perhaps he could do things beyond merely giving them their money back.

And really, could any of the town's men doubt that Mohammed Hasan would pay back every single afghani that he owed, when he commanded such respect from the Americans? Couldn't they all see that it was foolish to bother him about small amounts now or about beginning payments on the larger loans right away? A man who receives such friendly attention from a force as powerful as the American army is not a man to be bothered over a few million afghani here or there, even though the sum amounted to thousands of U.S. dollars.

What would such a thing cost, if a man had to pay for it himself: four men in two jeeps, who drive hundreds of kilometers to take you away to some important place, in order to speak with your burned daughter over a telephone to

America? And then after you are finished talking to her, they actually *bring you back home* the next day? A man who can command that kind of attention from military forces of such destructive power is not a man to trifle with over the details of when he plans to assume payment on his outstanding loans.

Hasan knew that he could gain extra patience from his creditors this way. He knew that wise businessmen in the marketplace pretend to forget what they are owed, while making sure to thicken the bonds of friendship and silently prowling for opportunity. Wise businessmen know that as long as they are close enough to the source of such power, it is only a matter of time before they receive a share.

Or so they might be allowed to think. And if there was an opportunity in this for Hasan to protect his family by delaying the day when he might have to choose between making loan payments or feeding his children, then he would do anything he could to help his friends and neighbors believe that there was potential for great good in showing patience to Hasan, regarding his outstanding loans.

12 🌿

It was like playing inside a cave or within some silent section of her ancient village's ruins. All the world dropped away. Her hearing still worked, but inside of her head there was quiet and stillness. Her feelings still worked, but the anxiety and the sense of frantic distraction were gone. Now she realized that the tightness around her chest wasn't entirely due to the scars from her burns and surgeries, but that most of it came from the deep tension settled around her heart. It was her daily companion and tended to grip her at any given moment—but for now she could feel the tightness melting away.

Throughout Zubaida's life, she and her family had remained rooted in the practicalities of daily survival, where a stroke of good fortune is celebrated but not questioned. There is no reason to ask why good fortune arrives, because then you will have to ask why so much ill fortune also arrives, and one of the basic components of poverty is its quality of rendering philosophical questions into just so much irritating nonsense.

There had never been a means for her to question her life because there was no other set of rules and no other point of view to apply to it. To question one's life implies that there is something that can be done about it, even if the great Answers arrive. Zubaida knew that such personal choices didn't exist in her future or in the future of the women she knew back at home.

She didn't feel any urge to understand what was making her feel different; she just fell into the rising sense of physical and mental comfort out of a lifetime of habit, then she moved along with it the way a natural dancer will instinctively move to music.

"To this day," Peter would say much later, "I believe that Zubaida was suffering from a variant of Attention Deficit Hyperactivity Disorder. Her reaction to the medication was a validation of that. The change in her for the better was immediate and dramatic."

Peter was still at the hospital for the day when Rebecca happened to walk past Zubaida's bedroom, glanced inside and saw to her utter surprise that Zubaida was sitting quietly by herself, reading—and that she seemed to be engrossed in the book. The thing that made the sight a jaw-dropper was that up until that day, Zubaida only did her homework with difficulty, and avoided unnecessary contact with books. Her joy in learning seemed to come mostly from classroom discussions and the personally interactive nature of lessons with other kids in a schoolroom.

Now here she was at home, on her free time, and not only was she reading by herself but she was so engrossed in the book that she didn't even look up when Rebecca peeked in on her. She continued to sit quietly, not pouting, not angry or frightened or sad, just amusing herself by reading a book and practicing her English.

Rebecca had recently been wondering if she could really see some progress coming from Zubaida's therapy sessions or if she only saw signs of change because she wanted them. Either way, there was no mistaking the dramatic shift that was taking place at that moment, right there in front of her. With the ADHD symptoms under pharmaceutical control, it was obvious that the Concerta was balancing out Zubaida's brain chemistry in ways that she needed in order for her to relax and concentrate. In that state she could experience enough calmness to feel her own basic enjoyment of living while still remaining alert to the world.

If the best possible effect was realized from the medication, she would also find that her calmed, focused energies would allow her schoolwork to proceed faster and with less effort.

When an old friend unexpectedly taps you on the shoulder in some faraway place and pulls up a chair beside you, the joy of their presence and the gratitude for the renewed relationship can prevent you from wanting to question the appearance too much. You understand that questions and answers can suck the heated air out of the balloon while it is still carrying you on your happy surprise ride. Such things are well avoided.

Zubaida greeted the old friend's return the same way she reacted to any emotionally risky situation; she shut down her feelings and lifted up her chin and pretended that there was nothing going on that she wasn't familiar with already and that she couldn't handle perfectly well.

Even so, it was too much of a surprise for her to completely conceal. Her heart speeded up so fast and beat so loud that she could hear the sound of her heartbeat coming up out of her throat and between her parted lips. Her breathing became ragged with excitement, even though she made a deliberate effort to take ordinary breaths. She put to work every bit of self-control that she could muster, using her deeply engrained knowledge of the marketplace, to avoid the foolish vulnerability of showing shock or reacting with surprise. In any unpredictable situation, she knew that it could be a mistake to reveal anything about her true feelings when others could easily use such knowledge to take advantage, or even to do harm.

She reacted the same way she would respond if a beautiful and rare bird perched right on Zubaida's windowsill, and she wanted to avoid scaring it away. Only this time, the rare bird was Zubaida's music—in the new quiet of her mind and the new ease to her thoughts, the former sputters of returning music were replaced with a full dose. The long-gone music simply reappeared inside of her, just as if it had come rising up out of a low fog. She didn't want to make a single move that might scare it away.

No big deal. She had learned the American words well enough to console herself with their sentiments. Tense up and music tends to disappear; relax and it gets better. No big deal at all.

Following her own advice, she relaxed all the way down inside, spreading all of her physical energy evenly through her body so that every muscle was relaxed, even though she remained poised to move at the same time. She took deep, even breaths to keep herself calm and balanced, and then let her old friend move through her in waves of music that she heard inside like a radio that comes from everywhere.

Parts of the music were slippery and just moved through her in the form of musical sounds, but other parts were sticky and grabbed at her feet or her legs or her hips or hands until they had to move in response. She kept the movements small, nothing to startle off her welcome visitor, just letting the music run back out of her while she undulated slightly to the rhythm in her brain.

She couldn't jump around much or do any fancy twists, but she could let the music flow through her and trace the motion of its waves with her body. She needed to avoid exuberant moves until she was better healed, but she would have avoided them anyway, at that moment, just to keep from seeming too happy about the return of her music. The ways of the marketplace were clear enough in her memory—she knew that the best way to prevent anyone from taking away something as precious as this newly regained ability to dance, to ride invisible waves of music, was for her to keep all of her emotions to herself until the coast was clear.

Before too long, she found herself eavesdropping on Peter and Rebecca while they talked about how much this new medicine was helping her. She picked up enough of their English to understand that they were saying that they both thought she seemed happier and more content, and that they thought it was because of the doctors and the medicine and all of the therapist's talk, talk, talk.

She didn't see it that way at all.

Zubaida's personality was better because the music was back again, constantly running through and reminding her that she was herself. And she was better because the surgical scars around her torso were finally healing enough for her to move her body along with the music, so long as she kept things gentle. This much was enough to remind her of why all the astounding events of this painful journey were worth doing in the first place.

Amid all the uncertainty, she knew that as long as she had her music and she could send its ripples through her body, she could be Zubaida in this world. No matter if the circumstances were familiar or completely strange, she could remain strong when strength was needed. She could endure all sorts of trials and remain composed throughout, because with her music and dance she carried a potent weapon against despair. Perhaps this weapon would, one day, even provide some kind of protection against developing that deadly cold blue depression which so often gripped her mother—who did not dance.

Zubaida knew that without her music, she would be of no use to anybody because in such a case her spirit would be so low that no one would want her around, anyway. Who could blame them? She wouldn't want to have to live around somebody who was dead inside, and that is what she would be. Not that most of the men would concern themselves with that as long as she kept up with her chores, but it would be very hard to have female friends if she was dead inside, unless they were dead inside, too.

The idea of a bunch of dead friends caused a shiver to run up her spine. She shook off the fear that accompanied the shiver by incorporating the movement into a series of waves that she sent up and down her spine in time to the melody. The instant that she shook off the fear-wave, a rush of elation filled her.

This was it. She had just demonstrated it to herself, although without intending to; this shiver-dance was an instance of her *power* in action. It allowed her to pass a burst of fear all the way through herself, without taking any harm from it, by translating the fear into physical motion and then playing it out in time to the music.

Now while she looked out from inside of the beautiful silence where her rampaging thoughts used to be, she could sense the attraction that she was feeling to all sorts of details about life in this world. Sources of fascination seemed to shine at her from every direction. She was content to wait until later to break out into long leaps over large pieces of furniture and throw the high kicks and the twisting jumps that she had always loved to hurl at the world with her body.

Such things could wait, for the time being, because she was certain that they were coming back to her. She knew it now. And she was sure that the hour for all of that wasn't so far away, either, because she could already sway and slowly spin to the music in her head. She could carve the air with graceful hands and fanned fingertips. And that was enough to prove to her own doubts and fears that she still had strong reasons to be glad inside of her heart.

She knew that she would be all right because not only was her music back, but also she was already such a surgical veteran that she had inherited a little bit of Peter's ability to see three dimensional objects and people through the fourth dimension of time—she could visualize her own healing process. And she could see herself steadily regaining her movement, her power, as time went on.

A quiet sense of happiness spread all through her. This one wasn't so strong that it made her feel any need to run and scream and jump around. She didn't feel compelled to stomp her happiness all around the house or to shriek it in the face of anyone she came across. She just let the happiness run through her until she felt all smoothed out inside.

It was as if she had just stepped outside and met the rest of herself out on the street—and brought her back home to live. With that, it occurred to her that she hadn't been seeing the other girls from school very much lately, so she wandered out of her room to go ask Rebecca if she could arrange for a visit with Emily, who still got depressed sometimes about the dog bite scar on her forehead. Zubaida figured that Emily could probably use a little cheering up.

She grabbed a phone and gave Emily a call, just to see what she was doing.

Later that same month, she asked Peter to take her to the Father-Daughter dance at school. She seemed so proud to have her dad accompanying her along with the fathers of the other girls and looked so adorable in her frilly dress that Peter would later describe it as a turning point in their relationship, in terms of a new level of trust and comfort that she demonstrated with him.

❊ ❊

John Oerum, the Foreign Service Officer at the UN Assistance Mission in Kandahar, was initially unsure of what to make of the story told by a man calling himself Mohammed Hasan and claiming to be from the village of Farah, out in remote Farah Province. Hasan was requesting—no, demanding—that Oerum find some way to make a telephone call to the United States and talk to some American doctor who supposedly had Hasan's ten-year-old daughter living in his home, while he operated on her over and over.

Calls went out.

It was a heady list: Raymond Short, the head of Military Civil Affairs in Afghanistan; Central Command in Florida; the charitable Non-Government Organization who sponsored her; and the U.S. State Department. Word ricocheted around that Mohammad Hasan was beginning to have anxiety attacks about his daughter's fate while she was out there among the Others. His concerns were not so much over her medical condition, because he had been provided with postsurgery pictures a few months earlier. And he said that the last time that he spoke to her on the phone, she sounded well and strong. His fears centered on nightmares of having lost her to a foreign world.

And while Hasan wanted his daughter to learn everything about America that she could, and to learn to speak English well, he was lately beginning to fear that the longer she stayed away, the less likely she might be to find her way back home to them. He feared that the temptations of the Western world might permanently estrange her from the family and from her own culture.

Since Hasan couldn't provide phone numbers, his query didn't go directly to Peter and Rebecca's house or to the Grossman Burn Center. It was routed through military channels to the NGO. But Hasan's simple telephone query about his daughter's condition sent the domino chain into a series of concentric loops.

Now the NGO became officially nervous. They wondered what kind of loose cannon Hasan might turn out to be, recalling that Dr. Mike Smith told them about having to work to keep Hasan from bolting off to explore, back in the U.S.—apparently, Hasan only remained under control because Smith convinced him that if he created an international incident, his daughter's welfare would be severely jeopardized.

But with Zubaida ensconced in her recovery process off in America, Hasan had discovered that it was much easier to accept the idea of losing his daughter for an entire year than it was to accept the hard reality of the Zubaida-shaped hole in his life. Worries were beginning to plague him, and back at home in Farah he was far from any source of information, and left with too much time on his hands.

From the NGO's point of view, the major problem with Mohammed Hasan was that the man was so proactive. He was liable to just show up at any American military or embassy office and start telling whatever story he wanted to give out about his daughter's unique charity situation. With the press hanging around looking for scandals to decry, it was only a matter of time before some sort of major uproar commenced, with voice after voice crying out, "What about me?"

The experienced humanitarian workers at the NGO realized that this would be a surefire guarantee of turning a beautiful expression of human concern into a political firestorm. It could limit cooperation between international Non-Governmental Organizations by adding elements of mutual suspicion that could only slow down the flow of victim relief—and ultimately do no good for anybody.

❧ ❧

Once Zubaida got the chance to speak with her father from Kandahar, after so much time without any communication from home, she felt less homesick and was able to jump back into her new American schoolgirl life with a lighter heart. She was glad that Peter had talked her father and all of the other American adults out of making her go back home right away. Even though she felt anxious to see everyone in her village, when she thought about going back home right now, she knew in her heart that it wasn't time. Peter hadn't even finished doing all the work that was necessary for her to have full physical range of motion yet.

Her English was much stronger, but she still understood it far better than she could speak the language. The thin, reedy American words seemed to stick in her brain when she tried to put them together. But she could sit back and listen to a conversation and get most of it, when adults were speaking, and she usually understood everything that the other kids said. She confused her words often enough, but she knew that she could do a lot better at it, given a little more time. And she could sense that the language might help her in countless ways. Such a thing would surely be a real addition to her power.

She talked over all of that with her father, basking in the messages of goodwill that the family sent through him. But despite the gregarious traits among her country's women, it was not in Zubaida's own nature to talk about her feelings very much, so she said very little about Peter and Rebecca, other than to assure Hasan that she was being treated well. She kept to herself her feelings of relief that she would have several more months with her surrogate parents and with her new friends. The feelings of relief grew stronger when Peter and her father agreed that she could go home in June or July, which would allow her to finish the year at school and to keep on polishing her English. She was also glad that her father assured Peter that her mother understood and agreed.

This would give her more time to enjoy this new feeling of being so much more smoothed out than she used to be, and to share those feelings with all of her new friends at school, or with Mom and Dad at home. And it didn't strike her as being the least bit strange to refer, in that way, to Rebecca and Peter or the house where they all lived.

Later, she sat on the floor in front of the sofa while Rebecca sat behind her and brushed her hair. For once, she could let someone get that close behind her and not feel overwhelmed by a creepy feeling of having one of the Others in your weak spot. But the whole set of bad feelings that went along with the idea of the Others was beginning to crumble into ashes. The Others seldom ever even got close to her, she realized now. They were out there, all right. But this new home was a safe place. She accepted that, all the way down into her most suspicious marketplace self. Whatever Mom and Dad were, they were not the Others.

Zubaida was busy learning, just as she had been instructed to do on behalf of her family. And what the simple fact of her second home and family here in America had taught her, by making it inarguably evident, was that there was yet another kind of human being in this world. Even though this kind was not of her people, they were also not among the dangerous Others.

How to explain that?

This kind of human being could be trusted, for some reason. Zubaida had no answer as to why people would do such things as Rebecca and Peter and all of them had done for her, other than that they were obviously dedicated to living lives of decency and honor, for some reason or another. And as much as possible, they also wanted to live their lives in peace.

All of that was as easy for her to accept as it was to take a breath. The idea of a peaceful but determined warrior is built into every Afghan's consciousness by the stories that are told to children from their earliest days, and by their constant exposure to people's spoken references to their long tradition of re-pelling foreign invaders. Zubaida could easily picture this other kind of human being in that form.

Maybe Peter and Rebecca, her doctors, her teachers, her friends at school, were all part of this newly discovered group of people. What else could explain it? This presented her with the same eye-opening revelation that has greeted so many, because the people inside of her newly discovered group came with all kinds of different faces and skin colors—so how was she supposed to tell them from the Others?

"I'm so glad that you can stay here until summertime and finish your school year," Rebecca said while she brushed at her hair. "Even though I know you miss your parents and all your brothers and sisters."

"I not going back," Zubaida quietly said.

Rebecca looked around to her face and saw a dreamy-looking smile playing on her face. Ordinarily, she would have thought that the expression was simply the result of Rebecca's gentle hair brushing, but despite Zubaida's fondness for saying shocking things, these strange words caught Rebecca's attention.

"Well, actually, we have about three months left, then you're going back home to Afghanistan."

"I not from Afghanistan anymore. I American now."

"But what about your family?"

"They can come here."

"They can't come here, Zubaida. We can't even keep you here after your last operation is done. We all know that, right?"

Zubaida turned away, made her face go blank. "I know."

"And you do want to see your parents and your—"

"Yes!" Zubaida yelled, trying to close her out.

"Then what can we—"

"You and Peter come back to Afghanistan with me!"

"You mean go back there to live?"

"Yes!"

"But Peter has to work here, for all the other people who need his help like you did. And our home is here. All of our families, our friends . . ."

Zubaida's shoulders slumped while she watched the happy picture of hav-

ing Rebecca and Peter live next door to her family in Farah crumble like campfire ashes.

On March 18, 2003, Zubaida turned eleven years old with forty of the kids
from school and about twenty sets of parents, at a giant backyard pool party
and general picnic blowout, American style. By this point, her English was
good enough to allow her to barrel right into the day's activities along with the
other kids without communication glitches. She had mastered a style of dress
for herself that took in the local California schoolgirl look but gave it her own
colorful twist, the same way that the women of Afghan tribes had done to ac-
cent their appearances for centuries, before religious rule.

To a stranger, it could have easily appeared to be an ordinary outdoor party
for any American girl's birthday celebration. Since Zubaida saw herself most
clearly in the way that others reacted to her, she had already perfected the subtle mannerisms of the local girls, right down to the same rolling of the eyes
whenever a grown-up said something incredibly stupid. This helped her to
guarantee that the feedback from the other girls remained as positive and ap-
proving as possible. She knew that approval was like gasoline in her engine.
She could feel it feed her and make her stronger. With enough approval, she
felt certain that she could do pretty much anything she wanted to.

Photographs of that day show a girl who appears to be completely at home
and assimilated into the American culture, even though it is so different from
her own. And the pictures seem to completely disprove any notion that on
that day she had been in the United States for only eight months.

❧ ❧

Two days, later, on March 20, forces of the U.S. military, coupled with British
combat soldiers and a smattering of smaller support troups from other allied
countries, invaded Iraq. The goal was to remove Saddam Hussein from power,
dead or alive, along with his entire administration and governmental system.
The answer to the question of what to do about the human condition was thus
expressed in the form of hundreds of tons of high explosives, delivered with
astonishing pinpoint accuracy most of the time.

Zubaida's future plunged back into a desert sandstorm of dangerous possibilities. If the Taliban forces who were holed up in the caves of Afghanistan's huge and rugged mountain ranges regrouped for an assault to retake Afghanistan while the United States was busy in Iraq, Zubaida's village could disappear overnight, especially if the Taliban decided that they needed that strategic location. Like everyone in her village, Zubaida knew that Farah sat on the ancient "Silk Road" convoy trail between the historic cities of Kandahar and Herat.

Even if they didn't destroy the village, the resurfacing of Taliban rule would completely negate the purpose of rebuilding Zubaida's future. Since her face would never be one hundred percent normal again, she would still have negligible social value if she were prevented from securing her education. Everyone involved in getting her to the United States was eager to see her safely returned home, and to finally be out from under the huge political risk that she represented. But it was also generally agreed that she could not be simply dropped back into the arms of antifemale tyrants. There was nothing to do but wait it out.

Eight days later, on March 28, Zubaida was back at the Grossman Burn Center, again under the fictitious name of Sarah Lewis to conceal her from curiosity seekers and tabloid paparazzi. She complained to Charles Neal again about the sleeping gas and hoped out loud that he had done something to make it smell better this time. She grudgingly accepted his apologetic explanation that he needed to use the medicine that was in the funny smelling gas, and that he could only promise that she would be asleep very quickly and wouldn't smell it for long.

The sun was barely up that morning before Peter Grossman began the day's procedures with Zubaida. Before he was done for the day, there would be four separate surgeries plus another three sets of steroid injections, dozens in each set, delivered to the worst of her scar areas.

He began with a fine-tuning release of her right earlobe with a two and a half square centimeter flap cut and rotated under the ear to give a more normal appearance. Moving to the second procedure, he performed a set of two Z-plasty cuts that allowed him to rearrange sixteen square centimeters of the lower right side of her neck. He then adjusted the pull of the scarring on her left forearm as a result of being separated from the torso scars, rearranging some twenty-nine square centimeters of flesh.

The last of the day's surgeries involved releasing the pull of scarring around her navel, and the rest of the day's work consisted of the artful placement of dozens of tiny injections of steroid solution into the places where the scars might tend to thicken, assuring the continued breakdown of the scar tissue and denying it the chance to develop further.

After she awakened from anesthesia, he made sure that she was in good condition and then sent her off to the recovery room to finish waking up. Since she was still too groggy for conversation, he wouldn't know how she was really feeling until she was back in her hospital room and he walked in the door.

Then he would see if she was going to acknowledge him or if he would have to coax her out of her anger once more over how these things still hurt her in recovery, in spite of all of Peter's magic. She might climb into his lap and call him Dad and be a needy little lovebug. She might pretend that he wasn't in the room. Or she might cover herself with that invisible turtle shell of indifference that was already familiar to him, the one that surely worked well in the village marketplaces to prevent others from observing feelings and spotting vulnerabilities.

Peter's mother, Sandy Francis, was divorced from his father back when Peter was in his early teens, and she had long since married her current husband, Mitch, but the couple lived close enough to visit regularly with the new threesome at her son's house. Since Sandy had been married to one surgeon and was the mother of another, she especially appreciated the high level of risk that her son assumed when he took on Zubaida's case. Sandy didn't need anyone to tell her how easily this noble experiment could get off track, and not just because of anything that might go wrong; there was enough danger from the suspicions of those who merely *thought* that something might be wrong. She knew that whenever any case gets wide public attention, there will always be a percentage of troubled souls who will project their own inner demons onto what they believe that a child such as Zubaida is actually experiencing. Such people are capable of seeing themselves as heroes ready to sacrifice anything to see in-justice thwarted, without realizing that they are projecting the troubles that they see. It doesn't matter. Such people sometimes find lawyers to represent them for free, just to give the attorney a crack at a "deep pockets" surgeon and his medical practice.

And so her delight existed on a number of levels once she had a chance to get to know Zubaida and to see for herself how well Peter was managing Zubaida's recovery, and how thoroughly he was documenting every surgical and medical step that was taken. It was enough to convince Sandy that not only was Zubaida safe, but also, for the time being, so was her son.

Before long, Zubaida became comfortable enough with Sandy to lovingly refer to her as Grandma Sandy, even though she had a conceptual problem about what to call Mitch. Since Zubaida came from a land virtually without divorce, a step-parent was a rare and unusual thing.

Zubaida and Mitch got off to a rocky start the first time he walked into the room. He had just begun growing a beard, and when Zubaida took her first look at his whiskered face, she ran to Rebecca whimpering in fear that he was Taliban. She remained upset by his appearance and didn't calm down until he left.

Mitch decided to go home and shave, saving the whole beard thing for some other time, and Zubaida decided that the name Mitch fit him better than Grandpa, which she reserved for Dr. Richard. With that mutual understanding established, Zubaida was able to relax in Sandy's presence and to feel safe in coming over to her house for private visits with Grandma Sandy. Zubaida had no compunction about constantly flattering Sandy with remarks about how young-looking and beautiful her Grandma Sandy was, in order to make sure that the snacks kept coming. Grandma Sandy wasn't above keeping quiet about the fact that Zubaida would have gotten the snacks anyway—a little flattery never hurt.

One night when Zubaida was there for a sleepover, Sandy finally realized how deeply the girl had bonded with Peter and Rebecca. During one quiet mo-ment of conversation, Zubaida leaned close to Sandy and confided, "You know, Grandma, Peter is a *Jew*." She said it as if she were sharing a dangerous secret.

Sandy felt her heart sink. Could anti-Semitism have already made such a large impact upon this young girl? She felt her chest tighten when she responded.

"Yes, I know that he's a Jew."

Zubaida nearly whispered it. "They don't like Jews in my country."

Sandy's heart sank a little further. "Is that true?" She waited for the anti-Semitic remark, whatever it was going to be.

"Yes," Zubaida affirmed with a confident nod. Then a little smile moved across her face. "But don't worry, I take care of him."

She didn't appear to be bragging; she simply spoke with the same quiet depth of determination that carried her through the process of surviving her burns. Sandy had already heard about Zubaida's proposal that she and Peter and Rebecca should all go live in Afghanistan together. So from that point of view, it only made sense that Zubaida stood ready to defend her Jewish second father.

Sandy stared back at her in open wonder at the mixture of forces that were playing upon this one child, who could seem wounded and frail in one moment and then like a block of iron in the next. She reached over and hugged her.

"I know you will."

She couldn't think of any other response that seemed to matter.

13 ❧

Zubaida's mother was well aware of the nagging question about her daughter's education. What real chance would she have to continue to learn, once she came home? Once the Taliban forces were overwhelmed in Afghanistan and their hold on the government collapsed, schools throughout the country were technically free to open, whether they had mosque affiliation or not. They were also free to once again include females among their students and to teach nonreligious subjects.

The reality was not so simple. Most of the qualified female teachers had long since fled the country, and the profession was ignored by most males, so that the personnel shortage was acute. Throughout the country, there was scant availability of texts and learning materials, and the wrecked national economy didn't bode well for a quick fix on that front. Rural areas such as Farah would be the last to receive attention from the government, and the mosques could offer little more than the rudiments of religious instruction. Science, mathematics, history, geography—the fields that challenge and develop young minds and train them for better livelihoods—none of that was going to be available in Farah for many months, perhaps many years.

There was nothing for Bador to do but endure the frustration of seeing her children continue to grow up uneducated. Everyone was free to go to school, provided that they could get themselves to one. But even if she cared to test the relaxed restrictions upon a woman's public movements, what was she to do about getting her children to school? Even if she went mad and gathered them all up and walked them many miles to the nearest school and enrolled them there, what were they to do, then? The city is not their home; they have no relatives there. Were they supposed to sleep in the streets and beg for their meals whenever they were not in class?

With the Taliban gone, Bador could start making craft objects and take them to the marketplace to sell, but the time that it would take for her to create an inventory and then accumulate enough money to do anything with it would be a long stretch, during which her children would continue falling further and further behind. It was especially true for her daughters, who otherwise had only the tiniest grasp of control over their lives. It meant that they would be slipping further into the likelihood that their time in this world would be a lot like Bador's, existing upon a diet of rocks within the life of a woman who must serve.

That was absolutely unacceptable to her, even though her world allowed her nothing to do but live with it. Her generation of women had been assaulted by a combination of religion, politics, and warfare in repeated waves during their lives, and forced to exist under enforced ignorance. There was no way that anyone could reverse the effects of that, simply by changing some faraway government authorities and coming out here to post a different set of laws. The law and new set of rulers was the latest of the dozens and dozens of new proclamations of general law that the trade route areas of Afghanistan had witnessed down through the centuries, always coming from that never-ending parade of foreign invaders.

With the scant tools available to her, Bador couldn't form any sort of effective plan as to how to overcome those dark forces that any mother in her position could sense, pushing her children toward insecure and undignified lives of servitude—and taking her old age and her husband's final years right along with it. But it was not her place to figure it out.

She knew exactly how her daughters were going to feel, once they realized that they were trapped inside of their own servant situations, living day after day and year after year as women who must serve. Bador realized that her husband was in no position to secure some kind of important job that would allow them to move to a city where schooling would be available, and she would not harangue her husband to achieve something that he had no capacity to do.

Still—Bador also knew that her husband was a private man who seldom confided everything that was going on in his life, not to her or to anyone else. And clearly, something very big was going on in the life of Mohammed Hasan, son of Darwish. Perhaps as a result of his long trips to Kandahar?

Bador had a whole set of remarkable new events to consider. Did she not see with her own eyes that the American military sent *four* soldiers in *two* jeeps, just to bring her husband someplace for a telephone call to the United States? And did she not see her husband safely returned to her the following day, glowing in his face and telling of how he had spoken with their daughter and of how he could assure all of her health and happiness? He heard with his own ears that she missed the family and would be happy to come home.

And was he not escorted back to his village like a tribal chief?

Bador Hasan was married to a man who obviously knew a lot more than he was telling. He had somehow managed—through his sheer tenacity and stubborn, unyielding willpower—to find hope for renewing Zubaida's life. He brought this gift of their daughter's salvation back home to Bador in honor of their family, and in so doing he saved his wife's heart from permanent despair, just as surely as he had saved his daughter.

Now she entered the marketplace for a little food shopping and it was all she could do to keep from smiling. But since the one public place where Bador and the other women were always allowed to go, even during the worst of the Taliban years, was the marketplace, there was nothing dull or rusty about her marketplace sensibilities. Any woman of the house knows that in the marketplace, when you receive an offer, you must always be confident that the giver has more to offer, if you can extract it. In the marketplace, all the other market-goers are your opponents. If you do not study the arts of bluffing, pushing, and haggling, you cannot hope to beat the other opponents and you will have failed yourself and cheated your family.

For centuries, millions of people have believed that an honorable woman never willingly squanders the smallest amount of the family resources in that way. What she does is to develop a highly refined sense of opportunity and, when opportunity is detected, she will press to get the necessary action out of whomever is allowed to go out and deal with it.

Her husband had done so well for the family on Zubaida's behalf, but Bador did not run her household by being a fool, and so she could not fail to realize that there was more, that there had to be more, behind all of that. So her Mohammed was just going to have to do much better.

She had no idea how he might achieve such a thing, and no particular interest in the details. Those factors are for the men to work out on their own, all the more so since they often regard their family matriarch as a woman who lies around the house and waits for something to do.

Bador knew that she couldn't achieve anything by confronting Mohammed and attempting to make demands upon him. Any direct confrontation would only cause him to plant his feet and do nothing at all for her. As usual, her power was best expressed through the wielding of mood. With fangs so thin that victims seldom felt them at all, a woman who must serve can inject silent poison into the victim's day. She needs only to deny the victim, in this case her husband, any peace or satisfaction in his home life.

The mastery that such a woman displays will be most evident in the fact that she continues to appear to be doing her best to move from one task to the next in the proper manner. Nothing, however, will ever be quite as it should be. Nothing will arrive on time, nothing will be warm enough to eat or cool enough to drink or soft enough to sleep on or clean enough to wear. Nothing will sit quite straight or stand without falling over.

And for all of those reasons, there would quite simply be no peace for her husband, Mohammed Hasan, son of Darwish, proud veteran of the Soviet war, until he found some way to get something done about educating their sons *and* their daughters. But every one of her relentless inflictions of minor pain would be carried out with a smile, and with the appearance of being one of those women who must serve who never does anything other than busily go about her work with the best of intentions while keeping a sharp eye out for even more work to do.

Bador was already familiar with the blessing of that lesson, that revelation, really, which will eventually come to all women who must serve: *There are many different kinds of power. All of them have their uses.*

☾ ☽

Throughout the first half of April, Zubaida could feel herself moving in a steady, upward curve. It wasn't as if her nightmares or her waking fears disappeared, but she became steadily stronger when it came to dealing with them. The sense of strength itself caused some of her fears to recede, and even though the ones that remained still seized her from time to time, she was usually able to pull herself out of a truly dark mood before it gripped her for long. Usually, the daily drama at school had nothing to do with her and was just something that some other girl whipped up. That gave Zubaida the chance to join the rest of the girls in speculating as to what the troublemaker's problem was, and whether anything might be done to help her.

Rebecca watched Zubaida's rapid progress with growing excitement. She decided that Zubaida was doing so well at adapting to American life that she would take her on a "girls' trip" to Texas to visit Rebecca's mother and a couple of childhood friends who still lived there. Zubaida's school had a week of spring break coming up during the third week of April. It gave them the perfect chance to spend time alone together in a variety of situations that would be unique to the two of them, and, she hoped, leave Zubaida with a set of memories that would continue to reinforce the message that Rebecca was truly on her side and committed to her well-being.

While she saw to it that Zubaida's experiences in California were stimulating and varied, she was still aware of how far those experiences differed from the more ordinary sort of middle-American life that Rebecca knew as a child. She had tried to impress upon Zubaida how much diversity there was among the population in Los Angeles, but the reality of Zubaida's time was that she seldom had any chance to mix with anyone outside the kids she met at her school.

With so little time left before Zubaida would be going back home, perhaps never to return, Rebecca felt obligated to give her the broadest experience of American life that she could. Perhaps Zubaida could continue to learn from it whenever she played it back in her memory during the years to come.

They arrived in Dallas on April 19, to visit with one of Rebecca's old girlfriends. Rebecca was interested to see how Zubaida would do with the company of children she met in Texas. They couldn't possibly have been given the level of preparation that Zubaida's classmates got, in terms of knowing how to handle themselves with her. If Zubaida could hold her own among them, she might be closer to being able to hold her own back inside of her culture.

Rebecca got a case of butterflies in her stomach at the thought of how uncomfortable it could possibly become, but she was determined to stop any antagonistic situation before it became too difficult for Zubaida, anyway—and after all, they would be leaving Texas after a few days. There wouldn't be time for any conflicts to get out of hand. It seemed like a perfect way to let Zubaida sample some variations on ordinary American life.

April 19 was a Saturday, so Rebecca's friend threw them a little potluck party at her house. It was a good excuse for her daughter to invite a bunch of her friends over and introduce Zubaida to them. The "test" was a nonevent; before long the girls were laughing and playing together as if Zubaida were a longtime neighbor. Rebecca had to marvel at this girl's ability to relate to strangers. When Zubaida was in one of her stable moods, she seemed to be able to ease her way into any new or novel situation and quickly find some way to meet it eye to eye. Even when she was quiet and nonconfrontational, Zubaida's matter-of-fact sense of herself as some kind of alpha personality imbued everything she did. It gave her an innate authority around other children, sometimes even around other adults. Most of the time, she didn't seem to consciously realize that she had it, she just radiated it and then reacted to the effects that it had on people around her. Throughout the afternoon, she displayed so much playful charm that by the time evening rolled around, she and a group of girls had decided to stay late and hang around together.

Zubaida's English was good enough for her to muddle through conversations without any help now, and it was such a thrill for Rebecca to watch this child, who ten months earlier had no idea of what America or its people were like. Once dusk settled in and obscured Zubaida's scars, it became impossible to tell her from the other girls running and jumping around the yard.

It seemed like a miracle, all on its own, separate and aside from the magical restorations that Peter had been performing over the months, that a child so monstrously injured and lost to the world should now be playing tag in a backyard in Texas with a bunch of American girls at a spring evening picnic.

Two nights later, they stopped in East Texas to spend the night with another old friend. Zubaida romped around during their visit to a wildlife preserve, marveling at the unfamiliar animals and abandoning herself to the day. She had a good time posing in front of a fenced camel while repeatedly insisting to Rebecca that there is nothing that hits the spot like a good camel sandwich. Rebecca ended the day without knowing whether she was making that up or not. Photographs of the afternoon show Zubaida mugging and posing for the camera without any shyness or inhibition. The wounded puppy aura that she projected a few months earlier was nowhere to be seen.

The final two nights were spent in Austin, capital since Texas's statehood in 1846. It put Zubaida smack in the middle of the American Old West, a distant past for the United States, but one that happened long after the ramparts of Zubaida's home village of Farah were already melted by age.

Before she met Rebecca's mother, Zubaida tried to listen to Rebecca's explanation of her family history, but the details were overwhelming. Nothing in her background knowledge of what it means to be part of a family could have prepared her for stories like the ones Rebecca told her, or the stories that so many of her classmates at school had to tell about their own situations at home. She understood the words, but the pictures that they formed were things from an alien world. Rebecca told her all about how she and her brother grew up without a father, and with a mother who went out into the world to work every day and who was able to carry the little family on her shoulders alone, without being reduced to begging or to a forced marriage.

She could only listen and then shrug off such stories. People might as well have been talking to her about the secret lives of cats and dogs, cute little tales that had nothing to do with her, beyond presenting some future topic of idle conversation about the way that people do things in America.

But when she listened to Rebecca describe her own way of creating a sec-

ondary family around herself with her teachers and her fellow students by being actively involved in all sorts of social activities, Zubaida felt the zing of familiarity. She had already experienced enough of what daily schooling was like
to be able to picture how she would approach her life if she could stay in
school, year after year. She knew that if she could, she would also replace some
of the attention that her overtaxed parents often couldn't give her with the
comfort and support of a circle of friends and a full-time school environment.
Rebecca had told her how she was even allowed to work while she was still in
school, to earn extra money. In her spare time, she used to run off and do extra
sports and social activities.

Zubaida tried to imagine what it could be like, for a girl still in high school
to have so much freedom—to walk the streets alone without being called a
whore and to earn her own money, which she could spend as she wanted. That
was a form of wealth that a personality like hers could understand. It was petty,
day-to-day freedom received as an embarrassment of riches. She had to
wonder—how does a girl handle the constant barrage of choices all day long?
And how does a woman raise children alone and still have a good job with dignity and never have to beg for anything?

How much does a woman have to know, to be able to do that?

Once Rebecca's mother arrived and Zubaida had the chance to be around
her for a while, she began to get a sense of where some of Rebecca's strength
came from. This woman, who had worked all of her life and raised her children
alone, spoke with quiet assurance and a gentle Southern manner that contrasted with the straight posture with which she carried her somewhat delicate
frame.

To Zubaida, she was otherwise like most other American adults that she
had met so far; her conversation was the same sort of pleasant adult stuff that
Zubaida was learning to handle by rote. But it was confusing; Rebecca's
mother appeared poised and healthy and was obviously an active person. How
could that be, given her life as a sole provider? And she certainly looked far
younger than any of the woman from Zubaida's village who were mothers of
grown women. How could she be so strong and healthy after a life alone?

And Peter's mother, Sandy—she looked young enough to be his older sister, even though her family was broken, too. So, were broken families the rea-

son that many of the women in America look so young and healthy? Was this why Peter's and Rebecca's parents look as if their legs are strong and their backs are not hurting? Most of all, did all of this mean that if Zubaida stayed in school after she went back home, so that she got a usable education to carry with her into adult life, that she would have to break her family into little pieces in order to be happy and healthy and strong?

Was that some kind of hidden secret behind American success?

She hated the way that it made her feel, to even think about watching her family break up into little groups and move away to different parts of the country, while everybody then goes on through life practically alone. To consider, even for a moment, what it would mean to live as a single entity in this world filled her with a sense of dread, the same kind of dread that used to hit her in the stomach back at home, when she bent over to peer down into a deep desert well.

Toward the end of the trip, Rebecca noticed that Zubaida was becoming withdrawn and moody. She tried to get her to talk about it, but Zubaida wasn't in enough pain to make it worth the risk of exposing her vulnerabilities.

14 ❧

The uncertainty about how to react to overall daily life in America followed Zubaida home. It didn't throw her emotions into overdrive the way that such things used to do, however. Now with her appearance nearly restored and with the effects of the medication and the therapy sessions, the grip of her inner torments no longer had claws. She let the conflicts run through her thoughts and sorted through them before deciding whether to react or ignore them. The process took up a lot of her energy and didn't leave her feeling sociable, but she was able to keep it to herself, most of the time, and to handle the worst of it when she was alone.

Life in America was easiest when she took it all as an elaborate form of play and adapted to the dominant rules of the play as quickly as possible. If she didn't focus on Peter's overall goals for her surgeries, and if she ignored the big picture questions and simply concentrated on playing out each moment of this American pageant as well as she could, then she could feel the relaxation that came with moving in harmony to the social expectations of those around her. The game did nothing to make her larger fears and anxieties go away, but it distracted her attention well enough that she could ignore those feelings and keep them packed away, out of sight and out of mind, while she tried her best to imitate behavior that met with expectations of the Others.

But did that word feel right, anymore? The "Others," as she had been taught about them, were corrupt people. They might not be corrupt like the Taliban, but they were just as dangerous. The Taliban were corrupt because they were so sure of their ideas of truth and decency that they didn't care if they abandoned both and used violence to enforce their rule. But the Others were corrupt because they are so sure that truth and decency didn't matter that they seldom bother to use violence to make people cooperate. Instead, lacking respect for life, they love to destroy with temptation.

America was supposed to be full of the Others, if not the very Land of the Others itself. But Zubaida hadn't met any of the Others, yet. She had already recognized that therefore, there had to be least *one other group* besides her people and the Others. Whoever they were, she still didn't know what to call them. She had no way to even describe or define them.

The trip to Texas sharpened Zubaida's dilemma; there were so many kind and friendly people. How was that possible? And with her English developing enough that she could participate in conversations and understand most of what was said, the people she met now seemed even less foreign to her. Although their lives were greatly different from hers, in terms of the available physical comforts, her lifetime of living as a part of an extended family made it easy and natural for her to recognize warmth and hospitality and to react well to it. The very core values of her own culture, far older than any form of religious control, had survived long enough to be handed down over the centuries, for no other reason than that they fit human survival so well: hospitality to a stranger, generosity to a friend, fidelity to one's promises. No one who showed her such clear demonstrations of those very qualities could be dismissed as an Other.

Now things were growing increasingly complex because she kept running into more of them, the not-Others, whatever they ought to be called.

When Rebecca took her to Texas, she had painted Zubaida into a tiny little corner by showing her so many who were not the Others—so that proved that it wasn't something special about Los Angeles. There were too many not-

Others to ignore any longer. She had to somehow learn to recognize them, per-haps through some trait that they all shared.

Zubaida recognized the feeling of being pushed into a corner, for different reasons. She had watched her entire village's female population struggle to ex-ist in the tiny corners of their own. All of them were either women who must serve, or, like Zubaida, girls who were expected to grow up to that existence.

The images of these women and girls had made such an impact on Zubaida that even here in America, so many thousands of miles away and in such a dif-ferent world, she could still sense them inside of herself. That old cornered feeling throbbed inside of her. Meanwhile, contradictions clashed between the world of the Others as it had been described to her, and the simple world that Peter and Rebecca were showing her each day. Each point of view battled to become the truth in her eyes.

She was doing her best to follow her father's directive and learn everything that she could while she was in America, but he had not told her what she was supposed to *do* with all of that information, other than share it with the others in the family, once she returned.

But what about after that? What happened the day after Zubaida finished telling them everything she knew about life in America and everything she knew about reading and writing? What was she supposed to do, then—go find a corner to occupy and watch it slowly grow smaller and smaller while the years pass?

Her loyalty to her family and to the familiarity of her old life was solid in-side of her. Homesickness was a constant nagging feeling in the back of her mind and the pit of her stomach. But as the time to return back home began to close in on her, the question of what she was returning to was becoming diffi-cult to ignore. Just because she was a master of maintaining a nonchalant atti-tude even when confronted with amazing things, she was only human, an eleven-year-old girl. The opportunity to go shopping with a bunch of girl-friends in a mall conveyed messages far more potent than simple challenges about greed and the worship of material things. These messages were far more ominous in terms of their capacity to affect her.

This kind of experience taught her how to exercise personal choice, how to consider her own style of dress, and how to devise her own way of presenting her personality to the world, instead of hiding it under veils. Were these the corrupting forces that the Taliban clerics railed against? Because they didn't make Zubaida feel corrupted; they made her feel stronger.

Where was she supposed to put that strength, once she brought it back home with her? What would her family think about that? What could they possibly expect from her?

She certainly couldn't see any way to leave it here, and since everybody kept assuring her that she was going to be allowed to go home, where could she hide her education back in her homeland? Where could she hide her cultural awakening and her sharpened personality and her personal strength?

Was there any veil thick enough to keep all of that hidden from disapproving eyes whenever she was out in public? At home, were there walls thick enough to restrain her curiosity?

Her father had asked her to become someone that her own world didn't know how to understand and accept. On the other hand, Peter and Rebecca were showing her a life that she wasn't going to be allowed to live with them in America. It was as if she had become some kind of a ball, and now everyone was taking turns at batting her this way and that, without anybody saying a word to her about where she was supposed to eventually land.

⚜ ⚜

Kerrie Benson spent the first two weeks of May watching Zubaida slowly withdraw into long silences. She still participated in classroom work, but she was beginning to have daily spats with various classmates. They were always minor issues, things that were quickly resolved, things that any other girl might suddenly find to be of concern. The difference with Zubaida was that she was having more of those moments and they were getting in her way at school.

When she and her best friend Emily got into a spat, Benson finally took Zubaida aside and quietly told her that she had been noticing some changes in her behavior. This argument with Emily was causing Benson to wonder: Was something going on that she should know about?

At first Zubaida gave her the standard look-away-and-clam-up routine, but when Benson asked when her next surgery was taking place, Zubaida suddenly looked as if she were about to burst into tears. Then all her concerns burst out of her like a flash desert sandstorm. Yes, her final operation was coming up in a couple of days, on Friday, May 16.

Even though it was the last one, she dreaded the hospital and the anesthesia. Most of all she dreaded another recovery. And this time, she knew that after the recovery period, she would be returning back home to Afghanistan. She missed her family and wanted to be back with them, but she also couldn't imagine what sort of a life she was returning to, now.

Or perhaps she could imagine it all too well. It struck Benson that Zubaida didn't say a word about having any problems with the idea of leaving behind her American comforts. She accepted those things as part of this whole experience, but also as unique to this part of her life; she didn't appear to have any concerns at all over leaving material wealth behind.

The things that were bothering her went deeper than that, and presented Benson with a dilemma that she could neither fix nor teach Zubaida how to resolve on her own. Not even Zubaida's dread of yet another surgery or her relief at having her health restored or even her enjoyment of school and friends was enough of a distraction to keep her from being haunted by the question—whatever was going to happen after this final surgery and the final recovery period?

Peter and Rebecca had assured her that she could stay long enough to finish out the school year, since they saw it as an important milestone for her to add in with the entire experience of being in America. It only extended her stay a couple of extra weeks, and her father had also agreed to let her finish the school year with the rest of the class. But she also had to wonder whether her last day in that elementary school would be her last day of schooling in this life.

Kerrie Benson could only respond to Zubaida by reminding her of her strong inner qualities, which had frequently impressed Benson. She pointed out that whatever direction Zubaida's life took, those same qualities would ultimately determine how well she adapted to whatever new challenges were going to confront her back at home.

Zubaida nodded, saying that she understood. But as usual, she kept most of everything masked with indifference until she could go off someplace by herself and try to figure things out.

There wasn't going to be a lot of time alone for that. The surgery was coming up two days later, when Dad/Peter/Doctor Grossman would change her body, one more time.

※ ※

For this final surgery, Peter Grossman had to again project his imagination into the future—not only to set the healing process in motion in the best way, but also to choose the particular adjustments to Zubaida's remaining scars so that she would retain maximum function over time, even if she was unable to receive the periodic adjustments that she would get if she could stay in America. His work had to push her ability to absorb so much surgery within a compacted time against the possibility that this might be the last effective surgical intervention that she would have, or at least until she was old enough to travel on her own and to make her own decisions—if that day was ever to come.

Once his team had her prepped for surgery and placed under anesthesia, he began the first of the day's four procedures. The main task of the day was to give back as much range of motion as possible to the heavily scarred areas beneath her left arm. He used two large Z-plasty cuts to open the areas of skin contracture, then refolded the skin flaps to allow the flesh a maximum capacity for stretching. He rearranged the tissue in layers, stitching the deeper muscle layer first, then stitching the skin covering again. The length, depth, and angle of each cut were vital to success of the operation, and would control how much motion that the remaining scars would allow her to have.

The next three procedures consisted of several dozen injections of a dilute steroid solution into the swollen areas of scarring on her torso, on her left arm and shoulder, and across her face. These were the final steroid treatments that he would be able to administer to her scars, boosting the process of smoothing them out. This final adjustment to her new suit of skin consisted of sixty separate injections to her body and face.

A couple of hours later, the work was done and Zubaida was transferred to the recovery room. Peter planned to bring her home as soon as possible this time, knowing that her morale would be higher in a safe home situation.

And with that, his official job came to an end.

He was finished, a year and a half after first being contacted by his brother-in-law and told all about an Afghan girl, burned beyond recognition, whom a bunch of soldiers and army doctors wanted to help out. He had performed the miracle of restoration that they had sought from him, and which he promised both to her father and to her. Video and still cameras had thoroughly documented the process of restoration, and future medical students or doctors would have it available as a reference case if they found themselves presented with a similar disaster.

Ordinarily, there wouldn't be much left for him to do. Check with his assistant of many years, Stephanie Osadchey—who began working at the Grossman Burn Center back when it was run just by Peter's father—and make sure the record keeping on the case was up to date. Then, after a few follow-up visits to check on the patient's healing, ordinarily, the case would be over.

Now, however, the last surgery meant that he was finally going to shift from being Dr. Peter—who repeatedly carved on Zubaida as if he were whittling wood, each time leaving her bandaged and sore—to just being Dad. Then he could focus on doing whatever he could to help the girl who had become his surrogate daughter to begin getting ready to make the transition out of her temporary American home, back to an environment that had utterly changed while she was gone. With the fall of the Taliban rulers, there was talk about new levels of freedom for women, perhaps even access to schools. But there was also chaos among the local warlords throughout the country, so that existence was still carried out on a very provisional day-by-day basis.

Peter knew that when it came to helping Zubaida prepare to face that world, so much of what was going on lay beyond the control of any individual. The best thing that he and Rebecca could do was to continually impress upon her how close to her that they had come to feel. They made it clear that they were determined to stay in touch with her after she returned home.

Zubaida lay half awake in the recovery room, balanced on the line between waking and sleeping. Her thoughts also balanced themselves; half of her awareness realized that she was coming out of anesthesia after another surgery. That part knew the score well by now, and was waiting for the first pain to hit. But the other half of her was still fading in and out of the place that dreams and nightmares come from, borne along on a flood of distorted images.

The half of her who knew that she was in the hospital and had a fair idea of what had happened felt completely cut off from the half of her who still wandered in a dream state. In dreams, she looked for herself and couldn't find anything. Who was she, anyway? She had been Zubaida as she knew herself to be, then the fire dunked her in hell for months and brought her back out melted like candle wax. Who was she then, when strangers stared and the cruel ones laughed?

Who was it that her father fought so hard and so long to find help for? Was that Zubaida? Was Zubaida that monstrous piece of beggar bait, drawing coins from sympathetic palms in the marketplace? If so, then Zubaida was gone, now.

But this person that Peter carved back out of her melted flesh, was that Zubaida? Because as that Zubaida emerged, over time, she also allowed herself to be transformed by the Americans and their lives and their friendship. Her friends at school became a partial reflection of her, as had her wide range of experiences in this place. She had been forming an American version of herself, one who loved playful mischief and who delighted in having little adventures with friends in public places. That Zubaida also was deeply impressed with the kind of freedom that women have in America, and with the kind of personal power that they can casually employ, practically everywhere they go.

She formed her rapport with the other girls at school by rapidly developing an Americanized persona that they found easy to accept. When she was in her most American mode, she tried not to think of her family or her home village, because she could sense how odd her behavior would look to them. She knew that her father would be alarmed at the changes in her. But when her American girl act became so natural to her that it didn't feel like an act anymore, then was that the Zubaida that she was, now?

Whatever was supposed to happen to the American side of Zubaida after she returned to Afghanistan? If she hung on to it, would she be seen as corrupted by her journey? Or if she tried to hide it, could she keep it under the veil forever? She was a caged bird who had tasted freedom over the treetops, and who was now expected to meekly fly back into her cage and voluntarily close the door on herself.

But then there was her family, and her ache for them. There was her hunger for the warm and familiar sense of sitting around the house with everyone after dinnertime and listening to their conversations buzzing around her ears until the sounds lulled her into sleep. Even the firm feel of the sleeping pallet was an old and welcome embrace. The fine beds at Peter and Rebecca's house might be far more comfortable once people get used to them, but they could never have the comfort of being associated with a lifetime of experience at the way a familiar sleeping surface feels. At home, when she curled up on the folded blankets, the familiarity of the sensations did more to comfort her than the most expensive mattress in the biggest American home.

That small and personal level of familiarity was the thing that called out to her with the most compelling voice. The smell of her mother's hearth, the feel of her native clothing, the sound of her family's voices, all such memories filled her with a homesick ache that sometimes nearly bent her over. A million tiny memories of such things were all a part of who she was, who she had always been.

But such things came from the memory of a girl who had never fit the profile of a docile Middle Eastern girl in the first place. Now, with her eyes open to countless possibilities that she could not have dreamed of a year earlier, how was she supposed to be able to confine herself to that tiny little corner of the room that she would be expected to occupy in her parents' home? Where was she supposed to exist after she was married off to some man who might or might not decide that her tiny corner of *his* house should be even smaller than it was in her parents' home?

The questions swirled inside of her until she was so dizzy that the bed seemed to spin. The part of her that knew where she was realized that the aftermath of anesthesia usually left her dizzy and nauseated until the chemicals cleared out of her body, but the part of her that was still lost to dreams and nightmares continued following behind the characters that were floating through her brain. Some of the characters represented family members, fellow villagers, and the glaring Taliban enforcers. Others reflected her recent experiences with images of Peter and Rebecca and the burn center staff, friends at school, her teacher. But every one of the rest of her dream characters was a variation of herself and all of them were trying to imitate the real Zubaida.

She was eager to see what they would find, so that maybe then she would know which Zubaida she was supposed to be, after she finished waking up and went back to Peter and Rebecca's to recover.

And which Zubaida she should be once she returned to school for the last weeks of the term.

And which Zubaida she should be when she returned again to her side of the world.

15 🌿

By the time that the maximum restorative effects of Zubaida's many surgeries started to show, the little fits and starts of publicity that previously ran through various news media turned into a steady stream. Quickly, a storm of media interest came to dominate Rebecca Grossman's days. Finally the phone/fax/e-mail queries overwhelmed her. Before long, she and Peter had to stop taking any media calls at all. They sat down to sift through the offers that had already come in.

The first thing to consider was the potential impact that media exposure might have on Zubaida. Had her self-esteem been bolstered well enough that she could enjoy such attention, or would she just find the scrutiny intimidating?

They decided to test the water by allowing *Los Angeles Times* reporter Steve Lopez to do a piece with the family, since there was no stress on Zubaida in a newspaper article. She seemed happy enough about the little interview, and an American newspaper wasn't of much concern to her. Beyond that, there was one offer, though, that seemed like a safe way to start with something where she would actually participate, but would still be easy on her. They could postpone deciding about the other requests until after they saw how she reacted to this one.

So they accepted an offer from a Los Angeles radio station that broadcasts in Farsi and has a large immigrant audience. They invited Zubaida to come in for a morning show interview. It seemed like a perfect setup; she and Rebecca would be together the whole time, sitting at a table across from the radio show host, and Zubaida would be wearing a headset and answering call-in questions in her own language from the listening audience.

Zubaida not only agreed, but showed real interest in the idea of talking to a lot of people over a telephone at a radio station. She was so intrigued by the opportunity that once Rebecca escorted her into the station and everyone gave her a few minutes to get oriented, she answered all of the host's initial interview questions without any apparent difficulty.

Rebecca couldn't follow the exact conversation, but she delighted in seeing how Zubaida came to life at the opportunity to tell her story in her own words. She could interpret Zubaida's voice, body language, and gestures well enough to follow along while Zubaida told the listeners all about dancing her way into the fire, and about the nightmare months, and about her present-day amazement at this second new life.

For Rebecca, the indelible image of that day was the sight of Zubaida perched happily next to the large radio mike with her head engulfed in the earphones, answering the first call with the cheery words, "Hello, Zubaida here!" and then glancing over at Rebecca to raise her eyebrows and flash her a grin before turning back to the microphone and taking the call.

For the next hour, Zubaida spoke without hesitation to the call-in audience. Rebecca visualized this girl's life in the mud-brick ruins, followed by only a few brief months in America—much of which were spent in the hospital or in recovery—and then she tried to grasp the enormity of the cultural adjustment that she was seeing. She didn't have to understand the process to be elated at witnessing this moment of glory for the little girl who called her Mom.

So she and Peter decided to take another step, and allowed local TV reporter Linda Alvarez to do a feature piece on their little family. All Zubaida had to do was to sit down for a brief interview with Alvarez, and then let the cameras follow her around for a while. Once again, she took to the whole experience. By this point it was plain that there was something appealing to Zubaida in this kind of attention. Instead of being intimidated, she clearly regarded all of it as an adventure. Peter and Rebecca watched her adapt to these media situations, minute by minute. She blossomed under the attention as if the spotlights invigorated her, like strong sunshine.

That left them wide open for a trip to Chicago and then to New York, as a threesome. They did a brief TV appearance in Chicago, although Zubaida didn't have a chance to get warmed up before the segment moved on. She did, however, very much like the long black limousine that took them to and from the studio. The concept of having free fruit and soft drinks available from the moment that you step into a car seemed like a fine idea to her.

She stood up to the intensity of downtown Chicago at rush hour while the trio posed for pictures beneath the skyscrapers. While she didn't like the noise any better than Peter or Rebecca did, she didn't shrink away from it either, and walked along happily between them.

She showed the same casual acceptance of big city environment when they reached New York City, and happily posed for pictures on the streets in Manhattan.

She was curious, however, as to why the limousine sent by the TV studio in Manhattan was not as long as the car they got in Chicago.

※ ※

On a number of nights, Peter and Rebecca sat up late talking over what they should do about Zubaida. Her impending departure was a giant weight hanging over them. They were a married couple hoping for a child of their own, and in many ways it was as if Zubaida was a strange fulfillment of that desire. As the day of her leaving approached, they finally began asking themselves one central question: *How can we send her back to that?*

Peter and Rebecca now faced the dilemma of many dedicated foster parents. The problem, of course, was that Zubaida was her parents' child. Questions of life and livelihood or of health and safety or of education and possibility had to take a backseat to the simple fact that Zubaida was the daughter of another man and woman. So long as she desired to return home and her parents were actively interested in having her come back, the only decent thing that Peter and Rebecca could do was to gracefully let her go. The pain of separation was only an unfortunate side effect of the yearlong experiment.

Zubaida often talked of her family, about missing them. Once she abandoned the fantasy of having Peter and Rebecca come back to Afghanistan to live next door, she was able to accept that their lives and their families were in America, just as hers were in Afghanistan. She knew that to return to her own people was to leave Peter and Rebecca, to leave her American friends, her school, and perhaps never to attend a formal school again. But she needed to go. Peter and Rebecca both saw that in her. She needed to continue to feel herself as a part of the Hasan family and of their extended family as well. That feeling of wholeness was worth more to her than any material temptation that her life in American had to offer. While it was plain to both of them that Zubaida returned their feelings of love, and that she had bonded with them as much as they had with her, they also saw the animation in her features when she talked about her family. It wasn't just that she missed them in a general way; she worried about how they were, without her. She seemed to feel a strong need to be back with them once again as a functioning member of the family. She needed to be needed. Every time that Peter and Rebecca talked about Zubaida's future, they had to face the blunt truth: *She had been like a daughter, but all along, she was another family's child.*

Zubaida knew that as long as she stayed on this side of the looking glass, everything made sense. She seemed to be pulled in two directions when she actually tried to compare her need to feel her mother's embrace and her father's warmth with the realization of the tiny space waiting for her. It wasn't that she didn't know how she was going to live in that tiny space—for her that was second nature. There were plenty of images stored in her memory of other females doing just that.

Not one of them knew what she knew of the world, of course. Not one of them ever saw anything like the things she had seen already in her short life. None of them ever felt how it is to interact with the world as she had done.

For women she had already known in Afghanistan, their small corner of the house was a large portion of their known world. They did not have the sense of possibility that had been awakened in Zubaida. They were not tormented by discontent when hope brushed up against reality.

She was only able to continue learning in America and to remain involved with her friends by ignoring the sizable difference between her life in California and the life she would be expected to live at home. But eventually, the day of departure began to haunt her. She longed to feel herself as a snug fit inside of her original family, but returning to Afghanistan brought its own bundle of concerns.

Zubaida participated in the school's year-end ceremony with her classmates, and Peter and Rebecca threw a big backyard farewell party for her and her friends from school. Home videos from that day show a bunch of girls playing happily together, with Zubaida holding her own among all of them. The kids also had two huge boxes filled with presents that they collected at school to send back to the other children in Zubaida's family. The task fell to Rebecca of seeing to it that the articles actually arrived halfway around the world, to a town with no mail service.

Pictures from that day are also mute testimony to Zubaida's spirit as well as of the acceptance and openness of the other kids. Her classmates had been given a language of tolerance and support to use with this strange girl. Teacher Kerrie Benson, with the help of the class parents, used it to find a familiar and accepting way for the students to look at her, while Zubaida's drive to be an active part of a group carried her into the good graces of the others.

Peter filled his off-hours in going over logistics with Rebecca, setting up Zubaida's return to her family. The State Department offered to arrange for an escort to accompany her back home, but Peter determined that after coming so far with her on this journey, he would finish it with her as well. By this time, the NGO that helped to bring Zubaida out of Afghanistan had moved on to other cases, so Peter and Rebecca took on all of the planning necessary for Zubaida's return themselves.

So far, Peter had taken the enormous risk of insisting that his father agree to expose their practice to the kind of scrutiny and criticism that was virtually guaranteed if anything unexpected went wrong during her time here. Then, with the surgeries well under way and the medical risk finally shrinking, he and Rebecca took her into their home and spread the risk to their personal lives. No doubt they would have come under attack if any sort of major accident had befallen Zubaida while she was under their care, or if she had been interested in making good on her threats to harm herself.

Over the course of a year, they ran that gauntlet with nothing worse than day-to-day difficulties. Now there was one more risk that Peter felt he had to take, and that was to personally escort her home to hand her over to the parents who had entrusted her into his care and eventually into his home. The trip actually presented a series of risks, not the least of which was the simple fact that Afghanistan was still a contested country dominated by Muslims, some of whom were extreme in their fundamentalism and in their hatred of all things Jewish.

So of course they would love to meet a man on their home turf with the last name of Grossman.

But he needed to look Zubaida's mother and father in the eyes while he gave them back their child, so that they could see for themselves that Zubaida had never been without care and protection. He and Rebecca hadn't intended to become surrogate parents at the outset, but it was as if events were designed to push them into it. Now with the bond between them and Zubaida as strong as it was, they wanted to offer a clear gesture to the Hasan family that they hoped Zubaida would always be a part of their lives, and that they had no intention of abandoning her just because they were returning her to her homeland.

If Peter and Rebecca could impress that message deeply enough upon her parents, perhaps it would cause them to use extra care in how they handled this next phase of Zubaida's life. Now that the Taliban were gone from power, schooling was legal for girls again, provided that the parents had the will to secure their education. Perhaps if the Hasans were going to be interested in keeping up the relationship with their generous American friends, they would think carefully before allowing Zubaida's continuing education to fail, and especially before allowing her to be traded off to a husband.

Since Peter was dealing with a set of parents with whom he shared no common language, he felt certain that the strongest message he could give them was his own presence, when he and Zubaida stepped off the plane back in her country. He got a message to Mohammed during Mohammed's last scheduled call from the embassy phone, telling him to take his wife to the closest city of Herat, where Peter would arrange for them to pick up tickets to fly to Kabul and meet them. There, Peter would leave Zubaida with her family, who would fly back to Herat together and then ride in a hired car for the seven-hour trip back to their home.

Rebecca would have been glad to endure the long trip with both of them, but she wasn't supposed to be flying, at that time. After years of disappointment in their quest to have a baby—and after discovering a small taste of the joy and burden of parenthood through Zubaida's unexpected presence in their lives—Rebecca had just learned that she was pregnant.

On June 24, three days before their departure, Peter and Rebecca allowed a camera crew from ABC's *Primetime Thursday* to move into their home. The crew had also arranged to accompany them on the trip and film the highlights for their show.

Zubaida had become so indifferent to camera by that point that she ignored the crew's presence most of the time, as if all the commotion was just part of life in America. If they wanted to interview her, she was usually willing to talk, unless they caught her in a bad mood. After she talked to them, she went back to whatever she was doing and ignored them again.

Peter and Rebecca both surprised themselves with the impact that having to release this girl and send her away was having on both of them, and they could do little more than hope for the best. After the appearances on national television, the burn center's Web site had been flooded with hundreds of small donations from individuals who were moved by Zubaida's story. Peter and Rebecca immediately used the money to establish a fund that could help pay for her education in Afghanistan, or someday bring her back to the United States if she needed more medical treatment. But they still had no clear idea of how to actually get that money into her hands. An aggressive black market and the country's chaotic state made money transfers difficult. And with no mail delivery to the village of Farah, and cash being the only usable medium of exchange, they were left with the prospect of trying to send funds halfway around the world into a war-torn country that was overrun by warlords and hungry people. The idea of dispatching a messenger cross-country to deliver a bag of cash to the Hasan family was absurd, and even once the funds could be delivered to them, how could anyone in America guarantee that the money would be used to further Zubaida's education and not some other purpose?

And so there was nothing else to do but for Peter to go over to the other side of the planet, so that Mohammed Hasan would know by Peter's very presence that he had come just to look him in the eyes.

Two days before leaving, Zubaida had to say good-bye to her best friend Emily, whose family was moving out of the state. She openly wept when it was time for Emily to get back into her mother's car, and the two girls hugged like sisters being torn apart. Zubaida's ability to present an extroverted personality despite her scars and injuries had served as a beacon leading Emily away from her own self-consciousness about the scar on her forehead. No matter what sort of self-doubts that Emily might suffer in the future, she would never have to wonder whether having a visible scar was enough to ruin her social life or prevent her from being accepted. Adults could speak encouraging words all day long, but Zubaida actually personified that lesson right in front of Emily's eyes throughout the course of the school year.

Zubaida grieved for their parting as she would for any beloved member of her clan. She hated to think of life without Emily. Now the reality of leaving hit home with her, and there was no way to ignore it. Her feelings were already in turmoil over the prospect of losing Peter and Rebecca.

Even if they weren't her real mom and dad, they were at least a mother and father figure inside of her clan of loved ones. In similar ways, so were her friends from school, and Peter's and Rebecca's parents, and even the familiar and attentive staff at the hospital. They were her American clan, and Zubaida could no more leave them behind without feeling the pain of it than she was able to leave her own family behind while she was in America. Each member of her American clan was represented by a tiny image in her memory, and each helped to form her concept of herself in ways that nobody could have predicted before it all began.

It seemed to Zubaida as if these Americans had some kind of Pashtunwali of their own, even though she knew that the members of her American clan came from different religions and that several were born in far-off countries. The Americans nevertheless seemed to share some common ideal that guided them, similar to the way that her culture guided its people with teachings based on ancient customs of the desert tribes.

And for all of those reasons, she reached her last day in America without ever having met any of the Others, and having no idea how she could explain that to the villagers back at home.

16 🌿

When Rebecca drove Peter and Zubaida to the Los Angeles Airport and the three huddled together inside the terminal for a quiet good-bye, Zubaida couldn't have known how close her reactions were to Rebecca's own. Even though Rebecca couldn't keep the tears out of her eyes while they all hugged, she held herself to a few sniffles and a catch in the throat. Neither of these two females was willing to come off to the world as sentimental, and both avoided maudlin behavior. But soon afterward, Zubaida was sitting at her window seat, alone with her feelings. While the plane took off and she watched the ground fall away, Rebecca was making the long drive home from the airport, alone with hers, moving north along the miles of Pacific beach line and back to their beautiful empty house in Hidden Hills.

When Rebecca arrived back home after dropping Peter and Zubaida at the airport, she found that no amount of focusing on all of the good that had been accomplished during that past year was enough to lift her heavy sadness. The triumph that Zubaida had made of her entire stay in America was real cause for joy, but the sharp sting of loss remained. She also felt her sense of isolation being sharpened by her fears for Peter's safety in the Middle East. He was traveling to Afghanistan on a purely humanitarian mission, but that often failed to dissuade zealous assailants. Peter was going to a land where Jews are openly hated.

It took nineteen hours for Peter and Zubaida to fly from California to Dubai, in the United Arab Emirates, and Zubaida repeatedly turned to Peter and said that she was going to miss Rebecca very much. She didn't elaborate, but after being quiet for a while, she would come back around to remarking again on how much she was going to miss Rebecca.

In the oil-rich architectural wonderland of Dubai, the pair stopped over just long enough to go have dinner in town, then they returned to their hotel for a short night before returning to the airport early the next morning. After the three-hour flight to Afghanistan's capital city of Kabul, they would find a place to stay near the airport and meet with Zubaida's mother and father there at last.

It was on that last leg of the trip that Peter found his own emotional weight beginning to feel heavy. The tightness in his throat grabbed him the hardest when he realized that he had been wondering whether he would be relieved to finish his mission with Zubaida, because of how difficult and unpredictable she could sometimes be. But now as their time together drew to an end, he was hit by the full force of the strong bonds between them.

They landed at the Kabul International Airport to find that the sole terminal was a shabby, two-story building with a six-story control tower. The entire place had been heavily damaged during the fighting to repel the Taliban forces, who made Kabul one of their last strongholds. Now, compared to the fresh-built opulence of Dubai, Kabul was the bombed-out ugly sister. Cracks and potholes dotted the tarmac. Ceiling tiles were missing inside the terminal building and signs of disrepair were all around.

The differences between this place and the place that they left earlier that morning were so dramatic that Peter had the perception of having stepped back a few decades in time. It was, he realized, the first level of the time travel process that Zubaida was about to undergo once she returned, progressing backward while she and her parents traveled out and away from the small city and back toward the isolation of a remote desert village whose physical walls and cultural ways were all built upon the silent remains left behind by centuries of anonymous generations.

Peter was relieved when they were greeted inside the fractured terminal by a small team headed up by John Oerum of the United Nations, who would help them get through the chaotic baggage claim process. The airport's single baggage carousel was out of order, so a mob quickly formed at the mouth of the baggage chute, where everything landed in a heap that the passengers had to straighten out themselves. Peter chose to hire one of the swarm of men who were there peddling freelance services, then let them battle the crowd. At least they could holler back and forth in a shared language.

As soon as the bags were retrieved from the dead carousel and Peter picked up his first suitcase, another crowd of men began shouting for his attention, pushing each other back and forth for the chance to carry it for him. The entire team was dogged by a mob of would-be helpers all the way out of the airport. Despite Peter Grossman's youthful appearance and athletic build, these men were determined to do anything short of breathing for him, in return for a few coins. If anyone in the party had indicated that they wanted to ride out to the taxi stand, two or three of the men would have gladly tossed them into the nearest chair and carried it overhead all the way to the curb.

This aspect of the instant change from the opulence of oil-rich Dubai in the United Arab Emirates to the overwhelming poverty in the capital city of Afghanistan hit like a thunderbolt. The fact that they were Westerners, people known to have money in their pockets, moving among throngs of those who did not, made them live bait for anyone desperate for opportunity. In that broken place, money didn't just talk, it shrieked.

Official estimates at that time put Afghanistan's population at between twenty-five and thirty million, and most people were existing from hand to mouth with limited success. Clearly, there was no possibility that Peter and his group could go anywhere in such an environment without attracting desperate individuals.

There were men of all ages and sizes, and several racial groups in the airport throng. The one obvious thing about them was that there were no criminals or vagrants or terrorists among them. Too much time is lost in such work, for a zealot to tolerate the inactivity.

These had to be local men, surrounding Peter and his group—husbands and fathers and grandfathers, family men left to carry out hardscrabble survival struggles after the decade of war with the Soviet invaders, the years of internal anarchy, and the Taliban takeover of the country. Things had grown progressively worse for these men over the years.

As soon as Peter and the team were clear of the airport, the first landmark that he noticed was the local airplane graveyard—uncomfortably convenient in relation to the airstrip. There were too many planes and sections of wreckage lying around to count them all. The bluntness of life and death were far more apparent in this place, everywhere he looked. He and Zubaida and the rest of the group rode off into Kabul, which Zubaida found just as fascinating as Peter did. They both marveled at the contrasts. The streets were congested with European vehicles driving along in a purely random fashion among sheep, camels, water buffalo, and the shepherds guiding their herds through the city.

They immediately sought out a UN ticket office to take care of the plane tickets for Zubaida's parents, then went to secure a room and found a clean but very basic guest house that was secular enough to allow both American and Afghan guests. Then they ended the day with a meeting between Peter, Zubaida, and members of an Afghanistan-based charitable NGO that had been set up by an Afghan-American friend named Captain Daoud, to begin discussing possible options for Zubaida's future.

Peter had hoped that she would enjoy translating for him. They made a deal before they left California, that she would be his interpreter in Afghanistan since she could now communicate well in Farsi and English. She had gained experience at dealing with Farsi-speaking people during her journey because they are so much easier to find in America than speakers of her native Dari. Her Farsi skills had grown along with her English, so that when Peter first brought up the idea of her being his translator, she seemed eager for the chance.

But once inside the country, she became very clingy and nervous, refusing to speak Farsi at all. She told the people in their greeting party that she didn't remember any Farsi although Peter recalled her knowing a great deal of it a week earlier in California.

He recognized the withdrawal behavior as part of her frequent reaction to overwhelming circumstances, and felt sure that if he didn't press her about it she would even herself out on her own. So they bid good-bye to Captain Daoud and others and made their way back to the guest house, then got into their beds early for the long rest that they were both going to need, to be ready for the following day.

The next morning, they did a little touring around and sightseeing, mostly to help the time go by until her parents arrived later in the day. There were plenty of sights to distract them; newly opened schools were being held in bombed-out buildings, while commerce was being reborn inside of hundreds of large metal cargo containers—all of them had been turned into tiny shops that peddled every sort of merchandise. The makeshift storefronts lined the streets of the bazaar.

After lunch, right about the time that the distraction factor of the marketplace commotion was beginning to wear thin, it came time for Zubaida's reunion with her parents. To avoid drawing a crowd, Peter arranged for a car to take Zubaida's parents from the airport back to the guest house, where they would all meet in the private courtyard. Captain Daoud, UN officer John Oerum, and a translator were there, along with a small crew from ABC television. By the time that Mohammed and Bador Hasan arrived at the guest house and were escorted into the garden, Peter and Zubaida were already there waiting.

He noted that Zubaida was beginning to fall into her familiar state of quiet detachment in the presence of strong emotions, as the excitement and anticipation began to overwhelm her. This time, the overwhelming emotions were felt by everybody there. The moment that her parents stepped into the courtyard and Zubaida made eye contact with them, everyone fell silent. Peter watched the reaction build. At first, father and mother could only gasp in delight and disbelief at the recovery of their daughter's features and body. But then came the cries of relief and tears of joy. And those quickly gave way to open wailing by both Mohammed and Bador, while Zubaida silently embraced them and buried her face against their shoulders.

Peter found himself overwhelmed by emotion. Mohammed stepped to him and brought his hand up to his heart in thanks, then embraced him. Peter looked him in the eyes as if to say, *here she is, I have kept my promise to you.*

Then he cried along with her parents while they embraced him and poured out their joy and gratitude through the translator.

It all went on that way for another forty-five minutes or so, then everyone left Zubaida and her parents alone. Peter had rented them a room where they could go to be in private. Zubaida decided to move into their room right away. He watched while, during that first hour, she already began her metamorphosis into her Afghan identity, returning to her place as a living cog in the family machine. She took the role of responsibility in their presence, making sure that her mother had enough to drink and otherwise felt well and content. Peter stayed on at the family's request and watched while Zubaida excitedly pulled out every item in her suitcase and showed them to her parents, some of which had to be carefully explained.

While she lost herself in the excitement of having both of her parents there with her again, both giving her their full attention, Peter looked on and felt the heaviest pang of the separation blues hit him. He could see that he was no longer so important to this little girl who, only one day earlier, had been unwilling to leave his side. In that first moment, he couldn't help but feel like saying, *remember me?* But the urge passed as he realized that he was seeing a good and healthy thing; there was no other direction for her but straight ahead, and she was taking the first step with both feet.

Peter and Rebecca had been determined to see firsthand that Zubaida arrived safely and was back in her parents' care, and that she was able to embrace the next important radical change in her life. Now it was plain to see that she was home again, not just back in her home country, but back in the embrace of her family. Through all the months of Zubaida's American experience and all of her exposure to luxuries she never knew existed, she also never lost the desire to be back with them. Peter reminded himself that no matter how well she adapted to life in America, Zubaida was an Afghan. No matter how harsh her home environment might appear to Western eyes, it was the familiar reality of her life, and the scene in front of him proved that her need to be back among her family was strong.

Over the next couple of days, Peter and Mohammed had a series of meetings with the Coalition for Human Assistance, a charitable Non-Government

Organization, to discuss Zubaida's future. The reality of her school situation was that the nearest school to Farah was at least a one-hour walk in each direction. In the 110-degree heat of the desert summers and the subzero cold of the harsh Afghanistan winters, daily round-trips of that size were unrealistic. There were some funds available from Zubaida's small trust of donations, but even if they could be stretched to build a new school in her hometown, the permits would have to be sought through the Ministry of Education's bureaucracy, an unlikely priority for them at this stage in the country's war recovery. But Peter left feeling that at least the dialogue had been started, and the CHA represented a local organization with the ability to reach Mohammed in Farah, in order to help maintain follow-up for Zubaida. The big questions weren't going to get answered on this short trip, but the structure to pursue them was set in place.

On day four, everybody but Peter got ready for the flight from Kabul to Herat. Peter would say goodbye in Kabul and return to the United States, while the family would make the long drive over war-shattered roads back out to the village of Farah.

They reached the airport terminal through the chaos of street traffic just in time to hear the announcement that the flight had just been cancelled. There was nothing else to do but reset themselves emotionally and go back to the guest house for the night. For Peter, it was both a reprieve and an extension of his emotional torment. He could see that Zubaida was sad to leave him, but he also saw her high level of excitement at the prospect of going home and seeing the rest of her family. As painful as the impromptu "dress rehearsal" for the next day's departure might have been, it also allowed him to witness her final, necessary transition within her own mind while she stepped back into her family fold and her cultural world. He watched that transition play itself out right in front of him. All of her attention was riveted on them. While she kept up a stream of happy chatter, she lapsed deeper into the rhythms of the Dari language and the subdued body language of a preteen Afghan daughter. Her adaptability was only surpassed by her strength of will. *What a life she could have!* he marveled.

Or what a life might be slowly extinguished in this place.

He was now free of his formal responsibility to her, but he was also losing the control of events around her and giving up the chance to protect her. He wondered what a modest trust fund could actually achieve for this girl, inside of this environment. How could such a thing even be administered, with her isolated in that remote village on the other side of the world from him?

His best and perhaps only real hope was that Zubaida would be allowed some sort of an individual future in the world, that her education would be completed and her intelligence and personality would be further cultivated. But that was now in the hands of her father. Peter trusted that after the man made such heroic efforts to find help for her, surely he would not just raffle her off to some warlord as a curiosity piece. Such a thing would be permitted in that environment. There were sure to be those around Mohammed Hasan in the marketplace who would hiss their opinions into his unwilling ears and warn him to take a fair bid for his Scarred Miracle Daughter right away, while the public awareness of her was fresh in people's minds. She would be twelve in a few months, an accepted age for marriage to an older and established man.

The following day, July 3, was the fifth one there, and it turned out to be the last. This time their plane was ready to board as scheduled and prepared to depart on time. In the confusion of getting everyone into a van that would taxi the passengers out to the plane, everything seemed to speed up. There was barely time to say good-bye. Peter hugged Mohammed and Bador, and when it came time to hug Zubaida he felt tears welling up as he told her that he loved her. She looked him in the eye and said, "I love you too, Dad." And that was all. Zubaida spun around to join her parents and jumped into the airport van. She waved while they rode away.

He went back to the guest house feeling a Zubaida-sized void in his heart. Usually, the objectivity of the work in the operating room kept him from getting emotionally involved with a patient. In Zubaida's case there had been no holding back. Her very presence somehow compelled that sense of concern and interest in her which most people seemed to feel. Even those who had been put off by her manic emotional behavior during her worst periods of stress nevertheless acknowledged that her ability to charm was as strong as her ability to disrupt. Her absence would leave a lasting void.

Peter felt like he had no more emotions left; he was facing another heartache that he hadn't told Zubaida about. In the tense hours before leaving, he had received a phone call from Rebecca, bringing him the crushing news that their baby had been lost to a miscarriage. There would be time enough to tell Zubaida later, if she needed to know at all. For now, Peter wasn't going to tell her anything that would distract her from her reunion with her parents.

But after the Hasans were gone, Peter learned that there was no way to catch an early flight home—the next flight back to the States wouldn't leave for another two days. Not only was he prevented from being with Rebecca, but he was stranded in Kabul. His head throbbed and his stomach churned while he tried to offer Rebecca whatever consolation that he could from so far away, but there was only so much that talking could do. He just needed to be home.

Then at last on July 5, his flight arrived and, after a round of servicing, was finally ready to depart. But just before boarding, he got a call from the nearby military clinic, asking if he could take a look at a burned two-year-old boy. Peter couldn't delay this trip back to Rebecca, so the clinic arranged to rush the boy to the airport. In the final minutes before departure, he was able to examine the boy behind a makeshift curtain while curious onlookers shuffled around trying to get a peek.

He made some suggestions for treatment, offering to help them clear the bureaucratic red tape if they would contact him through his office, then raced to his plane to depart. There was no way for him to follow up with that particular patient, but he could see that it was another case where the future of the child would only be bright to the degree that somebody made it a point to find the proper help and make it happen.

Even the few days that he had spent in Kabul had shown him that the country was host to a generation of amputees and burn victims, mostly resulting from the millions of land mines planted throughout the countryside. Only the most determined and resourceful among them received any meaningful medical treatment. Against that background, the depth of determination that Mohammed and Zubaida both showed during the long months of their search for help was all the more extraordinary.

Once the plane went into its final taxi, lifted off, and began to climb, Peter felt a palpable sense of relief. He never felt personally threatened while he was in Afghanistan and had been treated with the kindness and respect for which Afghanistan's people have traditionally been known. But a strong sense of foreboding had accompanied him at every moment. While the frequent kidnapping and beheading of Westerners in the Middle East had not yet begun, he still sensed the cold emotional winds that blew in the area. He knew that they can change direction in an instant, and just that quickly, a place that was safe becomes deadly.

Zubaida had reassured Peter's mother that there was no worry about Peter's safety in her homeland, that she would take care of him, and she had. The greetings he received while they moved about the city together, whether on the open street or in the few meetings that they had with various officials, were all done with high regard. Sometimes that was because the people there already knew something of the story. Other times, it was just the reactions of people who take their cue from the Afghan girl's obvious familiarity with, and affection for, the American doctor. Thus even in situations where Peter might have been vulnerable under other conditions, the American with the Jewish name was never threatened and suffered no harm.

It was so good for him to be able to take a deep breath and let it all go, to let the plane carry him home while he rested up and tried to restore some of his energy. He needed to be with Rebecca as badly as she wanted him back at home. If desire could have fueled the plane, the flight would have landed much sooner.

❧ ❧

It had been two years since the girl that they once knew had been consumed in fire, and now she was home again after more than a year in America. The story of what had been done to restore her was enough to occupy the gossip networks of the entire region.

The local people who were old enough to have survived the decades of war were also people who had seen more than twenty years of constant raids and retaliations, beginning with being "taught a lesson" by the Soviet invaders for failing to convert to Communism, to the backbreaking "tributes" demanded by the feuding warlords, and finally to the nonstop demands of the Taliban enforcers. So far, however, even the oldest and wisest of the villagers knew nothing more about these Americans than the fact that their soldiers were currently in the region.

Out in Farah, the local people had only seen U.S. soldiers when their jeeps drove in and out of the village to deliver messages to Hasan about his daughter. All the villagers heard his stories about the kindness of the American soldiers in the ancient city of Kandahar, and of how well they conducted themselves toward Hasan and his daughter even though the residents of Farah were only common people. These American soldiers behaved like common people themselves, and they supported Hasan and his daughter out of their own soldiers' pay, for weeks at a time, before the military hospital began to help them. *How could they do that? Are all American soldiers rich?*

Beginning with those first American soldiers, then the civil affairs people, then the military doctors, then the political powers that be, the villagers heard Mohammed's story time and time again, all about how more Americans kept getting involved until the miracle was at last made plain, there for all to see, and Zubaida Hasan walked among them once again. She was whole again. The burned thing that she had once been was long gone.

One after another, the villagers got their chances to speak with Zubaida. Sometimes when they asked her questions she would ignore them, pretending that she couldn't hear anything that anyone said to her. But at other times, when the mood struck her, she would tell long stories that were very hard to believe. When she spoke out that way, it hardly mattered what she told them. She became the medium and the medium was the message. They heard her clear voice and they saw the same old spark in her eyes while she wove her story.

Even though it was impossible for them to conceive of how much her frame of reference was forever altered by her unique journey, none could fail to see that she stood up straight among them, now. She looked them directly in the eyes, even though she was still not yet twelve years of age. They looked back at her and saw that she was Zubaida Hasan returned to them, not some imposter. There was no trick.

They knew that she had come home voluntarily, too, even though she was said to have lived in American splendor. They knew that she had been alone, a single small female child in the land of the Others, and that with her parents' consent she had been held in that country with its strange, Western ways all through the year.

Nevertheless, here she was back with them. Not only was she healed and restored to a degree that looked more like the product of witchcraft than mere science and medicine, but she had survived a year among the Others and come away unharmed. Most heartening of all for the villagers—and living proof that the so-called irresistible lure of America is a myth—she was home again with her family, right there in Farah. Anyone could see that she was in good shape and all was well.

Zubaida herself had no particular message to give to the people who pressed her with their curiosity and their endless questions. She was, after all, the message itself: an "alive and well" message, able to do whatever she wanted and free to make mischief. So amid an Afghan culture that reveres generosity and heroism, when Zubaida's amazed visitors looked at her and remembered how she had been, they saw touchable evidence of the American heart.

17 🌿

Zubaida was a tiny dancer who specialized in dancing on a tightrope, now. But she moved with levels of self-assurance she had never known during all the strange days since the fire. She was filled with energy by the overflow of amazement and delight from her family and neighbors. To be among the old faces and places of her hometown made her feel happy down inside of herself, in countless little ways that no foreign country can ever offer to a guest who has left a loving home behind.

The tightrope part of her act was to keep herself within bounds of the social restrictions placed upon girls of near-marriageable age, especially among women who must serve, and to find those isolated times and places when it was safe for her to set the energy loose and let it pour through every bit of her, the way it's supposed to for a woman who must dance.

There really wasn't anyone to stop her, after a certain point. If she was out with her sisters or brothers, she could wander their area's familiar turf with far more ease than formal customs might demand. There were no Taliban enforcers now, and the village men had better things to concern themselves over than rambunctious girls, and so she could get away with all sorts of things, provided that she followed fairly close to the limits of accepted behavior.

She could break away from a walking group and hop up onto a thick mud wall and dance on the balls of her feet from one crumbling brick or stone to the next, until she leaped into the air and landed squarely on balance and then scooted back into place with the rest of them. Usually nobody tried to stop her. She realized that a dignified young Muslim woman is not expected to do such things, but most of the time those things weren't enough to prompt a dangerous reaction, and so that thin margin between what will be tolerated and what will not became the tightrope itself. She danced along its edge everywhere she went.

The elders made a real fuss over her when she first arrived, crying and shrieking with joy and disbelief. Many stared at her as if they were seeing a true miracle, utterly astounding to their eyes. She came home to the loving embrace of everyone in sight, each one eager for anything she chose to tell about her journey. This sudden diet of concentrated attention was a nectar to her, and the affirmative responses from everyone around her were strong enough to send her energy level spiraling.

All of those things fueled her tightrope dance, energizing her constant process of testing the borders without stepping too far beyond them. She was sustained so well by that self-imposed challenge that she made it through the intense homecoming period with ease, stepping back into her family and her town and her civilization.

The dancing itself was good—easier than ever, with her last scars healing well. Throughout those first days after her homecoming, she loved to surprise people with how much she had grown in the past year, as well as how well she could move, now. The reactions were so strong that it was like showing people unbelievable magic tricks. They cried out in happy disbelief. In turn, their reactions turned everyone else's attention to her, to the point that it felt like warm light shining through her, all the way inside and back out again.

It filled her so perfectly that whenever she had the opportunity to give in to the urge to move, the contentment set her free within herself. If she chose, she could shrink her spirit down to a tiny version of her body—a copy of herself, perhaps half an inch high. With her spirit comfortably seated behind her own eyes, she could let her body do the dancing. She could stare out from the huge eye-windows and watch the room swirl away around her, until everything dissolved into a musical blur.

❧ ❧

Rebecca had spent less than a year in the very sort of parental role that she craved, but she already went through the "sending her off to college" phase when she had to release Zubaida at the airport. In the days and weeks afterward, she found herself suffering the same types of withdrawal that an empty-nester feels when the last young one has left home.

She went through the stage of pacing through the house and suddenly noticing how big and empty it feels, even though the empty nest should have been years in the future. She passed by the room that she and Peter had always called the guest room before Zubaida arrived; it had become her room the moment that she filled it with her presence. It was still Zubaida's room.

But it was during those first few days at home alone, while Peter was still off in Afghanistan, that she suffered the miscarriage. At that point, the feeling of isolation and loss was overwhelming, leaving her angry and hurting. Within the space of a few days, she had bid goodbye to Zubaida without knowing if they would ever see each other again, sent her husband off to a very dangerous part of the world, and now, experienced the crushing defeat of losing her unborn child with her husband far away. There was nothing else to do but call him and deal the same blow to him. They would each have to go through the initial shock and disappointment separately before they could be together and deal with the blow as a couple.

"It's true, I'm not one to sit around and cry," she said later. "My way of handling stress is much more to work it off by throwing myself into things." There was plenty to do with all the correspondence generated by Zubaida's recent media appearances. More than just fan mail, among the correspondence were scores of small donations sent in by people who heard of her story and wanted to contribute in some way toward helping guarantee a future for her. The account for Zubaida's foundation was steadily growing, almost entirely on small donations from ordinary people all over the country. Peter would come home to find her in motion. Like Zubaida, it was the state that she preferred.

* * *

July 6 was the first day back together for Peter and Rebecca. Since it was a Sunday, at least they had that little window of time to themselves before he had to take up his work again, early on Monday morning. The day was theirs, away from everyone else now, from the public and the patients and the non-stop obligations, and they both agreed that after coming so close to parent-hood, they did not want to quit. They would try for another child as soon as possible.

After that, the days began their march through the unending tasks and ob-ligations that bordered them, played out against a backdrop of separation pains that were prone to strike without notice. They both continued referring to the guest room as "Zubaida's room." Rebecca found herself occasionally waking up with a start, fearing that she was late for getting Zubaida up and off to school. She and Peter would be walking somewhere together and they would both spot girls who, from a distance, looked just like her.

There was no longer such a thing as a simple trip to a department store; in-stead it was a place mined with those sudden pangs that stab into the chest and snag like fishhooks. A clothing display for young girls had just the right outfit for the one who was not there. An innocent visit to a restaurant produced a menu with just the right dish for the one who was not there, and still more op-portunities to mistakenly see the one who was not there at a distance, in the crowd of strangers.

Since the process of grieving can't be measured, there is little more to say than this couple had to learn their own territory as they worked through deal-ing with the loss of two children: one who became a part of the family as they got to know her, the other who began as part of the family but whom they would never know.

Peter persuaded his father to donate the satellite phone from his boat, then he had it specially adapted so that it could only call their home number. He left it with Zubaida as a way of assuring her that she would always be able to reach them. All three of them were surprised at how much the brief, static-laced conversations came to mean to them. It was also a real test of Zubaida's English, to have to express herself to them over the phone without the aid of facial expressions and hand gestures to speed them through a conversation.

* * *

Slightly more than two months later, events took another sharp turn—Rebecca learned that she was pregnant again and she and Peter excitedly began to plan once more for their first child by birth. Rebecca decided that she should be the one to tell Zubaida, since she wanted to be as careful as possible to present it to Zubaida as gaining another sibling for her, and as with any other sibling, Zubaida would not be replaced in their hearts.

When Rebecca decided the time was right and told her the news, it was at a point when she and Peter already knew that they were expecting a girl. Rebecca explained that it would be almost like a having a sister in another part of the world, that there would be just that much more of a secondary family waiting for Zubaida if the time came that she was able to return.

It was always hard to gauge Zubaida's emotions in the immediate moment. Over the long-distance line, it was even more so. She responded quietly, congratulating them in a tone of voice that might or might not have been enthusiasm. To Rebecca, it sounded like a slight extension of a voice tone that she had been noticing in Zubaida for the past couple of weeks, long before the news of their baby was a factor. She tried to get Zubaida to tell her if anything else was wrong, but Zubaida's struggle to put emotions into English, plus the crackly connection and Zubaida's tendency to minimize emotions until she had time to sit with them for a while, all combined to leave Rebecca with no idea of what Zubaida's real thoughts or feelings about having an American "sister" might be.

Perhaps, she hoped, Zubaida had just been feeling sickly over the past couple of weeks, adjusting to the change in the food, the water. Nothing more serious than that. Perhaps she was fine about the news and would even sound contented and strong again, when they spoke the following week at the arranged time.

Peter had noticed the shift in roles with Zubaida as soon as she and her parents were reunited—she immediately began her old middle child role from her days before the burn, running around taking care of them, making sure her mother had a soft place to sit, something warm to drink, explaining as much of everything that she could. It was a moment of triumph for her and she was animated by it.

She fell into the behavior automatically. Once again she was going to be indispensable to the family and not merely a drain upon them. There was no reason to hide her face anymore, neither for injury nor for shame. Then, and in the days to come, she relished her revitalized role in the family even more than they did. Even though she performed chores all day long there that were far more difficult than anything she had ever been asked to do in America, she felt as much energy in those first days after coming home as she had ever known while she was away.

In every phone call, she assured Rebecca and Peter that it was good to be home. And while she missed seeing them and missed her friends from school, she never said a word about wanting to leave her home in Afghanistan and return to California. She was a child of her clan. There was no long vacation in Wonderland that could erase that from her past, remove its power from her memories, cancel it out of her very way of seeing the world. She still thought that it would be very nice if Peter and Rebecca came to live next door to them, but she was a child of Afghanistan and despite her brief flirtation with declaring herself "an American, now" back in the United States, she was an Afghan. She made it clear that she could feel that within herself.

The problem began to appear when she danced along the tightrope, pushing the social rules for every scrap of rambunctious energy that she could get away with expressing—watching her reflection in people's reactions. The tightrope began to feel thin. What was really shrinking was her own tolerance for the limitations placed on her, back inside of a Middle Ages level of existence in the village of Farah, in the middle of Farah Province, on the high plains of Afghanistan.

There was no problem with rejoining her family; they were familiar with her outspoken personality and they adapted to her easily enough, in their way of being together. And there was no real problem with finding opportunities to dance and be musical and feel glad to be alive.

It was everything else.

The only other girls who were there as companions for her were girls who had never seen anything more sophisticated than whatever sights they spotted during quick family trips in and out of Herat. It was the closest city, seven hours away by car—when there was a car—or a few days by camel if the weather was good. Their frame of reference for conversation was so tiny by comparison to Zubaida's that she discovered that friends and neighbors, whom she loved as much as she always did in the past, nonetheless had become boring. She knew it was unacceptable for a girl in her society to feel that way toward others, that it would be considered arrogant and disrespectful toward the gifts of friendship that these people represented. She didn't doubt it.

But her eyes had seen, her ears had heard, and her lips could speak the language. She had spent a year of her life deep inside of the land of the Others, and not only lived to tell the tale, not only come home unscathed and miraculously healed, but she never even came across any of the Others. The evils of America failed to materialize, even though she was there for such a long time. What did materialize, however, and with increasing frequency during every day that she spent in America, was choice. Choices, actually.

Choice after choice after choice, everywhere she looked. One hundred different varieties of anything you can think of—and not just choices in merchandise, either, since the addiction to material things can be switched off with a simple change in attitude and expectation. The choices that tormented her were in the nature of acceptable behavior and of personal expectation. The casual everyday freedom of behavior that she enjoyed with her friends on a typical California weekend was something that she took for granted, at the time. She was so busy acting as if nothing astounded and confused her that it took all of her concentration to hide how astounded and confused she was, so that she tended not to notice how much of herself she was free to express, until she arrived back in her home village and felt the constraints slip back into place.

They were not excessive restraints, compared to other girls her age. Nobody was out to punish her for anything. But the choices were gone, those choices of behavior and most importantly, the choices available to her future. Before the fire, the future was too remote for her little girl's frame of reference. She lived from day to day with the other children of her village and tried not to think about a future that could not hope to be anything but grim. The future of a woman who must serve. Zubaida touched that future every time she felt her mother's strong grip and calloused hands.

At least, back then, she had been able to make the choice to ignore any thoughts of her future, whenever they loomed. Now even that humble choice was gone. She couldn't ignore thinking of her future because she had *learned how*. And now she was learning what a tough skill it is to un-remember.

Leftover American choices tormented her like voices from dreams. Choices that she never fully thought through and choices that she had only heard other people mention—casually, she recalled, how casually they contemplated obtaining this or that next miracle in the parade of miracles that were their lives.

Most of all, she felt tormented by the loss of the choice to spend her life helping other people in some way, doing something similar to the way that she had been helped. No one had to tell her how vital such a thing would be, how important to the world, to herself. The choice was gone now and Zubaida could feel its loss.

She tried to keep up her spirits during her phone calls to Peter and Rebecca. Her gratitude to them was so strong that she wanted to maintain the appearance of being worth all the effort. But try as she might, the energy in her voice was lower each time, her pauses were longer, she had less to talk about—there was simply less to do, to talk about in the first place.

Fall came, and her father was unable to secure some form of transportation to get her and her sisters to the nearest school, miles away. She was facing the prospect of missing another year of school.

Her English began to slip away. Since there was never anywhere to practice it, and the weekly calls were awkward and brief, the new words were beginning to leave her. Now when she paused on the phone, it wasn't because she was too shy to express a certain thought or emotion, but often just because she couldn't think of how to say what she was thinking.

It wasn't just as if she had gone back through to the other side of the looking glass; it was more like she had slipped into a many-sided looking glass world where there was not just a single alternate reality, but where there was one strange world after another. Even though this was not the land of the Others, it wasn't the familiar old homestead, either. The place hadn't changed; what she felt was the depth of the change in herself, much of which she wasn't even aware of until the walls began to feel like they were pressing inward and the heavy feeling began to pull down on her.

Now, although nothing had become completely foreign to her, nothing was truly familiar anymore, either. There was the warm familiarity of her caretaker role at home, and the family was glad enough to have her there in that way. But now when she went though the daily motions of this or that essential activity she found it strangely unsatisfying. The sense of fulfillment that she should have gained from her own sense of usefulness was barely there. She felt as if she was trying to scratch her back with a short stick—one that used to fit her long ago, before she grew so much.

When despair began to follow her, she dealt with it by becoming as small and as focused as she could. She avoided thoughts of the future. She avoided the temptation to ask herself what she was going to do with her life, now that even the rural school in Afghanistan was denied to her. She made her attention span so tiny that there was only room for one little moment, then the next moment, then the next. She went from one little task to the task after that, trying to soak whatever joy she could from each passing moment without stopping to stand up and look around. The view was too grim, and nothing in it seemed to have enough room for her.

Without the satellite phone, it would have begun to seem that somehow her entire journey in Wonderland among the Others was nothing more than some sort of dream, unreal as a desert mirage. The phone, at least, saved her from that.

She knew that Peter was wise to have the phone fixed so that it was only good for calling their phone number. With the part of herself that knew the ways of the marketplace, Zubaida saw the way that the village's struggling people eyed that wondrous thing. They might not know how much it was worth, but they knew it was more money than they had, and Mohammed Hasan owed a number of people a great deal of money, after all. The satellite phone would have walked away by now, she had no doubt, if she and her father had not been so careful to spread the news far and wide that this was a special phone, made by the people who did this thing for Zubaida, and it would only call them, nobody else. The villagers were not so desperate as to dare to steal it in spite of that rumor, so the phone stayed with her.

The calls sustained her, paltry as they were. They kept her from the fear that there was no longer anybody on earth who understood her. With Peter and Rebecca, she didn't have to retract any of herself. The principal obstacle became her failing English. Zubaida could listen to them, even without the words for complex thoughts, and she could feel the way that the very sound of their voices was meant to be greatly reassuring to her. But she found that the reassurance couldn't sink in anymore, and the voices did nothing to make her feel any safer. Every one of their soothing words was cancelled out by a growing sense that she was slowly being extinguished.

By now she had been given plenty of time for the message to sink in. There had been warnings, before, but she had paid no attention. Sometimes you can sneak by an angry Taliban bully and he won't notice you or choose you for trouble. The trick is to go on about your business as if you don't feel any danger and don't have any reason to feel danger, so that they don't smell your fear. And you never make eye contact. If you make eye contact, you fall into their realm, you invite them to deal with you instead of melting away unscathed. She had been sneaking by the warnings well enough that she managed to forget that the danger was out there. It was a sound course of action, in terms of getting through a potentially stressful situation, and it had served her well in America. It served her well enough back at home, at first, and for a while. But of course that did nothing at all to actually protect her.

Some of the warnings were so clear to her, now. She looked back at them and they screamed at her, *We were right there! How could you miss us?*

Back in America, she had seen a beautiful model of a tiny sailing ship, perfectly detailed, sails unfurled and set to run with the wind. It was captured inside of a glass bottle barely big enough to hold it. The ship was fully rigged for tacking through powerful storms on the high seas, but it would never know a drop of the water it was created to sail, or put canvas to a single puff of breeze. The beautiful sailing ship was really nothing more than a thing of curiosity, trapped inside its tiny space.

She had known her predicament back then, looking at that model ship, but until recently she managed to keep herself from seeing or feeling what she saw in the back of her mind—that there was no way out.

18 ❧

What Zubaida could not have imagined was the way that her story had affected many of the millions who saw her on television. She had no way of conceiving of the power of the Internet, where hundreds of people all over America—and in translated versions, other countries around the globe—spontaneously searched out Zubaida's foundation online. Donations and offers of service began to come in, and quickly became a mountain of generous energy expressed in twenty-five-dollar and fifty-dollar and one-hundred-dollar amounts. The amount of cash being held on her behalf grew in excess of fifty thousand dollars. That money had a great deal of buying power in Afghanistan, far beyond its European value.

That knowledge was overwhelming, at first, and more than a little intimidating because Peter and Rebecca had only begun the foundation thinking that it might raise enough to send occasional aid and supplies to the Hasan family in support of Zubaida's schooling, and to one day raise enough to pay for her trip back to America, if she wanted to pursue more education here. They hadn't had the chance to visualize further than the hope that all of this might encourage her father to prevent her from being pressured into any unwanted marriage situation until she was old enough to support herself and make her own decisions about her life.

Suddenly, there was this fortune. Not only was it an unexpected plot twist, but it was like the evil twin to the other twist of her sinking tone of voice during their phone calls, and her clear despair over the lack of continued schooling. They hadn't expected such a steep drop in her spirit and such a strong need for some kind of effective intervention on her behalf.

But the sheer size and complexity of such a thing towered before them. How was anyone to achieve any sort of effective end, using American money that would have to be delivered across hundreds of miles of unpoliced terrain amid a country full of struggling people who lack technology and basic communication infrastructure, half a world away? How was it to be done, to send what would be considered a massive amount of aid, and direct it at one specific girl without simply putting her in an impossible social situation amid the jealousy and envy of family or neighbors?

Her status, after all, was only that of a woman who must serve.

Peter and Rebecca went into the holiday season full of joy for their impending arrival, but still apprehensive about Zubaida's fate. She was sounding so much less alive during their phone calls, now. It was getting hard to find something positive to say to her about her situation. The very aliveness of the holiday season with the bright lights everywhere and the traditional expressions of cheer served to drive them to do something about the deteriorating situation in Zubaida's life.

Using contacts at the office of the Provincial Reconstruction Team in Herat, Afghanistan, they checked and found out that her foundation account was enough to buy a good, modern house for Zubaida's family inside the city of Herat, with enough money left over to stock the house with basic appliances. There it would be far easier for Mohammed and the older brothers to get work, and best of all, Zubaida would have a choice of schools available within walking distance, as would all of her siblings.

That single boost upward could guarantee a fighting chance for a new and much better life for the entire family. The city is only two hundred miles from Farah, but it's a world away in terms of opportunity. With the fall of the Taliban, inside of Afghanistan's three major cities, a woman with an education can live a life that is once again filled with choices.

The bureaucratic process was a slogging nightmare of red tape and official permission-seeking. Simple questions took days to answer. Simple forms took weeks to get.

On February 10, 2004, they received this e-mail from an analyst at the National Security Council in Afghanistan, advising them on his progress at helping them find out how to move money into an unstable region:

> I have just called a man in Herat, a money changer. He said it would be difficult to transfer money directly to Herat but the way to do it is to get the money in Dubai, over in the United Arab Emirates, and then send it to Herat using Hawala. I think I have told you about Hawala (an ancient tribal system of money transfer. It is based on good faith and verbal contracts, and is usually safe. It has been in place for centuries). He is supposed to call me back soon and let me have the information we need. He said they can do it within a week.

The offer was put to Hasan: Let Zubaida's fund buy your family a good house in the city. Move the entire family there and seek employment there, making sure to put Zubaida in school and keep her there. If you want the foundation's support, you will see to it that your daughter gets an education and never allow her to be taken away in marriage against her will.

As soon as Hasan received the offer, he was eager to cooperate. There were countless e-mails and letters and phone calls to secure permission to take on this project while the creaky wheels of Afghanistan's battered bureaucracy turned. Peter and Rebecca eventually found an ally who was a compassionate soldier in the area, named Shannon Para, and eventually Shannon found them an ally in a local man named Latif, who worked as a facilities manager with the Provincial Reconstruction Team in Herat. Shannon was their reliable local contact for as long as he was in the country, and when he was transferred out, he made sure to bring Latif up to speed on how to work with the Grossmans, the Hasans, and the local authorities. That thin line of contact would be all that linked them.

* * *

On May 31, 2004, Rebecca and Peter came to the end of a healthy pregnancy when she gave birth to their daughter, Alexis. But despite the aura of joy and celebration at their house, Rebecca decided that this wasn't the time to tell Zubaida that there was another child in the house where Zubaida had once held their sole attention. Peter and Rebecca both wanted to be sure to get the message across to her that no child could replace Zubaida and that she would never be forgotten by them. Rebecca decided that a better time to tell her about her new sister would be after Zubaida's foundation funding made it possible for her family to move into the city and her continued schooling was arranged. Then, with that living proof that she had not been abandoned by them, Zubaida would surely be feeling much stronger and hopeful, able to see the arrival of baby Alexis as a happy thing that was safe to celebrate with them.

So by July of 2004, Zubaida was still unaware of her new American sister, but a small contingent of people in Afghanistan began helping Zubaida's family find a new home. They were ready to bring Hasan to Herat after several previous scouting trips, to finalize a deal on an available home in the right price range. There were a number of false starts—and the disappearance of five thousand dollars in "earnest money" on one particular house—but eventually a modern, nine-room house with electricity and running water was found for a final cost of just over forty thousand dollars, plus the add-on costs of essential utilities and appliances. For less than fifty thousand dollars, the entire Hasan family would have a ground-floor start in a relatively urban city, where the men could have a better chance of finding work and all of the young ones could go to the new public schools.

Zubaida's school would only be a quarter of a mile away from their new home, paid for one fistful at a time from the pocket money of ordinary Americans who joined themselves as links in a long, long chain. Early in August, the entire family moved from their home village of Farah into their new home in Herat, where they remained among their people and their culture but were now in a position to participate in the best that their people and culture had to offer them.

The city was modern enough that it would have elements of the country's rebuilt infrastructure as soon as the new government's public works were under way, but Zubaida would remain in contact with her ancient culture, even in this place—high atop the cliffs over Herat there still stands a giant battle fortress. Huge, circular guard towers join thick walls that reach up several stories high. The walls are notched at the top for archers' battle stations, and fitted with extra slits for archers and spear throwers. The fortress shows a Roman influence in its grim efficiency. It was erected centuries ago by the mighty army of Alexander the Great, when it was their time to invade, conquer, and occupy.

The Afghan people got rid of them, too.

The move away from Farah was a well-timed event for Mohammed Hasan. His neighbors were openly wondering why he couldn't just pay back all his debts from his trips with Zubaida, since he had such powerful American friends. They only had to look at Zubaida to know that this was true. When the survival struggle is long and hard and social niceties fall away, people who are otherwise generous in spirit begin to wonder why one person should find favor over another. The Hasan family was beginning to live a fishbowl existence in a town of mud-brick walls. It was as if there had been a rumor about the Hasans having a box of gold hidden in their house, keeping it all to themselves while their neighbors struggled to feed themselves.

Mohammed Hasan now found himself in the position of living out the same struggle for survival every day amid fellow villagers who could not help but assume that he had access to some form of wealth and power that he was refusing to share with them, an especially powerful message in a land where financial dealings have always been matters of faith and of personal honesty. His biggest mistake was to panhandle the American soldiers whenever he was around them and gather up enough to make a few payments to his creditors. They got the taste of the money, and there was no choice but to presume that where there was that much, there had to be more. If he could get that much, he could repay them all, could he not?

However, it's likely that the same fear that prompted their suspicions ultimately protected Hasan in the long run. If he could summon such power from the American forces and even extract those small amounts that he had paid back to them so far, then he had proven himself too important to punish for his tardy payments. The trick would simply be to keep him on the string well enough that he didn't forget to keep paying, but avoid angering him with demands or intimidation. Because just as Hasan's possible value to the Americans could not be measured by the villagers, it was also impossible to know whether he might also have power to harness some of their soldiers on his behalf if he got angry with them. Such things had been the expected means of grabbing power in Afghanistan ever since the days of the long Soviet invasion: harnessing some measure of the dominate power's force and turning it to your own ends.

Could Hasan have something like that in mind? How could anyone in the province know what Hasan's resources were with these Americans, and what sort of secret plan he might be concealing? No, it was best to play Mohammed Hasan like a well-tuned instrument. Just pull a little music out of him, one or two songs at a time. No need to beat the instrument to death. In fact, leave it in good shape, to keep the music coming.

It was time to go.

Around the Hasan household, the arrangements to leave were kept quiet. They knew that the most peaceful departure would be the most unexpected one, free of too many gathered witnesses who might bring unpleasant suspicions along with them.

The female side of the family had just as much reason to be excited as the males; Mohammed and Bador agreed that the best way for the entire family to improve its fortunes was for all of the young ones to go to school. The couple didn't need to force themselves to go along with the desires of the Americans who were helping them; they both saw the compelling need to keep their children out of ignorance. That was the real implication of the opportunity opening up to them, since in their society their children's future was literally their own.

At last, on Monday, September 6, at the end of a long road of bureaucratic paper chasing, Peter and Rebecca received an e-mail from Shannon Para, their closest contact to Zubaida's family in Afghanistan. He confirmed that one month after the family's arrival in their new home, they were settled into the area and school had just opened. Zubaida and several of her family were enrolled and starting classes. Shannon personally drove them to school on that special day, but they would easily be able to walk the distance.

When Zubaida called Rebecca and Peter, the tone of her voice said everything they wanted to hear. It would take a while for her to relearn enough English to express it, but her voice showed that she felt it already—now the life that her American mom and dad dared to awaken in her was actually going to exist, all around her. This time it would unfold in her home world among her whole family, in a country that needs her kind of energy from its women.

※ ※

On that same September day, at a rally in Poplar Bluff, Missouri, President Bush said,

> Afghanistan, a country which has been brutalized by the Taliban, a country in which many young girls didn't get to go to school, a country in which their moms were whipped in the public squares because they didn't toe the line to these barbarians running the country, has now registered ten million people to vote in the upcoming election.

Two months later, when newly elected Afghan President Hamid Karzai was inaugurated, he expressed special gratitude to the country's newly freed women, who turned out to vote in numbers so high that the world's political commentators were floored with surprise. He told a story—one of many, he emphasized—of an older mother who came to a voting booth with two ballot cards, asking if she could also file a ballot for her married daughter, who was at home giving birth. The registrar explained that this was not allowed, that she could only cast her own. So she did, and went away, but a few hours later her daughter showed up carrying her newborn daughter and cast her vote anyway.

This was the social sea-change that was going on all around Zubaida while she began her new life in a world that not long ago had no place for a female with her outsized personality. Now the elected leader of the country was calling out to just such women, asking them to stand up and join in their society from a position of strength, to grasp the opportunities that education and personal freedom offered, at all levels of life.

❊ ❊

A growth spurt hit Zubaida not long after she returned to her country, and she quickly gained inches in height. It made her look more grown up, old enough to cover her hair with a light shawl, now that her undersized form was expanding into lanky adolescence. There was the temporary loss of coordination that comes with sudden new length in fast-growing limbs.

With adolescence also came a somewhat heightened sense of her own modesty and an increased desire to be taken seriously in the adult world, meaning that much of the dancing she was to do would be invisible now, dances of her own thoughts and imaginings. There was so much more to engage her mind. The lonely and dangerous celebrations of life that used to pour through her body in secret bursts of musical motion were no longer as necessary to her spirit as they once were, back when they were her only outlet for personal choice and expression.

In this new phase of her short and strange life, the future lay ahead full of possibilities and options. Now she was moving into that future with an opportunity for personal dignity that was more like the existence she had seen ahead for her friends back in America.

Thus, for the mere price of constant anxiety over whether or not she is making the right decision at any given moment, she would be rewarded by having those very possibilities and endless options available in the first place. Whether her time in this world was going to be short or long, her experience of being alive was going to take place inside of an existence that the tiny dancer who once played alone among the ruins could never have imagined or even dreamed.

Anyone who has spent time with Zubaida Hasan would understand that whether or not she is listening to the music inside of herself at any given moment, it is fair to picture a miniature version of the tiny dancer curled up behind Zubaida's eyes, looking out of those big round windows when her body moves through the world, and singing along now and then while she watches it all spin by in front of her.

Epilogue ✨

Every single human link in the chain had their own long list of Perfectly Good Reasons why they could not, should not, get involved. And the constant theme played out by each one isn't that those reasons were not Perfectly Good, it's just that sometimes there is truth that goes beyond the force of rules. As a thing made out of nothing more than individual acts of personal conscience, it was a fragile chain, thinner than smoke rings, but it held together well enough to reach halfway around the world and back again.

At the moments when each one of the people chose to get involved, they did so without having any idea of the sprawling tree of connections they were joining. They simply found something inside of themselves that was compelled to reach out in an extraordinary way to help, to make something decent and good come out of one very large tragedy for one very small person.

The staff sergeant who headed the Civil Affairs Team and took on the responsibility of keeping Hasan and his daughter supported through the long process of finding a doctor in America and getting approval to travel later went to Officer's Candidate School and graduated as a commissioned officer, to serve a full career. One of the men on his squad described him as "a big guy, capable of being fierce when he needed to, but friendly by nature. He tended to be kind of quiet. And in spite of his size and his lethal occupation, he was known among all of his men as having a good heart."

Dr. Michael Smith, the physician from the U.S. Army overseeing all of Zubaida's medical care, went on to reserve status with the military but continued to live overseas. He also remained active in the field of medicine, in both civilian and military affairs. Smith was the first one to write about the appearance of "divine coincidences" that seemed to run all through Zubaida's story, in an early note to Peter Grossman. His viewpoint was eventually shared by many of the people who were directly involved with the story; this was something that traveled under its own power. It was compelled, no matter how the nature of that compelling is be explained.

The force began with Zubaida's stark refusal to die, in spite of all the professional opinions, then it moved to her father's persistence in finding help for her, and then on to the very first American soldier who could not let Zubaida and her father pass in the marketplace without inquiring and who, once he had heard their story, was compelled to bring them with him. He had to tell dangerous stories to get them past the sentries and onto the base, then into the medical unit and under a doctor's care. The risks to his professional life and future weren't enough to stop him.

The military doctors who agreed to take her into their system, and who were well schooled in all of the Perfectly Good Reasons, surely had enough medical training to see that the amount of scarring over Zubaida's injuries proved that they predated the American presence in Afghanistan. They could not possibly have been caused by American "friendly fire." Even so, her case didn't quietly disappear as it should have. Mike Smith spoke of how he never liked the political risks of this endeavor, but he kept the medical side of her care in Kandahar organized for months, anyway. Then he followed through by personally flying to America with Zubaida and staying the week in Los Angeles with Mohammed Hasan, so that he could personally fly him back home.

* * *

Also of special note on the military side is Robert Frame, the commanding military officer in Kandahar. His story typifies the mind-set of every soldier involved with Zubaida's story. Frame was in charge of all of Mohammed and Zubaida's military contacts and clearances. Once Zubaida was into the military health system, everything that happened to her came through his office. Frame moved on to become chief of the Public Health Team in Baghdad, a reserve army officer in his mid-fifties with twenty-five years of service and numerous deployments.

On April 27, 2003, he and his Public Health Team were en route to the Ministry of Public Health to meet with representatives of the provisional administration when they were ambushed while driving a small convoy of two Humvees through the main marketplace.

The trouble began when the traffic abruptly ground to a halt all around them. Everyone in the two-vehicle convoy became alert to the possibility of danger, but at first there was nothing overtly threatening about the scene. Unlike many ambush situations, this particular area hadn't been cleared of the local people; the marketplace was crowded and activity appeared normal. Things remained quiet in that way, for the first few moments.

They could see the problem up ahead; a stalled bus had sealed off the road, choking traffic in both directions. That seemed to be reason to hope for the best. In the next moment, when two shots came from somewhere nearby, the men flinched. Still nobody panicked and started firing; a couple of random shots weren't necessarily abnormal, in a land where almost anything can be considered an excuse to celebrate by discharging weapons into the air.

Since the team was stalled in the middle of confused surroundings, they began to set up a defense perimeter according to their training. But while they were still trying to determine where the shots came from, there was a direct bullet strike on the Humvee. Frame was shot through his left upper arm by a rifle round of such power that his arm was almost completely severed from his body. Within a blink, the left arm was motionless in his long sleeve and everything around him was transformed into noise and motion. He and his team were being ambushed by organized shooters, firing from somewhere up at rooftop level. There wasn't time to get help for his massive injury; he secured the end of his sleeve to the belt clip on his gas mask to steady the useless arm, then returned pistol fire with his right hand whenever one of the ambushers stepped into range.

When one of the officers in the second Humvee opened fire with an M-16 rifle, it immediately drew return fire in a fusillade of bullets that rained down from the overpass and onto both of the Humvees. The men could see at least five attackers overhead. Within seconds, every one of Frame's team took hits to various parts of their bodies.

He quickly lost so much blood that he began to get light-headed. He saw that one of the men, a major, had been shot in the chest and was slipping out of consciousness; he could feel that it wouldn't be long before he followed. His senses were overwhelmed while his vision cut in and out and his hearing echoed after all the gunfire. He could smell the strong odor of gunpowder.

In the midst of the confusion, Frame slipped in his own blood and fell under the Humvee. Just at that moment the vehicle jolted forward a couple of feet and the wheel pinned his leg down. While he struggled to pull himself out from under the wheel, two young males, maybe eighteen or twenty years old, bolted out from the protection of the crowd and ran toward him.

This, it seemed, was to be the place where he would die—at the hands of young attackers. Instead, they ran to him, bent down, and began to pull him free from the weight of the thick Humvee wheel.

"I had no idea why they were putting themselves in harm's way. Bullets were flying all around us, and I couldn't even give them any cover fire, since I was already out of ammunition and couldn't reload with one hand."

The two young men managed to get Frame to his feet just as two of his own soldiers hurried over to help him into one of the vehicles. The team broke out to make their escape. By the time he got oriented again, the young men were gone. He had no chance to thank them or to learn whether or not they ever suffered reprisals for helping a man they didn't know, an American soldier.

The first to treat Colonel Frame was the deputy team leader, an old-school warrior who knew of a treatment that was seldom prescribed anymore because it was so difficult to apply, but done right could save Frame from bleeding to death. He tied a tourniquet around the underarm area and over the upper shoulder. The method is questioned by many physicians because of the risk of causing massive circulation difficulties, and because of the challenge of properly tying such a tourniquet. But Frame had already lost so much blood that any sort of risk-versus-benefit analysis would reveal that potential risks were the least of his problems.

The deputy team leader was right; the radical tourniquet slowed Frame's bleeding and ultimately saved his life. He and the other injured men were evacuated to the United States, while another colonel took charge of the Civil Affairs Team and the rebuilding mission continued.

Following Frame's hospitalization and surgeries, he was discharged in partial recovery to finish his healing at home. Despite the loss of the use of his left hand and some functional deficits, he returned to work at the Department of Veterans Affairs in Washington, D.C., as Assistant Under Secretary for Health and Dentistry.

The NGO that worked so hard to serve as liaison between the military and the doctors and hospitals is still quietly operating just below the radar. There are a host of other such NGOs in operation around the globe, never enough of them. The thing that these Non-Government Organizations share with the Civil Affairs branch of the U.S. military is that they both struggle to do their restorative work in places that are almost always environments of high risks. They are staffed by people with the same kinds of sensibilities as teacher Kerrie Benson—who continued her work with third-grade students even after the birth of her first child—and Patty Moayer, who has worked as a special education nurse for many years even though she could have a lifestyle of idle wealth if she were so inclined.

The Children's Burn Foundation continues to work on behalf of children who suffer catastrophic burns but whose families can't afford the needed care. They ultimately contributed nearly half a million dollars to Zubaida's case; even though Peter and his father volunteered their services, there were still mountains of costs, including the fees of the many other doctors, nurses, staff, medical supplies, and diagnostic procedures that were necessary to the process.

Peter Grossman, Richard Grossman, their entire staff, and all of their families know that Dr. Peter dodged a bullet with the case of Zubaida Hasan. Instead of meeting with catastrophe, he asserted himself as an independent surgeon within their practice. It would have surely dealt a deep blow to his relationship with his father, as well as his standing in the medical community, if things had gone off-kilter with Zubaida. The memory of a little girl taunting her nanny by pretending to jump out of a moving car was enough to drive that risk home. Even if she had mistakenly fallen out of the car while playing around like that, the tragedy to her, to her family, and to virtually everyone in Peter's life would have been incalculable.

Instead, in addition to maintaining the connection with his successful patient and surrogate daughter, his continued interest in the medical plight of Afghan women and of burn victims in that part of the world was acknowledged by the U.S. State Department when they asked him to become a member of their Department of Global Affairs Health Advisory Committee for the U.S.–Afghan Women's Council. He returned to Afghanistan again in 2005 as part of his ongoing efforts to support the establishment of a fully operational burn center there.

When Peter and Rebecca decided to take Zubaida in, they did it fully aware that they would be pilloried in the media if their gamble on Zubaida's behalf failed in some way. But the compelling force that seemed to congeal around her was already under way in their lives. The part of her journey that led through Peter's career, their home, and their hearts was something that had to happen, for better or worse.

Rebecca found that in Zubaida's absence, the process of keeping in touch with her and helping to guarantee that Zubaida had a chance in life also served to keep her motivated to continue working on behalf of Zubaida's Fund, as well as the Grossman Burn Center. She also continued working as a freelance writer focusing on health-related topics and serves on the board of advisors for *Westlake Magazine* in Los Angeles.

At the end of May 2004, she gave birth to a healthy and beautiful daughter whom they named Alexis. The parenthood that she and Peter had desired for so long finally arrived to stay and they began a sustained campaign to pack the e-mail addresses of everybody they knew with pictures of the baby girl they introduced to Zubaida as her newest baby sister. They felt overwhelmingly blessed that another sacred gift of life was bestowed upon them.

※ ※

In the end, any miracle that may have taken place in this story only began with Zubaida's surgical transformation; it moved through the transformation of her heart from its trapped condition in a prison of despair, through the return to its former state as a beating channel for the music she loves, and ultimately led her to an entirely different way to live her life as a young woman in the newly emerging society in her homeland.

There are still levels of humanity and decency that are recognized all over the world. By engaging one another at that level, beyond the reach of armies and politics and religious debates, we will stitch together whatever future lies ahead for us. The ride that we take when we follow Zubaida's long journey leads us away from a storybook mirror showing her restored reflection. It leaves each one of us alone in front of an internal mirror, challenged by our own.

Selected References

Alexander, Debra W., Ph.D. *Children Changed by Trauma: A Healing Guide*. Oakland: New Harbinger Publications, 1999.

Fontana, Vincent J. *Save the Family, Save the Child: What We Can Do to Help Children at Risk*. New York: Dutton, 1991.

Kean, Thomas H., and Lee H. Hamilton. *The 9/11 Report: The National Commission on Terrorist Attacks Upon the United States*. New York: St. Martin's Press, 2004.

Nafisi, Azar. *Reading Lolita in Tehran: A Memoir in Books*. New York: Random House, 2003.

Skaine, Rosemarie. *The Women of Afghanistan Under the Taliban*. Jefferson, N.C.: McFarland & Company, 2002.

Acknowledgments 🌿

The bad guy in this story was a can of flammable liquid. Everybody else who came in contact with Zubaida willingly gave up some part of their time, effort, and energy. Some went far beyond that, getting involved at considerable professional and personal risk.

I personally owe deep thanks to Martin Literary Management for believing in this book, and to my longtime screen agent, Lew Weitzman; their faith has sustained me. I will always be grateful to Peter and Rebecca Grossman for allowing me to tell their story and for generously submitting to a months-long barrage of questions. Through them, I was also introduced to Zubaida's father and Zubaida herself, so that I could gain their permission and verify parts of the story that only they could know.

Publisher Sally Richardson brought her full team to the table at St. Martin's Press, where *Tiny Dancer* was adopted by Thomas Dunne of the Thomas Dunne Books imprint. Editor Marcia Markland championed this book from the beginning, and, along with assistant Diana Szu, provided a gracious home for this project. She also brought a graceful and caring edit to the manuscript. Copy editor Norrie M. Feinblatt brought an eagle eye for chasing the devil through the details.

Deep thanks are due to those military personnel who can't be identified, as well as those who were able to speak on the record with permission from military CentCom: Col. Robert Frame, Dr. Mike Smith, Maj. Raymond Short, and Sgt. Benjamin Abel.

The doctors, nurses, and staff at the Grossman Burn Center, plus Peter Grossman's longtime assistant, Stephanie Osadchey, were extraordinary, both in their level of care in this case and in their willingness to provide needed information and interviews. That this lifesaving and hope-restoring facility exists is thanks to Dr. Richard Grossman, joined in recent years by his son, partner, and fellow surgeon, Peter Grossman.

Michael Gray, Dorothy English, and Sandy Francis provided valuable family insights to Peter and Rebecca's story, as did Mahnaz Terrah with her insider/outsider perspective—hired as Zubaida's interpreter, she also wound up providing personal care. Teacher Kerrie Benson's help and concern matched that of every other player in this story, and Patty Moayer began as a concerned neighbor and became the official project translator in my contacts with Afghanistan. Betsy Hegel agreed to have her daughter Emily's story told and they both added truth and beauty to the rendering of Zubaida's personality.

Since a story can't survive in the crowded marketplace unless the public knows it's there, we are all grateful to Suzanne Wickham-Beaird, publicist, to Joe Bolduc, and to Victoria Lang of Plus Entertainment for vital promotional assistance.

Parting Thanks to:

Woodie, feline calico companion of ten years with the mass of a cannonball, for teaching a living lesson via her complete lack of shame over total body fat of any amount;

Houdini, the Great Escapist, nasty orange tabby pulled off death row at the city pound on the morning of his scheduled demise (canine in his affection and persistent in his gratitude, he has rewarded my years of training efforts by finally learning how to type, although he still refuses to write what I tell him);

and

Grandma Ruthie Levin, eloquent in the consistence of her loving tolerance. And to Matthew Levin, who—at the age of three—named me Uncathy, because Uncle Anthony was too hard to pronounce.